Av

Compliance Management
for Public, Private, or Nonprofit Organizations

Compliance Management

for Public, Private, or Nonprofit Organizations

Michael G. Silverman

NEW YORK   CHICAGO   SAN FRANCISCO   LISBON
LONDON   MADRID   MEXICO CITY   MILAN   NEW DELHI
SAN JUAN   SEOUL   SINGAPORE   SYDNEY   TORONTO

To Liz and to all those I love . . .

. . . with a special thanks to Beatrice and Carl

Contents

Acknowledgments   xiii

Introduction   xv

Part I: Setting the Context

1 The Expanded Focus on Compliance   3
The Forces at Work   5
The Judiciary   6
The Legislative Response   10
The Expanding Role of Federal Agencies   12
State Governments   17
Government Examines Its Own Operations   18
The Nonprofit Sector   19
Private-Sector Oversight   21
Corporate Social Responsibility   21
Shareholders and NGOs   22
Global Telecommunications and the Internet   27
Summary   28

2 The Mandate for Compliance   31
Regulatory Compliance   33

Internal Corporate Compliance Systems 37

The Private Sector and Organizational Compliance 39

The Nonprofit Sector 47

The Public Sector 50

Summary 52

Part II: The Foundations of Compliance

3 Compliance and Ethics: Challenges and Approaches 55

Intertwined but Not Interchangeable Concepts 56

Motivations for Compliance 57

Barriers to Compliance 59

The Organization's Cultural Framework 61

Rules versus Integrity 63

Corporate Codes of Conduct 64

Creating an Ethical Culture: The Linchpin 70

Nonprofit Organizations 72

Public Sector 74

Summary 75

4 Leadership and Culture: The Foundations of Compliance 77

The Legal and Regulatory Underpinnings 79

Self-Regulatory Organizations: New York Stock Exchange 84

Boards of Directors 85

Nonprofit Organizations 92

Senior Management 96

Public-Sector Organizations 99

Summary 101

Part III: The Modern Compliance Organization

5 Managing Compliance: Goals and Structure 105

Designing the Compliance Program 106

Government and Regulators' Guidance   108
The Compliance Program Charter   110
Features of a Modern Compliance Program   113
The Compliance Structure   116
Outsourcing Compliance   124
Coordinating the Compliance Program   127
Staffing the Compliance Program   131
The Role of the Chief Compliance Officer   134
Budgeting for the Compliance Program   141
Small and Medium-Sized Organizations   144
Summary   149

6   **Policies, Communication, and Training**   151
Policies and Procedures   151
Communication   158
Training   161
Summary   173

7   **Hotlines, Whistle-Blowers, and Investigations**   175
Whistle-Blowing Programs   175
Instituting a Whistle-Blowing Program   179
Managing Information   187
Tracking Inquiries   188
International Operations   189
Related Issues   189
Conducting Investigations   191
Summary   197

8   **Information and Technology: Challenges and Tools for Compliance**   199
Federal Regulatory Requirements   200
State Regulatory Requirements   201
International Requirements   201
Technology Standards   202
The Challenge of Multiple Regulations   202
Creating a Multidimensional Compliance Framework   204

Privacy and Information Security   206
Third-Party Relationships and Outsourcing   211
Compliance Technology Tools   211
Education, Communication, and Training   213
Summary   214

9 **Compliance and Oversight: Risk, Monitoring, Audits, and Regulators**   215
Compliance Risk   215
Regulatory Requirements   216
Standards-Setting Organizations   218
Governance and Compliance Risk   219
Compliance Risk Assessment Process   221
Compliance Monitoring and Audits   235
Regulators   243
Summary   245

10 **Compliance and Controls**   247
Government Regulations   248
Internal Control Regulation and the Public Sector   251
Self-Regulatory Organizations: New York Stock Exchange   251
*Standards Setting Organizations: Committee of Sponsoring
   Organizations of the Treadway Commission*   252
The Internal Control Program   258
Summary   264

11 **Evaluating Compliance**   267
Criteria for Compliance Effectiveness   269
The Need for Evaluation   271
Techniques for Evaluating Compliance   271
Assessing Compliance Effectiveness   272
Postevaluation Actions   283
Summary   284

Part IV: The Future of Compliance

12 Compliance, Going Forward 287
Brief Retrospective 288
A Profession with Growing Pains 288
At the Crossroads 289
The Road Ahead 294

Resources 295
Index 299

Acknowledgments

I want to thank all those persons who freely and generously gave me their time, thoughts, and help throughout the different stages of this book: Steve Michaelson, Fred Dietz, Hans Decker, Joan Helpern, Laurie Zeligson, Kalisa Barratt, Sadie Koga-Kadish, John Lenzi, and Abigail Goren Matthews.

A thank-you to Freddy Trejo for his illustrations, and special thanks to Richard Goren.

I also wanted to acknowledge the number of people who spoke to me "on background" whose ideas, candor, opinions, and insights made this book possible.

Introduction

Compliance Management for Public, Private, or Nonprofit Organizations offers a comprehensive look at the role that compliance plays in our modern organizations. It examines not only the traditional compliance issues associated with law and regulation, but, equally important, the broader role that ethical behavior, organizational structure, technology, administration, and risk management play in developing an effective compliance program.

In the last two decades, the concept of compliance has become increasingly intertwined with the governance of our modern complex organizations. The failure of organizations, from Enron to the Red Cross, to comply with laws, regulations, codes of conduct, and ethical standards of good practice have heightened our awareness of these critical issues. Indeed, accountability, transparency, adherence to laws and regulations, ethical conduct, and standards of conduct and behavior have become as much a part of how organizations manage their affairs as their primary mission and operations. This simple fact applies to organizations in the public, private, and nonprofit sectors of our economy.

Why should organizations care about compliance and about developing an effective compliance and ethics program? The answers range from the obvious—preventing criminal actions and mitigating organizational and individual liability (ranging from fines, penalties, and sanctions to possible imprisonment) in cases of wrongdoing—to the more subtle implications, such as employee morale, customer disaffection, media scrutiny and, perhaps the greatest risk, the loss of public reputation.

To address these critical needs, compliance programs and staff have become a standard element in many of today's organizations. Yet, this is a nascent and evolving profession that is barely 20 years old. From its origins in the Federal Sentencing Guidelines for Organizations in 1991 through various court cases dealing with board members' responsibilities, Sarbanes-Oxley and other legislation imposing significant corporate governance obligations, and regulators advocating support for organizational compliance programs, we have witnessed the growth of a profession and its supporting industry of consultants, vendors, and suppliers. In fact, one of the industry's professional groups even requested the U.S. Senate to designate a "National Corporate Compliance & Ethics Week."

This book is designed for people who have the responsibility for compliance and ethics in their organization, or who want to learn more about this critical issue. It demonstrates how organizations, large and small, manage their compliance responsibilities. It examines such critical issues as identifying compliance risk, the relationship between compliance and governance, the role of the board of directors and senior management in promoting compliance, the relationship between compliance and ethics, the various barriers to compliance within organizations, and the elements of a compliance program that work best for organizations.

On an operational level, *Compliance Management* examines the strategies and techniques used by various organizations to establish compliance goals and plans, technology and systems, education and training, the role of risk assessment, ethics, internal control techniques, self-assessment, and staffing and budgeting requirements. Through an extensive examination of organizational compliance practices (both successes and failures) across the spectrum of the private, public, and nonprofit sectors, the reader will gain an invaluable insight into the workings of compliance initiatives and learn significant lessons that can be applied in today's organizations.

Compliance Management is divided into four parts that address the broad sweep of an effective compliance program, from its legal and ethical underpinnings to the role of the organization's board of directors and senior management, and the strategic and operational aspects of establishing an organizational compliance program.

The first part of *Compliance Management* examines the complex factors that have contributed to our focus on compliance. Chapter 1 reviews the diverse forces (judicial, legislative, economic, societal, and technological) that have shaped our enhanced focus on compliance. From the egregious examples of organizational misbehavior to the awakenings of corporate social responsibility and the advent of instant messaging, the world of organizational compliance management is a changed environment in the twenty-first century. Chapter 2 explores the issue of government regulation and its meaning for compliance. It identifies the key structures and techniques of modern government regulation (e.g., the growing use of self-regulation) and their implications for organizational compliance.

Chapter 3 examines the issue of compliance and ethics from a variety of perspectives: the challenges of managing compliance and ethics in a modern organization, the role of the manager in compliance and ethics, and techniques and strategies used by organizations to address issues of compliance and ethics. It provides guidance for developing an effective organizational code of conduct. Chapter 4 focuses on the major judicial and legislative actions that have emphasized the importance of organizational leadership (the board of directors and senior management) in modern organizational compliance. It explores the duties and responsibilities of boards of directors and senior management and the critical actions they need to take to create an effective compliance and ethics program.

Chapter 5 shows how to establish and manage an effective compliance program for large and small organizations. It examines the complex strategic and programmatic issues involved in establishing a modern organizational compliance program, along with setting realistic goals for the function, creating an effective working relationship with key organizational units, and staffing and budgeting for the compliance program. Chapter 6 examines three critical elements of an effective compliance program: policies, training, and communication. It describes how to write effective compliance policies; it demonstrates various techniques for compliance communication, ranging from newsletters to Web sites; and it covers establishing a comprehensive compliance training program.

Chapter 7 explores the sensitive issue of whistle-blowing and conducting investigations. It describes how to establish and manage an effective hotline program, and the techniques and strategies for conducting investigations into compliance-related matters. Chapter 8 looks at the role of technology in a modern compliance function. It examines this issue from two perspectives: the growth of information technology and its significant legal and regulatory compliance ramifications, and the role of technology in assisting a modern compliance program.

Chapter 9 looks at the key issues of compliance risk management, risk monitoring, and compliance audits. It examines the role of risk in managing compliance, and it explores modern compliance risk management strategies and their application in a modern compliance function. The chapter describes how to conduct an in-depth compliance risk assessment and a comprehensive compliance audit for an organization.

Chapter 10 addresses self-assessment and internal controls, and the critical role that internal control standards, such as those developed by such organizations as the Committee of Sponsoring Organizations of the Treadway Commission, play in managing compliance risk. This chapter describes the techniques for establishing an effective internal control program to address compliance risk. Chapter 11 explores the techniques and strategies that organizations utilize to evaluate the effectiveness of their own compliance programs. Finally, in Chapter 12, we explore some of the possible future trends for organizational compliance programs and the evolving profession of compliance and ethics specialists. As government regulatory approaches change, these changes may have a significant impact on compliance programs. The chapter examines some of these possibilities.

Finally, the resources section provides some important sources of information for organizations and people seeking further information on compliance and ethics programs, professional organizations, and other relevant topics.

PART I

SETTING THE CONTEXT

The Expanded Focus on Compliance

On July 22, 2003, Richard Thornburgh, the former U.S. attorney general who had been appointed bankruptcy examiner for the failed telecommunications company WorldCom, testified before the U.S. Senate Committee on Judiciary:

> *I believe that WorldCom's conferral of practically unlimited discretion upon Messrs. Ebbers [former WorldCom CEO] and Sullivan [former WorldCom CFO], combined with passive acceptance of management's proposals by the Board of Directors, and a culture that diminished the importance of internal checks, forward-looking planning and meaningful debate or analysis formed the basis for the Company's descent into bankruptcy. In many significant respects, WorldCom appears to have represented the polar opposite of model corporate governance practices during the relevant period. . . . A culture and internal processes that discourage or implicitly forbid scrutiny and detailed questioning can be a breeding ground for fraudulent misdeeds.*[1]

Thornburgh's testimony characterized, in many respects, the turmoil of the events that were portrayed daily in the media. Passive and ineffectual governing bodies, failure to understand risk, inadequate internal controls, inattention to compliance issues, excessive greed, accounting failures, conflicts of interest, and corporate cultures that were indifferent to unethical conduct were the hallmarks of many organizations. These failures, and the subsequent criminal indictments, fines, and penalties, involved some of the most prominent organizations in the United States. Organizations as diverse as WorldCom, Enron, the American Red Cross, United Way, Fannie Mae, Boeing, Citigroup, Global Crossing, and Arthur Andersen were caught in the maelstrom of wrongdoing. According to Tamara Loomis in the April 29, 2003, issue of the *New York Law Journal*, one of the lowest points was reached on April 28, 2003, when nearly every major U.S. investment bank, including Merrill Lynch, Goldman Sachs, Morgan Stanley, Citigroup, Credit Suisse First Boston, Lehman Brothers Holdings, JPMorgan Chase, UBS Warburg, and U.S. Bancorp Piper Jaffray, agreed to a $1.4 billion settlement covering their actions to defraud investors. Words like *compliance*, *governance*, *transparency*, *accountability*, and *ethics* became part of our organizational lexicon.

Events of this kind are not uncommon. The United States has experienced periodic waves of organizational wrongdoing and legislative reaction. In the 1970s, scandals related to some American companies' practice of bribing foreign government officials to obtain business led to the passage of the Foreign Corruption Practices Act. In the late 1980s and early 1990s, the Federal Deposit Insurance Corporation had to spend $100 billion in deposit guarantees for failing savings and loan associations and other financial institutions, many of which collapsed because of poor management, greed, and incompetence. Those scandals led to the passage of the Federal Deposit Insurance Corporation Improvement Act, which tightened financial institutions' internal controls (and which would later serve as a model for the Sarbanes-Oxley legislation), and the creation of the Resolution Trust Corporation to manage the failed savings and loan institutions.

The events of the late 1990s and early 2000s, however, went beyond these earlier incidents. The scope of corporate wrongdoing transcended a particular industry. Telecommunications, communications, financial services, and energy companies, to name a few, were involved. Moreover, the collapse of companies such as WorldCom and Enron affected not only their employees and suppliers, but the voluminous number of individual, state, municipal, and 401(k) pension plans that had invested in these companies. While Congress and the states passed regulatory legislation to address the situation, as they had done in previous cases of wrongdoing, what was unique about the events of the past decade has been the extraordinary amount of public and government attention focused on the issues of compliance and ethics. The concern was focused not only on corrective regulatory legislation or enhanced sanctions, but, equally important, on the issues of accountability, ethics, and responsibility in organizational management.

Yet these highly publicized incidences of organizational wrongdoing were not the only forces at work to focus attention on the issues of legal and regulatory compliance. A complex set of actions, some of them independent of these scandals and others a direct result of this wrongdoing, contributed to this movement. This chapter examines the range and interplay of the various forces that over the past two decades have been instrumental in focusing attention on the issues of legal compliance and ethics in organizations in the public, private, and nonprofit sectors.

The Forces at Work

The evolution of legal and regulatory compliance as a growing force in organizational life has been the result of numerous forces: judicial, legislative, economic, societal, and technological. While discrete activities to comply with legal and regulatory requirements were a longstanding fixture of many organizations (e.g., audit, legal, human resources, security, internal control, and financial control functions), their codification into specific compliance programs with a defined identity, organizational charter, and staff and endorsed by government actions is a relatively new phenomenon (see Box 1.1).

BOX 1.1   A Compliance Prototype

A prototype of an organizational compliance program is the Defense Industry Initiative on Business Ethics and Conduct (DII). The DII was created in October 1986 when 18 defense contractors drafted a program for self-governance. The initiative was in response to the Packard Commission, which was created in July 1985 by President Reagan after a series of well-publicized defense procurement scandals. The commission, in its June 1986 report, A *Quest for Excellence*, called for defense contractors to "assume responsibility for improved self-governance to assure the integrity of the contracting process. . . . Corporate managers must take bold and constructive steps that will ensure the integrity of their own contract performance. Systems that ensure compliance with pertinent regulations and contract requirements must be put in place so that violations do not occur." Among the commission's recommendations were the need for defense organizations to develop ethical standards of business conduct, increase the effectiveness of their internal controls, and enhance senior management oversight and employee training. Many of these features would ultimately be incorporated into the Federal Sentencing Guidelines for Organizations.

The Judiciary

An early catalyst for focusing attention on compliance was judicial activity at both the state and federal levels of government. The 1990s and into the twenty-first century witnessed a significant change in corporate governance and its impact on compliance. Boards of directors and senior management of organizations came to have an affirmative duty to implement internal corporate compliance programs to detect and prevent criminal misconduct by the organization's employees and its agents, and then to monitor those programs to be sure that they were working properly. These developments can be seen in the advent of the Federal Sentencing Guidelines for Organizations in 1991 and a number of judicial decisions.

Federal Sentencing Guidelines for Organizations

November 1, 1991, is a seminal date for compliance programs. It was on this date that the Federal Sentencing Guidelines for Organizations (FSGO) went into effect. The FSGO were developed by the U.S.

Sentencing Commission, an independent organization within the judicial branch of the U.S. government. The guidelines were developed to create a consistent approach to addressing wrongdoing by organizations and the punishment for their transgressions. As the U.S. Sentencing Commission explained in its *Guidelines Manual*:

> *These guidelines offer incentives to organizations to reduce and ultimately eliminate criminal conduct by providing a structural foundation from which an organization may self-police its own conduct through an effective compliance and ethics program. The prevention and detection of criminal conduct, as facilitated by an effective compliance and ethics program, will assist an organization in encouraging ethical conduct and in complying fully with all applicable laws.*

In brief, the FSGO require an organization to remedy the harm caused by its offense and to pay a monetary fine for the violation of federal law. The fine is calculated by applying a multiplier based on a "culpability score" to the "base fine." The culpability score is increased for factors such as the size of the organization, the number of years since any previous offense, violation of a previous order, and obstruction of justice. It is reduced by factors such as the existence of organization programs to prevent and detect noncompliance and the organization's self-reporting of violations, cooperation with the regulators, and acceptance of responsibility. These culpability factors can be further mitigated by an organization's having an effective internal compliance program. The FSGO prescribe seven key components for an effective compliance program that form the basis for organizational compliance programs in the United States.

The FSGO were significant for a number of reasons. From a public policy perspective, they defined a model for good corporate citizenship and created incentives for companies to take crime-controlling actions. This was a shift from a traditional mode of regulatory enforcement to a more interactive, "self-policing" approach. Moreover, the organizations affected by the FSGO spanned the full spectrum of the U.S. economy: corporations, partnerships, associations, joint-stock companies, unions, trusts, pension funds, unincorporated organizations, governments, and nonprofit organizations.

The FSGO were also instrumental in creating a major growth in organizational compliance programs and compliance offices. Organizations ranging from financial institutions to hospitals developed compliance programs and appointed persons to the position of compliance or ethics officer. A survey by the Ethics & Compliance Officer Association found that only 15 percent of the respondents reported that their positions had been created in or prior to 1991 (when the FSGO were first written), while 86 percent had been created after the guidelines appeared.[2]

Similarly, an industry of law firms, consulting organizations, and independent contractors developed to provide services to enable organizations to cope with the FSGO. Kimberley Krawiec, writing in the *Washington University Law Quarterly* in 2003, noted that a commentator wryly explained that the FSGO were "referred to by some industry insiders as 'The Ethics Consultants Full Employment Act of 1991.'"

Finally, the FSGO became the compliance model for other regulatory agencies to follow with respect to their own spheres of responsibility (including their contractors). Federal agencies such as the Environmental Protection Agency, the Department of Health and Human Services, the Department of Veterans Affairs, and the Department of Justice's Antitrust Division established programs and requirements modeled after the FSGO.[3]

November 2004 Amendments to the Federal Sentencing Guidelines for Organizations

A decade after the original Federal Sentencing Guidelines for Organizations were enacted, the United States Sentencing Commission approved significant amendments to the FSGO, which became effective on November 1, 2004. It had convened an Ad Hoc Advisory Group on the Federal Sentencing Guidelines for Organizations (the advisory group) to review the FSGO and propose changes to enhance their effectiveness. The advisory group's recommended amendments expanded upon what organizations must do if their programs are to be viewed as effective by the courts.

- The amendments expanded the role and duties of boards of directors, particularly directors' duties with regard to effective corporate governance. The amendments specify that boards of directors and senior executives must assume responsibility for the oversight and management of the organization's compliance and ethics programs.
- Organizations were required to promote "an organizational culture that encourages ethical conduct and a commitment to compliance with the law."[4] The 2004 Amendments to the Federal Sentencing Guidelines for Organizations, with their strong focus on organizational ethics and culture, shifted "the paradigm of compliance programs away from an exclusive rules-based approach toward a rules-and-values-based approach," Bowers et al. noted in their November 2004 report, *Organizational Sentencing Guidelines: The New Paradigm for Effective Compliance and Ethics Programs*. As a result, greater emphasis was placed on ethical awareness and training for all persons in an organization.
- Organizations were required to conduct periodic compliance risk assessments to identify potential areas of vulnerability. The results of these analyses had to be considered in the design, implementation, and modification of all other aspects of a company's compliance and ethics program— for instance, in its policy creation, training, and auditing activities.

In 2005, two U.S. Supreme Court decisions had potentially signifi-cant ramifications for the FSGO. In *United States v. Booker* and *United States v. Fanfan*, the court held that federal judges could consider the Federal Sentencing Guidelines as only "advisory" in nature. However, the consensus in the legal and compliance communities is that the FSGO are still considered "best practices" for organizational compliance and ethics programs, and their importance in determining an organization's culpability has not been diminished.

Court Decisions

Federal and state court cases also contributed to the growing attention being paid to organizational compliance and ethics programs. Among the more prominent were the 1996 Caremark case (*In re Caremark International Inc. v. Derivative Litigation*), which was decided by the Delaware courts, and several federal cases dealing with the role and duties of board members. These cases are discussed further in Chapter 4. The U.S. Supreme Court, in 1998, decided two matters involving sexual harassment in the workplace, *Faragher v. City of Boca Raton* and *Burlington Indus., Inc. v. Ellerth*, both of which had significant implications for organizational compliance programs. They created incentives for employers to create or enhance their existing compliance and ethics programs to address federal antidiscrimination laws.

The Legislative Response

For modern organizations, the focus on legal and regulatory compliance is fueled by the panoply of federal and state laws and regulations. In areas as varied as antidiscrimination, occupational health and safety, environmental law, money laundering, transportation, and health-care billing practices, government regulation dictates the form and manner in which many organizations operate. Increasingly, this includes specific measures that address organizational compliance requirements. However, the most prominent law dealing with corporate governance and compliance was passed in 2002: Sarbanes-Oxley.

Sarbanes-Oxley Act of 2002

On July 30, 2002, Congress approved the Public Company Accounting Reform and Investor Protection Act, more commonly known by its short title, the Sarbanes-Oxley Act of 2002. Reflecting the widespread corporate governance failures of major corporations in 2001 and 2002, Congress passed this legislation by overwhelming margins: it passed the House by a vote of 423-3 and the Senate by 99-0. Some have called Sarbanes-Oxley the most significant (or onerous) business reform legislation since the enactment of the Securities Act of 1933, the Securities Exchange Act of 1934, and the Investment Company Act of 1940. The July 31, 2002, issue of the *Cleveland Plain Dealer* reported that President George W. Bush hailed Sarbanes-Oxley for making "the most far-reaching reforms of American business practices since the time of Franklin Delano Roosevelt." The law's purpose is to rebuild public trust in America's corporate sector. It requires publicly traded companies to adhere to significant new governance standards that broaden board members' roles in overseeing financial transactions and auditing procedures.

The importance and impact of the Sarbanes-Oxley Act of 2002 cannot be underestimated. While the focus of the legislation is on publicly traded companies, its scope, power, and influence reverberate throughout the economy. For many corporate officials, "compliance" often translates into meeting the requirements of Sarbanes-Oxley. In brief, the legislation:

- Defines a higher level of responsibility, accountability, and financial reporting transparency for organizations.
- Enhances the legal status and responsibility of the organization's chief executive officer and chief financial officer, and of the audit committee of the board of directors.
- Affects auditors and lawyers and the role they play in internal corporate governance.

For boards of directors, the legislation establishes new responsibilities for the audit committee. It requires the committee to approve all services provided by the organization's external auditor. The audit committee must be composed solely of independent directors, and at least one member of the committee must be a "financial expert" (as defined by the law).

Senior management responsibility is significantly enhanced. The legislation requires the organization's chief executive officer and chief financial officer to certify not only the completeness and accuracy of the information contained in quarterly and annual finance reports, but also the effectiveness of the underlying internal controls that generated the information.

Auditors are not allowed to provide to a company, contemporaneously with audit services, nine nonaudit services (e.g., management consulting, information system design, and internal accounting) specified in the statute or the regulations.

Sarbanes-Oxley and its implementing regulations require companies to disclose whether they have adopted a code of ethics, and if they have not done so, why not. The code of ethics technically applies only to the organization's executive officer, principal financial officer, and principal accounting officer or persons performing similar functions. However, many companies have used the requirement to issue companywide codes of conduct applicable to all employees.

The legislation obliges public companies to install an internal whistleblowing policy for employees and others to report accounting, internal control, and auditing problems, and establishes protections against retaliatory actions. Finally, at the heart of Sarbanes-Oxley is Section 404. It mandates that a company assess its internal controls for financial reporting. This has been a source of great controversy because of the time and expense involved in conducting the analyses (although in 2007, the Securities and Exchange Commission gave some relief to smaller organizations).

Since its passage, Sarbanes-Oxley's audit, director, and internal control requirements have set the standard for best practices for corporate governance and financial oversight even for organizations that are not significantly affected by the law. As we shall see, in organizations ranging from hospitals, museums, cooperative apartment buildings, universities, and charitable organizations to the government itself, Sarbanes-Oxley has left its governance and compliance imprint.

The Expanding Role of Federal Agencies

Federal agencies have been increasingly active in providing compliance assistance and guidance to encourage organizations to self-police their operations. The range of federal activities has run from the extreme of threatening suspension and disbarment unless compliance programs are in place to offering proactive advice and guidance on best compliance practices. Federal agencies such as the Environmental Protection Agency (EPA) have created examples of model compliance programs and made them available through Internet sites and various publications. The EPA offers five different types of economic models to calculate compliance costs.[5] The Internal Revenue Service has promoted voluntary compliance programs and established amnesty periods for self-correcting violations in areas ranging from taxes on restaurant tips to employee benefits regulations.

Punitive Actions

The government's threat of suspension, disbarment, or prosecution for companies that violate federal laws and regulations has been a powerful force in fostering the use of compliance programs. Increasingly, regulators and prosecutors have incorporated compliance-related provisions in deferred prosecution or corporate integrity agreements. In the health-care industry, for instance, H. Lowell Brown, in a 2001 study in the *Delaware Journal of Corporate Law*, noted:

> *The real catalysts for the wide spread adoption of health care compliance programs, however, have been the [Department of Justice] and the [Office of the Inspector General of the Department of Health and Human Services]. These agencies have recently required all organizations settling health care fraud charges to adopt government-sponsored corporate integrity programs as part of the defendants' settlement agreements. These government-imposed compliance programs usually require corporations to commit substantial assets to compliance and involve government and private oversight.*

This study also found that in 22 administrative settlements in which companies entered into agreements with executive-branch administrative agencies to avoid serious repercussions for violation of law and regulation, the offending companies had to put in place a number of compliance program features such as written policies and practices governing the manner in which the company conducts its business, codes of ethics and business conduct, training, and mechanisms for reporting misconduct. Many of these features are consistent with the tenets of the Federal Sentencing Guidelines for Organizations.

Inspectors General

The Inspector General Act of 1978 created the position of inspectors general (IGs) within the executive branch of the federal government. The IGs' mission is to identify and eliminate waste, fraud, and corruption within their respective agencies, and many of them have been extremely active in promoting compliance initiatives. There are now 64 statutory IGs in agencies ranging from the Departments of Agriculture, Commerce, Defense, Education, and Homeland Security to smaller agencies such as the National Aeronautics and Space Administration, National Science Foundation, Small Business Administration, and Veterans Administration.

Illustrative of the IGs' influence in introducing compliance programs has been the work of the Office of the Inspector General (OIG) for the U.S. Department of Health and Human Services (DHHS). This office has been one of the most prolific and important catalysts for the introduction of compliance programs in the $590 billion health-care industry in the United States. Over the past decade, the DHHS OIG has issued extensive compliance guidance, modeled after the Federal Sentencing Guidelines for Organizations, for various sectors of the health-care industry, including pharmaceutical manufacturing, ambulance suppliers, nursing facilities, hospitals, "Medicare + choice" organizations, clinical laboratories, and home health agencies.

U.S. Department of Justice

Amidst the passage of Sarbanes-Oxley and the continuing revelations of corporate misbehavior, on January 20, 2003, Larry D. Thompson, former deputy attorney general of the U.S. Department of Justice, issued the *Principles of Federal Prosecution of Business Organizations* (the principles, sometimes referred to as the Thompson memo). The document provides guidance for federal prosecutors on whether or not to file criminal charges against business organizations for wrongdoing.

The principles list nine criteria that govern business prosecutorial decisions. Two of these factors directly involve compliance programs. They are "[t]he existence and adequacy of the corporation's compliance program" at the time of the offense and "the corporation's remedial actions including any efforts to implement an effective corporate compliance program or to improve an existing one." The principles mirror the tenets of the Federal Sentencing Guidelines for Organizations' requirements for an effective compliance program (e.g., encouraging the establishment of compliance programs and early identification of issues). They also call upon a prosecutor to ask a number of key questions regarding the management and oversight of an organization's compliance program. The principles are discussed in greater detail later in the book.

Federal Regulatory Agencies

Consistent with the compliance initiatives undertaken by the executive-branch agencies, federal regulatory agencies have been active in promoting compliance programs. Agencies ranging from the Securities and Exchange Commission to the Federal Energy Regulatory Commission have taken strong positions on issues of organizational compliance.

In one of the strongest statements on compliance, Joseph T. Kelliher, the chairman of the Federal Energy Regulatory Commission (FERC), which oversees the wholesale energy market in the United States and regulates interstate trade in electric energy, said in an October 20, 2005, FERC statement:

> *Our purpose is firm but fair enforcement of our rules and regu-*
> *lations. I want to be clear: the Commission's goal is compliance.*
> *We have a duty to be clear on what the rules are. Compliance*
> *should not be elusive, it should not be subjective, and it should*

be objective to the greatest extent possible. Our goal is to facilitate compliance—and to quickly identify and sanction noncompliance.

Similarly, the Securities and Exchange Commission (SEC) has taken a very public stance in promoting compliance initiatives. SEC Commissioner Cynthia A. Glassman, in an October 17, 2003, speech to financial executives, vividly stated her views on compliance:

If your goal is to get as much money as possible in the door today—even if it leaves shortly thereafter in the form of fines and litigation settlements—then you may be tempted to look the other way. I respectfully suggest that firms that cut corners on compliance jeopardize the long-term profitability—and ultimately viability—of the firm. A company's reputation is a valuable asset, and in the securities industry it is a firm's most valuable asset. Failure to safeguard this reputational asset with first-rate governance and compliance procedures is a serious failure in strategic thinking. Remember that although there are a lot of business risks inherent in running a securities firm, regulatory risk—which is manageable—probably poses the single greatest potential doomsday scenario, capable of shutting the doors of even the most prestigious firm forever.

Securities and Exchange Commission Leniency Guidelines. In 2001, the SEC issued its "Statement on the Relationship of Cooperation to Agency Enforcement Decisions" (also known as the Seaboard report), in which it cited 13 criteria that it would use in considering possible credit for "self-policing and self-reporting" for organizations with securities law issues. Like the Thompson memo, the Seaboard report lists several criteria that are applicable to an organization's compliance and ethics program, such as: How did the company discover the issue? How did the company handle the misconduct when it was discovered? Did it take prompt action to stop the action and punish the wrongdoers? What compliance procedures were in place to prevent the misconduct that has now been uncovered? Did the company adopt more effective internal controls and procedures to prevent a recurrence?

State Governments

While the federal government has been the predominant player in addressing the issues of organizational wrongdoing, it was certainly not the only one. For example, the Delaware court's ruling in the Caremark case had a significant impact on the role of directors in corporate governance. During the developing story of corporate wrongdoing in the early part of this decade, the states, through their attorneys general and securities regulators, played an increasingly active role in prosecuting organizations for wrongdoing. California, Massachusetts, and New York began to aggressively pursue corporate malfeasance. Even smaller states, such as Oklahoma, took an active role: in 2004, Oklahoma prosecutors filed a case against WorldCom for accounting fraud.

Perhaps the best-known state activist is New York Governor Eliot Spitzer, who in 2001, when he was attorney general, opened an investigation into Merrill Lynch's research department and its promotion of certain valueless Internet stocks. Spitzer won a $100 million settlement from Merrill Lynch, and then expanded his investigation to a number of other banks and investment companies. As a result of that initiative, and in conjunction with the SEC, the National Association of Securities Dealers (NASD), the New York Stock Exchange (NYSE), and other state securities regulators, a comprehensive settlement involving 10 firms was reached. The agreement forced the brokerage firms to undertake extensive measures to ensure the integrity of their research and investment operations.

In 2003, the New York State attorney general and the Securities and Exchange Commission negotiated a settlement with Alliance Capital Management for a case involving the illegal practice of market timing. The total monetary value of the settlement was $600 million. Alliance agreed to cut its fees to investors by 20 percent for at least five years and pay $250 million in restitution to resolve charges that it permitted market timing. In addition to the monetary settlement, Alliance had to implement substantial governance and compliance changes to safeguard against future harm to its shareholders. Among these changes were the creation of ethics and internal compliance committees, the installation of a company ombudsman, and the requirement that the company submit to an independent compliance review at least every other year.

On September 28, 2002, the California legislature enacted its own comprehensive state-level corporate disclosure requirement entitled the California Corporate Disclosure Act. The legislation authorizes the California attorney general to impose civil penalties of up to $1 million on California corporations that fail to notify the government and their shareholders of specified types of misconduct.

Government Examines Its Own Operations

While federal and state governments were busily promulgating guidance on compliance for a wide range of organizations, they were not exempt from the need to address the issues of compliance within their own operations. Traditionally, the role of compliance in the public sector's own administrative and financial operations has been taken by a myriad of functions and bodies, including the courts, the legislature, independent commissions that oversee both private and public organizations (e.g., worker safety and equal employment opportunity commissions), and even private agencies such as credit rating agencies, the media, and NGOs.

Indeed, the plethora of oversight agencies is staggering: comptrollers, inspectors general, internal auditors, ombudsmen, executive regulatory bodies (e.g., the budget office and the procurement office), and specialist regulatory bodies and functions (e.g., water compliance specialists and police boards).

The growth in the number of federal agencies with compliance responsibilities has been significant. The General Accountability Office (GAO), the Defense Contract Audit Agency (DCAA), and the Office of the Inspectors General are some of the most prominent.

Yet not even the federal government is immune from the impact of Sarbanes-Oxley. In a December 2004 memorandum, *Revisions to OMB Circular No. A-123, Management's Responsibility for Internal Control*, from the Office of Management and Budget (OMB) to the senior managers of federal executive agencies, the OMB defines management's responsibility for internal control in federal agencies. As the memorandum noted:

> *A re-examination of the existing internal control requirements for Federal agencies was initiated in light of the new internal control requirements for publicly-traded companies contained in the Sarbanes-Oxley Act of 2002. . . . [T]he policy changes in this circular are intended to strengthen the requirements for conducting management's assessment of internal control over financial reporting. The circular also emphasizes the need for agencies to integrate and coordinate internal control assessments with other internal control-related activities.*

The Nonprofit Sector

Organizations in the nonprofit sector are increasingly paying significant attention to issues of compliance, ethics, accountability, transparency, and internal controls. The passage of Sarbanes-Oxley and its focus on corporate governance have been a prime catalyst for this movement. While the legislation has only two provisions that directly affect nonprofit organizations, the law's requirements governing directors, auditing, financial control, and auditor provisions are being recommended as best practices.

The adoption of Sarbanes-Oxley best practices can be seen, for instance, in the activities of nonprofit associations and the advice and guidance that they are offering their members. Anticipating greater scrutiny by auditors, state agencies, the IRS, and other regulatory bodies, these associations are calling for greater attention to the issues of corporate governance in their member organizations.

The National Association of College and University Business Officers released a report in 2004, *The Sarbanes-Oxley Act of 2002: Recommendations for Higher Education*, which recommended that organizations in higher education adopt many of the audit and financial control provisions cited in the legislation. Similarly, Independent Sector, a leading organization for charities, foundations, and corporate giving programs, instituted an extensive program for its members dealing with organizational accountability and providing technical assistance in such areas as conflicts of interest, codes of conduct and ethics, audit commit-tees, and financial report certifications.

Enhanced Federal Oversight

In June 2004, the Senate Finance Committee staff released a draft white paper that contained a number of proposals to impose governance requirements similar to those required under Sarbanes-Oxley on the non-profit sector. An organization's tax-exempt status would be conditioned on compliance with these requirements, which include restrictions on governing board compensation, mandatory audits for organizations with over $250,000 in annual revenue, internal control certifications by the organization's CEO, and new governing board roles (audit, oversight, and so on) enforced by federal law.

Shortly thereafter, in January 2005, the Congressional Joint Committee on Taxation released a series of proposals prepared by the Panel on the Nonprofit Sector. Among the proposals was an increase in penalty taxes for misconduct by tax-exempt foundations and charities.

The IRS, which has significant oversight over tax-exempt organiza-tions, also weighed in with compliance-related requirements based on Sarbanes-Oxley. IRS Form 1023, the Section 501(c)(3) tax-exemption application, was revised in October 2004. Organizations must now declare whether or not they have developed and implemented a conflict of interest policy consistent with the IRS model. If an organization has not adopted such a policy, it must explain its reasons for not doing so to the IRS.

Enhanced State Oversight

State governments, such as those of New York and California, have stepped up their regulatory oversight of nonprofit organizations. California, for instance, passed the Nonprofit Integrity Act, which is based on requirements derived from Sarbanes-Oxley. The act became effective on January 1, 2005, and applies to all charities that do business in California, regardless of where the entity is organized. For charities with annual revenues of $2 million or more, exclusive of government contracts, a mandatory outside audit is required. The audit results are to be publicly disclosed. Further, an independent audit committee must hire the auditor and oversee the relationship between the organization and the auditor to ensure that there are no conflicts of interest.

Private-Sector Oversight

Compliance obligations and activities do not emanate only from government mandates. Increasingly, private-sector organizations, both U.S. and international, are playing a significant role in developing and overseeing programs, policies, and standards of behavior that affect organizational compliance. From the New York Stock Exchange to the accounting profession, private-sector organizations (e.g., standards-setting and self-regulatory organizations, credit rating agencies, and developers of industry codes of conduct) are increasingly focusing on legal and regulatory compliance and ethical behavior.

Corporate Social Responsibility

Since the 1970s, there has been an increased focus on corporate behavior and responsibilities. International codes of conduct governing corporate behavior have proliferated. There are now voluntary codes or standards in the European Union, the World Trade Organization, and the Organisation for Economic Co-operation and Development (OECD).

The result is an ever-expanding concept of corporate environmental and social responsibility. These codes identify universal, uniform standards related to conflicts of interest, discrimination, corruption, treatment of employees, and obligations to the community and to stakeholders. The 1990s witnessed expanded attention to corporations' role as "corporate citizens," not only compliant with legal and regulatory obligations, but demonstrating ethical and moral values and making a public commitment to responsibilities and obligations that transcend their financial concerns.

Initiatives such as Caux Roundtable's Principles for Business, the Global Sullivan Principles of Corporate Social Responsibility, and the U.N. Global Compact with Business illustrate this growing trend. By 2007, the U.N. Global Compact, for instance, had more than 3,300 companies from more than 100 countries endorsing its provisions and its commitment to nine principles of human rights, labor, and environmental sustainability.

Shareholders and NGOs

Along with the expanded focus on corporations as good corporate citizens, the recent decade has seen the role, power, and influence of shareholders and nongovernmental organizations increase dramatically in corporate affairs, especially in matters of corporate governance.

The Growing Influence of Institutional Shareholders

Of particular importance has been the growth of large institutional investors and their expanded focus on issues related to corporate governance and corporate behavior. The power, strength, and influence of these large institutional investors cannot be underestimated. According to Bengt Holmstrom and Steven Kaplan's September 2003 report, *The State of U.S. Corporate Governance: What's Right and What's Wrong* (European Corporate Governance Institute), in less than 20 years, from 1980 to 1996, large institutional investors doubled their share of ownership of U.S. corporations from less than 30 percent to more than 50 percent.

As boards of directors have been made more visible and have taken on greater responsibility for governance matters, shareholders have also become more visible and active in matters of corporate governance. While companies' financial performance and value have been, and continue to be, principal concerns, many shareholders have actively engaged corporations and their boards of directors to address issues related to ethics, human rights, investment practices, and board composition and operations.

Indicative of this growing pattern is the 2006 Institutional Shareholders Services' *Global Institutional Investor Study*. This survey, which involved 320 institutional investors in 18 countries with an aggregate of $10.5 trillion in equity assets owned or managed, focused on the growing importance that institutional investors are placing on corporate governance and compliance in the companies in their investment portfolio. According to the survey, 70 percent of these investors said that corporate governance is very important or extremely important to them. As the ISS report stated, "Most institutional investors face rising client expectations to monitor the corporate governance of their portfolio companies, and in some cases, to go beyond proxy voting and to engage companies on their governance practices."

A number of leading investment funds make a direct link between ethical and governance issues as risks and the value they are seeking as investors. State governments, e.g., those of New York, California, and Pennsylvania, with their huge pension investment portfolios, have taken an aggressive role with respect to the behavior of the companies in their portfolios. Reflecting this concern, a group was formed to restore investor confidence through better corporate governance. Led by state treasurers and pension funds, the National Coalition for Corporate Reform was created in 2003. In an article from the September 10, 2003, issue of *Social Funds*, a former New York State comptroller said at the time of the group's creation: "The best way to stop corruption is by instituting policies and structures inside corporations that prevent it or expose it early, by ensuring strong and effective regulation and oversight, and by suing when necessary to recover investors' losses and provide a deterrent."

Similarly, trade unions have taken an aggressive position regarding the corporate governance behavior of companies in their investment portfolios. The AFL-CIO, the largest U.S. trade union federation, publishes an annual "key votes survey" in which it tracks the voting records of fund managers of behalf of its members, whose assets are tied up in over $3 billion of pension fund assets. Key votes include such items as independent boards; international labor standards, including the use of child labor; redemption of, or shareholder voting on, "poison pill" anti-takeover defenses: equal opportunity reporting; and reporting on environmental liabilities.

The California Public Employees' Retirement System (CalPERS), which controls more than $247 billion in investment assets, has decided to introduce basic screening on social and ethical issues. Speaking at the Asia Corporate Governance Roundtable in 2001, California's former state treasurer, Philip Angelides, said that the policy "recognizes the correlation between political stability, human rights, and the long term stability and profitability of our investments."

In fact, CalPERS makes clear its corporate governance philosophy:

> The California Public Employees' Retirement System (known as "CalPERS") has long been a leader in the corporate governance movement. As the largest public retirement system in the U.S., CalPERS' Board of Administration has concluded that "good" corporate governance leads to improved long-term performance. CalPERS' also strongly believes that "good" governance requires the attention and dedication not only of a company's officers and directors, but also its owners. CalPERS is not simply a passive holder of stock. We are a "shareowner," and take seriously the responsibility that comes with company ownership.[6]

Nongovernmental Organizations

The expanding role of stakeholders in organizational concerns has not been limited to financial issues. The past decade has seen a dramatic increase in the number of nongovernmental organizations, sometimes referred to as "private voluntary organizations" or "civil society organizations," playing an increasingly visible role in monitoring organizational behavior. Organizations such as Corporate Watch, Transparency International, Rainforest Action Network, Amnesty International, Clean Clothes Campaign, and CorpWatch are increasingly influencing organizational behavior.

The number of NGOs is staggering. According to James A. Paul in the June 2000 issue of *Global Policy Forum*, some 25,000 organizations qualify as international NGOs (with programs and affiliates in a number of countries)—up from less than 400 a century ago. Amnesty International, for example, which has taken a strong stance on the role of corporate behavior and human rights, has more than a million members and has affiliates or networks in over 90 countries and territories. Its London-based International Secretariat has a staff of over 300 that carries out research, coordinates worldwide lobbying, and maintains an impressive presence at many international conferences and institutions.

Since the late 1990s, relations between NGOs and corporate entities and policy makers have evolved. While violent protests from some NGO organizations still make headlines, the reality is that both parties have entered an era of constructive dialogue. In 1999, thousands protested the policies of the World Trade Organization as it met in Seattle. However, in 2005, NGOs were given the chance to question three candidates for the position of WTO director general. This marked the first time in the organization's 10-year history that activists were allowed to have input in the selection process.[7]

In 2003, representatives of Amnesty International and other groups were invited to address the World Economic Forum in Davos, Switzerland. As Irene Khan, secretary-general of Amnesty International, said at that session: "Thank you for giving me this opportunity to speak to you today at the Public Eye on Davos. This is a very important forum. By its very title, this gathering acts as a reminder to the world leaders attending the World Economic Forum that international civil society is watching them. This community wants action, not words; it wants progress, not pronouncements. And it wants corporate accountability, not public relations."[8]

The effects of NGOs have been wide-ranging. The February 25, 2005, *Los Angeles Times* reported that Greenpeace International had persuaded refrigerator maker Whirlpool Corp. to use environmentally friendly insulation. Under pressure from NGOs, Home Depot Inc. and Lowe's Cos. agreed to stop buying lumber from Canada's environmentally sensitive Great Bear rain forest. Gap Inc. and Nike Inc. have collaborated with labor NGOs to address their manufacturing operations in Asia.

The growing visibility and credibility of NGOs as a force for institutional change can be found in a recent survey. According to the Edelman Trust Barometer,[9] a survey of 1,500 global opinion leaders, NGOs rank as the most trusted institutions in the United States, Europe, Latin America, and much of Asia. The biggest jump was in the United States, where the "trust ratings" of NGOs soared to 55 percent in 2005 from 36 percent in 2001. At the same time, public regard for corporate executives and government officials has diminished. According to the Edelman survey, chief executives and financial officers are viewed as credible sources by only 3 of 10 opinion leaders in the United States, Europe, and Japan.

The Equator Principles. One potent example of the NGOs' impact is the development of the Equator Principles, which were reached between NGOs and financial organizations in 2002. The Equator Principles are a set of voluntary environmental and social guidelines for ethical investment practices. The principles were agreed to by the financial institutions in response to NGO pressure based on the institutions' financing of projects viewed as unsustainable. In an article by Oliver Balch in the July 1, 2006, issue of *The Banker*, when the Equator Principles were first introduced in 2002, 10 banks had agreed to them. By 2006, 41 banks had signed, including most of the world's most powerful investment organizations, such as Citigroup, JPMorgan, HSBC, and Bank of America.

While there is cooperation, there is still skepticism and pragmatism. As Balch reports, one commentator from the banking industry noted, "Contrary to perceptions, bankers are not becoming tree-huggers. Their reasoning is far more down to earth. Banks are increasingly conforming to the view that social and environmental risks pose a threat to long-term shareholder value."

Global Telecommunications and the Internet

Contemporaneously with the increased focus on corporate governance and organizational compliance, a revolution in information and communications technology occurred. In the course of less than two decades, access to an extraordinary depth of information and the speed and ease of communicating with others have significantly influenced the increased focus on compliance issues.

In this era of WiFi, e-mail, instant messages, and laptops that are intrinsically part of our daily lives, it is astounding to note that it was only in 1991 that the first friendly interface to the Internet was developed at the University of Minnesota. Or that Delphi, the first national commercial online service to offer Internet access to its subscribers, first opened up an e-mail connection in July 1992 and added full Internet service in November of that year. It was soon joined by other Internet service providers such as AOL, Prodigy, and CompuServe. The transformation has been staggering. The July 10, 2006, issue of *Fortune* reported that 77 percent of American adults are online, up from 9 percent a decade ago, and that 700 million people are online worldwide.

Never before has such a wealth of information been so readily available. Information on organizational performance, activities, and entanglements can be found by someone sitting at a desk in almost any part of the world. Data that used to take hours, days, or weeks to retrieve can be found within minutes and then shared with others around the world shortly thereafter. The advent of e-mail and the Internet has given organizations the ability to mobilize their constituents swiftly and inexpensively. Moreover, the Internet serves as a unique source of technical information. For instance, one Web site, the NGO Café, offers viewers advice and guidance on the use of the Internet for purposes from information collation, to networking, to collaboration and partnerships.

Beyond its ability to allow access to information and mobilize others, the Internet is empowering individuals to voice their opinions, objections, and ideas to an audience never imaginable previously.

As John Pavlik eloquently stated in his book *New Media Technology: Cultural and Commercial Perspective* (Boston: Allyn and Bacon, 1998), "The internet and other media technologies are empowering members of virtual communities around the globe. They are providing a new electronic age printing press that costs little to operate and reaches audiences of millions in almost instantaneous fashion."

For modern organizations, the implications are daunting. Irate stakeholders, disaffected employees, aggrieved shareholders, and annoyed clients and customers can make their voices heard as never before. Organizations that once could hide behind a wall of secrecy and obfuscation are increasingly exposed.

The implications for corporate governance and organizational compliance practices are enormous. As David Kirkpatrick duly commented in the July 10, 2006, issue of *Fortune*, "Being a big company isn't what it used to be. Consumers and employees are bad-mouthing you on their blogs, tiny outfits on eBay are under pricing you with counterfeit or gray-market products, and competitors are appearing from nowhere and subverting your business model. With the web has come an unnerving and growing transparency." Yet it is this "unnerving and growing transparency" that is transforming modern organizational behavior and the importance of organizational compliance and ethics.

Summary

The focus on compliance in modern organizations is a complex set of forces that transcend a particular series of events or scandals. While these acts of wrongdoing may serve as a catalyst or a rallying point for legislative and regulatory action, there are other broader forces at work (societal, judicial, and technological) that are inexorably forcing our attention to issues of organizational behavior and compliance. Understanding the full spectrum of these forces provides us with a guide to help shape the modern organizational compliance goals, programs, and tools that we will discuss in later chapters.

Notes

1. Senate Committee on the Judiciary, Testimony of Richard Thornburgh, "The WorldCom Case: Looking at Bankruptcy and Competition Issues," *Hearing before the Committee on the Judiciary*, July 22, 2003.
2. Steven Lauer, "Pending Amendments to the Organizational Sentencing Guidelines: Changes in the Wind," Integrity Interactive Corporation, 2004, p. 3.
3. Paula Desio, "An Overview of the Organizational Guidelines," U.S. Sentencing Commission.
4. U.S. Sentencing Commission, 2005 *Federal Sentencing Guidelines, Chapter 8, Part B: Remedying Harm from Criminal Conduct, and Effective Compliance and Ethics Program, §8b2.1. Effective Compliance and Ethics Program*.
5. http://www.epa.gov/compliance/civil/econmodels/index.html.
6. http://www.calpers-governance.org/forumhome.asp.
7. Evelyn Intani, "From the Streets to the Inner Sanctum," *Los Angeles Times*, February 20, 2005.
8. Irene Khan, "Taking Stock: Corporate Social Responsibility and Human Rights," *Public Eye on Davos*, January 24, 2003.
9. Richard Edelman, *Edelman Trust Barometer 2005: The Sixth Global Opinion Leaders Survey*, January 2005. Details of the survey are located at: http://www.pressesprecher.com/media/edelmantrust-barometer2005.pdf#search=%22Edelman%20Trust%20Barometer%22.

2

The Mandate for Compliance

When prophets and comedians talk about the inevitability of "death and taxes," another category that might be added is the bewildering array of regulations, codes, and standards that fuel today's compliance requirements. The maze of regulatory demands imposes an enormous burden on organizations. In 2006, the *U.S. Federal Register,* which is the official U.S. government publication for rules, proposed rules, and notices of federal agencies and organizations, alone had more than 75,000 pages of regulations—and this does not include state and local government regulatory obligations! As a senior compliance officer for a major financial organization once said, the biggest challenge she faced was simply keeping up with the bewildering array of laws and regulations governing her operations.

Beyond the sheer volume of regulations, there are the often overlapping regulatory compliance jurisdictions. A classic example is a January 2007 report by the U.S. Government Accountability Office, *Federal Oversight of Food Safety,* that cited the "fragmented nature" of the federal food oversight system. There are 15 agencies that administer at least 30 laws related to food safety. Two agencies have the principal responsibility for food safety: the Food and Drug Administration (FDA) (food items exclusive of meat and poultry), and the Food Safety and Inspection Service in the Department of Agriculture (USDA) (meat and poultry).

Compounding the federal regulatory compliance burden is the complexity of dealing with state governments. In testimony before a U.S. Senate committee in September 2004, an insurance official, William McCartney, described the situation with respect to the state insurance regulatory system:

> [The] lack of uniformity and inconsistency are hallmarks of the state insurance regulatory system. The mere existence of different state regulators presents a significant problem for any company serving a national and highly mobile population. This problem is compounded by the fact that, even within each jurisdiction, there are often differing systems for different lines of business, making the process incredibly cumbersome and unresponsive to consumer needs. . . . [I]t is illogical to believe that compliance with more than 500 [state] filing and review requirements will lead to efficiency or consistency.

Regulatory compliance also transcends government regulation. Sidney Shapiro, in the November 2003 issue of *Duke Law Journal*, succinctly summarized the situation: "Regulation is not just for bureaucrats anymore. The government has increasingly relied on private means to achieve public ends, not only involving services to the public, but the origination and implementation of public policy as well. . . . Compliance mandates and obligations are increasingly being delegated to private organizations to issue standards of conduct and behavior, some of which have the force of law and others a moral-ethical imperative."

The challenges of regulatory compliance are daunting. Regulatory requirements address every facet of organizational life. They range from the crucial to the absurd, covering areas as varied as health and safety issues, environmental issues, wage and hour regulations, equal employment opportunity, antitrust considerations and competition, data privacy, fund-raising, and even personal hygiene. As to the last, a government office building in Washington, D.C., has posters in the lavatories describing the proper techniques for washing one's hands!

Regulatory Compliance

Regulatory compliance and its enforcement produce an ever-changing environment. They pose significant legal, organizational, and financial challenges for both the regulators and the regulated. For government agency officials, there is the never-ending quest for the most effective and efficient mechanism to ensure that organizations comply with legislative mandates. And for many of the organizations that are subject to these requirements, there is the perpetual quest to meet regulatory burdens despite limited resources, time, experience, and funds. A 2005 federal study, *The Impact of Regulatory Costs on Small Firms*, reported that the "annual cost of federal regulations in the United States increased to more than $1.1 trillion in 2004. Had every household received a bill for an equal share, each would have owed $10,172, an amount that exceeds what the average American household spent on health care in 2004 (slightly under $9,000)."

Regulatory actions are in a constant state of movement. Organizations struggle to understand and manage within this maelstrom of rules and regulations. A former chairman of a global telecommunications corporation ruefully referred to the "universe of regulation" that his organization had to constantly struggle to manage within.

Indeed, as Figure 1 points out, the combined forces of government regulations, voluntary codes, company policies, and self-regulating organizations have placed great pressure on our modern organizations. The mandate for compliance stems from multiple sources.

Like its stellar counterparts, regulation is also forever evolving in form and fashion.

The regulatory approach adopted by many governments, both in the United States and internationally, is a mix of regulatory strategies that dictate the requirements for "compliance." The Organisation for Economic Co-operation and Development (OECD)'s 2000 report on the

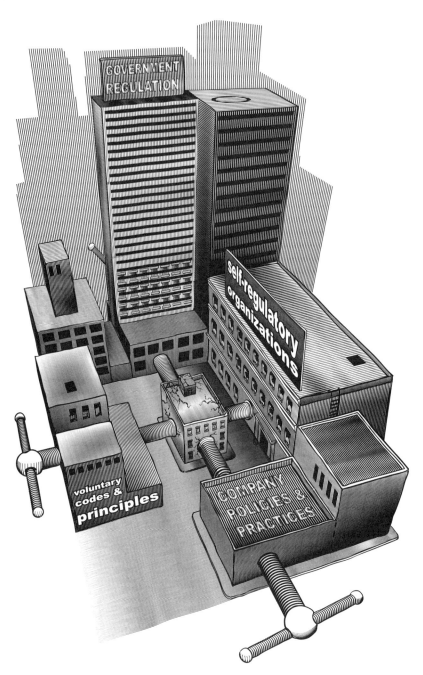

FIGURE 1.   Organizations Pressured by Compliance Mandate

issue, *Reducing the Risk of Policy Failure: Challenges for Regulatory Compliance*, summarized the situation:

> *A central theme of much of the current research on regulation is the idea that in order to understand compliance, we must understand how government regulation interacts with other forms of "regulation" such as self-regulation, internal corporate management and with the actions of other parties such as professional groups (e.g. auditors, lawyers, safety professionals), standards-setting organizations, contractors and industry associations. In particular, scholars are using the concept of "regulatory pluralism" to draw attention to the fact that the state is not the only source of "regulation."*

Self-Regulation

The complex nature of regulation can be seen in the shift from the classic form of regulatory compliance, "command and control," with its rigid standards of behavior, detailed regulatory requirements, and limits on permissible activities, to a more flexible and voluntary approach. In the latter, "responsible" organizations self-regulate, or police their own activities with minimal government oversight (some call it "cooperation-based compliance"), while government agencies use their increasingly limited resources to focus on noncompliers. It should be noted that under a self-regulatory scheme, government regulators still reserve the right to impose legal sanctions against individuals or organizations that violate the law or regulation.

This approach has been adopted by various government agencies ranging from U.S. Customs and Border Protection (its Importer Self-Assessment program allows trade-compliant businesses to have less regulatory oversight) and the U.S. Environmental Protection Agency (EPA) to the U.S. Department of Labor's Occupational Health and Safety Administration (OSHA). OSHA, for instance, introduced its Voluntary Protection Programs (VPP) in 1982 as a means of fostering industry cooperation in workplace safety and health initiatives, and at the same time refocus its regulatory oversight on other high-risk entities.

Eschewing the "1950s Paradigm"

The role of (and need for) self-regulation was illustrated in a series of widely publicized incidents of food contamination that occurred in the United States in 2007. The U.S. Food and Drug Administration acknowledged the need for the food industry to police itself. In an April 23, 2007, article in the *Washington Post*, the head of the FDA's food-safety group said, "We have 60,000 to 80,000 facilities that we're responsible for in any given year." Thus, for food manufacturers, this means that they "have to build safety into their products rather than us [the FDA] chasing after them. . . . [W]e have to get out of the 1950's paradigm."

A number of reasons (political, philosophical, and economic) help to account for the movement toward self-regulation. For instance, the government resources available for policing organizations have substantially decreased. In an August 2003 Urban Institute report, *E-Government and Regulation*, it was stated that between 1980 and 2000, the number of business establishments in the United States grew by 56 percent, from 4.5 million to more than 7 million. Despite this increase, the resources available to the U.S. Department of Labor for inspections declined. The number of wage and hour inspectors declined by 9 percent, and the number of OSHA inspectors declined by 29 percent!

The Federal Trade Commission (FTC) has also expressed strong support for industry self-regulation. In a 1999 report, *Self-Regulation in the Alcohol Industry: A Review of Industry Efforts to Avoid Promoting Alcohol to Underage Consumers*, it lauded the virtues of self-regulation:

> *For decades, the FTC has recognized the important role that effective self-regulation can play and has worked with many industry groups to develop sound self-regulatory initiatives. These programs complement the Commission's law enforcement efforts to stop "unfair or deceptive acts or practices." The net effect is greater consumer protection in the marketplace.*
>
> *Well-constructed industry self-regulatory efforts offer several advantages over government regulation or legislation. Self-regulation often can be more prompt, flexible, and effective than*

*government regulation. It can permit application of the accumu-
lated judgment and experience of an industry to issues that are
sometimes difficult for the government to define with bright line
rules. With respect to advertising practices, self-regulation is an
appropriate mechanism because many forms of government inter-
vention raise First Amendment concerns.*

Self-regulation has not been without its detractors. Critics fear that
the regulatory process may be co-opted by the businesses or organizations
that are the subjects of regulation. Other fears include weaker enforcement
when violations of law and practice occur, and that self-regulatory bodies
do have not the power or authority to command compliance that government agencies possess. There is also the "regulatory paradox." According to
this theory, if membership in the self-regulating organization is not mandatory, it may not be able to control risks, such as compliance violations,
because the violators are likely to be found disproportionately among non-
members. The regulatory paradox is that those who are regulated tend to
be those "responsible" parties that are least in need of regulation.

Internal Corporate Compliance Systems

A classic example of self-regulation has been the growth of internal
corporate compliance systems. The rise of internal compliance systems is
attributed to the Federal Sentencing Guidelines for Organizations.

Federal Sentencing Guidelines for Organizations

As discussed earlier, under the Federal Sentencing Guidelines for
Organizations (FSGO), organizations can reduce their "culpability
score" by having organizational programs in place to prevent and detect
noncompliance and by self-reporting of violations, cooperation with the
regulators, and acceptance of responsibility. These culpability factors can
be further mitigated by an organization's having an effective internal

compliance program. The FSGO prescribe seven key components for an effective compliance program:

1. Organizations must establish compliance standards and procedures to be followed by employees and agents of the organization.
2. The program must be administered and overseen by "high-level" personnel within the organization.
3. Organizations must ensure that substantial discretionary authority is not delegated to employees with a propensity toward criminal conduct.
4. Organizations must provide training programs and effective communications about their compliance standards and procedures.
5. Monitoring and auditing systems must be implemented, and a reporting system must be established through which employees can report wrongdoing without fear of retribution (e.g., whistle-blowing programs).
6. Organizations must provide incentives for employees and others to come forward to report issues and must establish disciplinary policies for those involved in wrongdoing.
7. After an offense has been reported, organizations must take reasonable measures to respond and prevent future incidents from occurring.

These seven elements form the basis for organizational compliance programs in the United States. They have been the mantra for compliance professionals, who can recite the seven steps with the same ease as they can recite their favorite sport teams' statistics. The November 2004 amendments to the Federal Sentencing Guidelines for Organizations added another level of complexity for internal compliance programs. As previously mentioned, the amendments expanded upon what organizations must do to have their compliance programs viewed as effective by the courts. These included a focus on ethics and culture in organizations, a redefining of the role and responsibilities of the organization's senior management in the compliance process and program, and an expanded view of understanding and managing compliance risk.

The Private Sector and Organizational Compliance

As the OECD noted, compliance obligations and activities are no longer solely the province of government actions. Private-sector organizations are playing an increasingly significant role in developing and overseeing programs, policies, and standards of behavior that affect organizational compliance. This section examines several examples of private-sector actions: self-regulating organizations, standards-setting organizations, credit rating agencies, and voluntary industry codes and the role they play in compliance.

Self-Regulating Organizations

In keeping with the precepts of self-regulation, self-regulating organizations (SROs) play a critical role in the structure of legal regulatory compliance and are a feature of a number of professions, including accounting, medicine, and the law. The government delegates considerable authority to SROs to design rules and regulations governing their members' practices, including disciplinary practices, licensing requirements, and certifications.

In the U.S. financial services industry, for instance, the Securities and Exchange Commission (SEC), which has primary responsibility for regulating the securities markets, delegates significant authority to such SROs as the New York Stock Exchange (NYSE), the Financial Industry Regulatory Authority, Inc. (which combines the former NASD and the regulatory functions of the New York Stock Exchange), and regional stock and option exchanges.

New York Stock Exchange Regulations. One of the most dramatic examples of an enhanced compliance obligation issued by a SRO is the 2003 governance and compliance regulations, *Final NYSE Corporate Governance Rules,* issued by the New York Stock Exchange for its listed companies. In some respects, these rules are more stringent than Sarbanes-Oxley.

NYSE-listed companies are required to have boards with a majority of independent directors; and the boards' audit, compensation, and nominating committees are required to be composed solely of independent directors. Additionally, the criteria for independence under the NYSE standards are stricter than those under Sarbanes-Oxley. Former employees of the company or of the company's independent auditor, and their family members, are not considered independent until five years after their employment ends.

Financial Industry Regulatory Authority (formerly the NASD). The Financial Industry Regulatory Authority, which regulates broker-dealers in the United States, also issued enhanced corporate governance standards in 2003. As Valentine V. Craig noted in the 2005 *FDIC Banking Review*, the NASD required listed members to have a majority of independent directors, a code of conduct for all directors and employees, and the approval of stockholders for the adoption of all stock option plans and for any material modification of such plans. As with the NYSE standards, audit committee members may receive no compensation other than their board compensation.

Joint Commission on Health Care and Accreditation of Health Organizations. Just as the SEC relies on self-regulation by stock exchanges and the Financial Industry Regulatory Authority, the U.S. Health Care Finance Administration uses an independent, nonprofit organization, the Joint Commission on Health Care and Accreditation of Health Organizations (JCAHO) to accredit hospitals for participation in Medicare and Medicaid. JCAHO evaluates and accredits nearly 15,000 health-care organizations and programs in the United States.

The National Advertising Division of the Council of Better Business Bureaus. The U.S. Federal Trade Commission lauds the National Advertising Division (NAD) of the Council of Better Business Bureaus as an "especially effective model of self-regulation that has stood the test of time." Started in

1971, the NAD investigates complaints by consumers or competitors about the truthfulness of advertising. An advertiser that disagrees with the NAD's conclusion may appeal to the National Advertising Review Board (NARB), which includes members from both inside and outside the industry.

Chemical Manufacturers Association's "Responsible Care" Program. The Responsible Care program is a voluntary program for reducing chemical hazards. It was started in 1985 by the Canadian Chemical Producers Association after the horrific Bhopal, India, chemical leak. The program was designed to improve the industry's environmental and safety performance. The U.S. Chemical Manufacturers Association (CMA) adopted a similar program in 1989. Participants in the CMA's Responsible Care program agree to adhere to a set of guiding principles.

Standards-Setting Organizations

The past decade has seen a growth in the importance of private organizations, both U.S. and international, that promulgate industry standards and practices. A number of these organizations have been active in developing standards that are increasingly playing a key role in compliance management functions. Sidney Shapiro, in his November 2003 *Duke Law Journal* article, noted that in 1988, "The Occupational Safety and Health Administration (OSHA) adopted 428 new protective health standards; most of the new regulations were adoptions of national consensus standards written by the American Conference of Governmental and Industrial Hygienists (ACGIH)."

This practice has become so ingrained in regulatory administration that in 1995 Congress passed the National Technology Transfer and Advancement Act, which requires federal agencies to adopt private-sector standards wherever possible, in lieu of creating proprietary, nonconsensus standards.

Internal Control Framework. In recent years, increased attention, as witnessed by the passage of Sarbanes-Oxley, has been devoted to internal control by auditors, managers, accountants, and legislators. A number of initiatives have been instituted to define, assess, report on, and improve internal controls. One of the best known of these initiatives is the internal control framework developed by the Committee of Sponsoring Organizations of the Treadway Commission (COSO) in the early 1990s. COSO is a voluntary, private, non-profit organization. It was formed by several professional groups, including the Institute of Internal Auditors (IIA), Financial Executives Institute (FEI), American Institute of Certified Public Accountants (AICPA), American Accounting Association (AAA), and Institute of Management Accountants (IMA).

The COSO framework defines internal control, describes its components, and provides criteria against which control systems can be evaluated. It offers guidance for public reporting on internal control and provides materials that management, auditors, and others can use to evaluate an internal control system. Two major goals of the framework are to (1) establish a common definition of internal control that serves many different parties, and (2) provide a standard against which organizations can assess their control systems and determine how to improve them.

COSO and Risk Management. The linkage of compliance and risk management has become increasingly important. The November 2004 Amendments to the Federal Sentencing Guidelines for Organizations, for instance, place great importance on an organization's identifying its compliance risks as a preemptive measure to combat violations of law and ethics. The convergence of compliance and risk has been reflected not only in the organizational structure of compliance operations (e.g., the shifting of compliance offices and staff to a corporation's risk management organization), but in the recognition that legal regulatory compliance is one of the key risks facing an organization.

Strategies to manage risk are becoming of paramount interest. In the fall of 2004, COSO released its *Enterprise Risk Management—Integrated Framework* (ERM Framework), prepared by the consulting organization of PricewaterhouseCoopers. The framework provides direction and criteria for improving an organization's ability to assess and manage risk.

Federal Reserve Board Governor Susan Schmidt Bies was quite succinct in her views on the integration of compliance and risk. In a February

4, 2004, speech to the Bond Market Association, she said, "A strong compliance program is an integral part of the risk-management function. . . . [W]e are overdue for a paradigm shift to an enterprise-wide compliance structure as we also shift to enterprise-wide risk management."

The International Organization for Standardization. The International Organization for Standardization (ISO) is a global federation of national standards bodies created to set standards for similar technologies in different countries. Two of its standards—ISO 9000, which deals with quality management, and ISO 14000, which deals with environment management—are probably the best known. The ISO program is voluntary.

Companies wishing ISO compliance certification go through an extensive process. They must be able to fully document each process, control, management responsibility, and systems specification. For example, in complying with quality management standards, companies must be able to demonstrate their ability to identify customer requirements, needs, and expectations; determine customer satisfaction; establish procedures for customer communication; and make employees aware of the importance of meeting customer requirements.

ISO certification is playing an increasingly important role in compliance operations, especially for environmental organizations. There has been a trend toward the government's offering incentives to businesses that self-regulate their regulatory compliance and promptly report and correct violations. The U.S. Environmental Protection Agency, for instance, has more than 40 voluntary programs. Many of these programs require organizations to establish environmental management systems and to self-police their environmental performance. Companies are considered to be in compliance with government regulations if they follow specific program guidelines. One self-policing program that satisfies EPA requirements is ISO 14001,[1] which by 2000 had more than 1,200 certified facilities in the United States.

The Basel Committee on Banking Supervision. Another example of a global standards-setting organization and its growing impact on compliance management has been the Basel Committee on Banking

Supervision (the Basel Committee). The Basel Committee was established in 1974 by the central bank governors of the Group of Ten countries. The committee's members include Belgium, Canada, France, Germany, Italy, Japan, the Netherlands, Sweden, Switzerland, the United Kingdom, the United States, Luxembourg, and Spain. It plays a critical role in setting standards in banking regulation.

In April 2005, the Basel Committee issued an extraordinary high-level paper, *Compliance and the Compliance Function in Banks*. In this document, the Basel Committee outlines the requirements for a compliance function in members' banking organizations. It requires that banking supervisors be satisfied that effective compliance policies and procedures are being followed and that management takes appropriate corrective action when compliance failures are identified.

Credit Rating Agencies

Credit rating agencies exert enormous influence in their role of assessing the creditworthiness of organizations in the public, private, and nonprofit sectors. The passage of Sarbanes-Oxley and its focus on internal control will have a significant impact on credit rating agencies' assessment of organizations' operations. This fact was reflected in a January 2005 report issued by Fitch Ratings, *Sarbanes-Oxley Section 404: Fitch's Approach to Evaluating Management and Auditor Assessments of Internal Controls*. Fitch states that the implementation of Section 404 requirements is likely to cause internal control problems to surface more frequently than in the past. As noted earlier, Section 404 requires management and its auditors to express an opinion on the adequacy of controls over financial reporting and disclosure. Should a weakness be disclosed or a new weakness identified, negative rating actions may occur if the disclosure and/or further discussion with management either reveals it to have a significant effect on a company's future financial standing or calls into question the data on which analysis has been based.

Voluntary Industry Codes

Another permutation of self-regulation has been the proliferation of voluntary codes of organizational conduct. From the International

Bottled Water Association and the American Sheep Industry Association to the U.S. Apparel Industry, codes of conduct have become a fixture of organizational compliance. In many respects, voluntary codes perform functions similar to those of government regulations. A March 2000 Canadian Office of Consumer Affairs report, *An Evaluative Framework for Voluntary Codes*, explains that codes are "designed to influence, shape, control, or benchmark behavior. Codes are unlike regulations in that they are not rules directly backed by the power of the state."

The Canadian report went on to describe the enormous breath and scope of voluntary codes:

> *Voluntary codes may be developed with or without any direct gov-*
> *ernment supervision or active encouragement. Codes may consti-*
> *tute agreements among industry or NGO [nongovernmental*
> *organization] members (or employees in a firm), which may be*
> *embodied in contracts, and commit parties to adhere to the terms*
> *of the code. Sanctions or other consequences may be provided for*
> *breach of the code, and mechanisms may also be included to deal*
> *with disputes or noncompliance, such as mediation or independ-*
> *ent third-party arbitration. There may even be provisions for inde-*
> *pendent auditors, competitors, community representatives, and*
> *members of civil society organizations to aid in code enforcement.*

Legal/Compliance Context. From a compliance perspective, it is important to note that voluntary codes exist within a broad legal context that includes statutes, regulations, guidelines, and enforcement and compliance policies. They are not without legal consequences for an organization. As the Canadian report just cited says, voluntary codes can be seen as "adjuncts to existing legal schemes, as substitutes for laws, or as a source of interstitial detail in a legal regime. The existence and content of a code can have legal implications, particularly in defining such concepts as 'due diligence' (the customary or expected behavior in an industry)."

Proponents of voluntary codes cite them as an effective alternative to government regulation in that they provide greater flexibility, recognize that achieving a desired state can be reached via many different practices

> **BOX 2.1 Alternative Approaches to Regulatory Compliance: Principle vs. Rule**
>
> A source of considerable discussion is the difference in regulatory philosophy (and its consequences for compliance) between the United States and other countries. In brief, this discussion centers on the view that the United States has a "rules-based" regulatory structure that imposes significant compliance obligations on organizations, as opposed to a "principles-based" compliance strategy, frequently used in Europe and the UK, in which organizations are given greater latitude to comply with regulations.
>
> This difference was aptly expressed by Alexander Schaub, director general, Internal Market, EU Commission, in a 2004 speech:
>
> > *The European approach to these challenges is to some extent substantially different to the one followed in the United States: it is a matter of 'comply or explain' versus law enforcement; principle versus rule based; bottom up versus top down. Concepts such as flexibility, subsidiarity, proportionality, mutual recognition and home country control are common language in an EU regulatory environment but somewhat alien in a US environment. Any idea to design a 'one size fits all' approach to corporate governance problems is rejected by market participants.*

or structures, produce the same (or more) protection at lower costs, and are less intrusive than traditional regulation. See Box 2.1.

While proponents of voluntary codes extol their virtues, critics cite their limitations. Principally, these focus on the monitoring and enforcement of voluntary codes. For instance, who audits and reports on the organizations' (and their suppliers') compliance with the code? What are the consequences and sanctions for noncompliance with the code? How are issues resolved with respect to violations (alleged or real) of the code?

Self-Regulation and Its Implications for Organizational Management

While self-regulation offers organizations enhanced latitude in their operations and freedom from burdensome regulations, it is not without organizational duties and responsibilities to ensure compliance. Explicit in the concept of self-regulation is the expectation that the organization and its leadership will devote the time and resources to address its compliance obligations.

A Commitment to Compliance and Ethics. It is incumbent upon the organization's leadership (e.g., the board of directors, the CEO, and senior management staff) to make a significant commitment to compliance and ethics that includes the allocation of resources (funds, staff, and time) to develop and maintain an effective compliance program.

Developing the Specialized Skills and Knowledge for Compliance Management. The organization needs to acquire and/or develop the staff needed to manage an effective compliance and ethics program and to address compliance issues. It may need to set up a specific compliance staff and/or dedicate current employees to this function and responsibility. It must empower the board, senior management, and compliance staff to address compliance issues on a routine basis, developing policies and procedures to identify and address compliance issues, and clearly defining an individual who has ultimate responsibility for the organization's compliance program.

The Institutionalization of Compliance. Ultimately, an organization has to make a commitment, in the words of Christine Parker in the 2004 *Australian Institute of Criminology Research and Public Policy Series*, that "The policy of detecting, preventing and correcting non-compliance is made an integral part of corporate objectives." This ranges from developing an organizational code of conduct (and setting up the necessary policies and procedures to enforce it) to training and communicating with employees on compliance-related issues, undertaking a comprehensive and regular program of risk assessment, and ensuring that the organization's compensation and reward systems recognize compliance and ethical behaviors.

The Nonprofit Sector

Like their brethren in the private sector, organizations in the nonprofit sector are increasingly paying significant attention to the issues of compliance, accountability, transparency, and internal controls. In light of the nonprofit scandals outlined in Chapter 1, federal, state, and local regulatory requirements and private funding agencies are demanding that nonprofit organizations accept greater accountability for their operations.

Self-Regulation and Compliance

Being cognizant of these issues (and wary of increased government regulation), many nonprofit organizations have increasingly adopted self-regulation of their operations. The Panel on the Nonprofit Sector, which was created in 2004 to bring changes in nonprofit governance, said in its *Draft Principles for Effective Practice*:

> *While well-crafted, well-enforced laws and regulations are crucial to protecting charitable organizations from individuals who deliberately use them for personal profit, a strong system of self regulation and education is critical to enable the people making up the nonprofit community—boards, staff, volunteers, and donors—to ensure that their organizations are living by the highest ethical standards.*

The growth of the self-regulation movement comes at a time when government oversight organizations simply do not have the resources to examine every nonprofit organization intensively. Susan Berresford, an expert on foundations, noted this concern in a 2004 speech, "Public Obligations of Foundations." She said, "At the core of the compliance issue are the minority of foundations that operate improperly. Some do so from disrespect for the law, and others hold to a mistaken belief that the money is 'ours to do with however we wish.' Finding and changing behavior of these scofflaws will be tough, given the currently limited resources of the IRS and State Attorneys Generals' charities bureaus."

Berresford's concerns about limited government resources were reinforced in a March/April 2005 *Foundation News & Commentary* article on self-regulation in private foundations.

> *Unfortunately, this ratcheting back of private foundation audits coincided with unprecedented growth in the number of foundations and in the assets they hold. The field grew from more than*

21,000 foundations in 1975, holding $30 billion in assets, to more than 64,000 foundations with $435 billion in assets (as adjusted for inflation) in 2002. At the same time, the number of private foundation audits by the IRS declined to about 60 or 65.

As in the private sector, compliance self-regulation in the nonprofit sector has come in two general forms: self-regulatory organizations and standards-setting organizations.

Self-Regulatory Organizations

Nonprofit organizations have created a multitude of self-regulatory organizations that oversee member organizations' compliance and have the authority to bring sanctions against organizations that fail to comply. Classic examples range from the National Collegiate Athletic Association (NCAA) to nursing homes to institutions of higher education. Although the specific requirements vary by field of service and by state, the organizations in these fields must meet well-defined standards in order to receive insurance coverage, recognition of degrees conferred, access to government funding, and other benefits required for successful operation. Failure to meet these standards will result in substantial penalties, which can even include being prohibited from operating.

Standards-Setting Organizations

Two major initiatives within the nonprofit community encourage accountability. First are the so-called watchdog groups, or those committed to increased transparency that provide information to the public about whether or not a charitable organization meets certain standards. Included in this group are such groups as the American Institute of Philanthropy (AIP) and the BBB Wise Giving Alliance. These groups cannot impose sanctions directly, but they are influential if their ratings affect the giving decisions of the public.

Second, there are programs that improve ethics within the nonprofit community through training and education. Some of the organizations offering instruction focus exclusively on a discrete area, such as board governance or fund-raising practices, while others have a broader mandate to assist with a range of issues. The use of these groups' resources is purely voluntary. Independent Sector, a leading organization for charities, foundations, and corporate giving programs, has instituted an extensive program dealing with organizational accountability for its members, providing technical assistance in such areas as conflicts of interest, codes of conduct and ethics, audit committees, and financial report certifications.

The Public Sector

The traditional focus of compliance for public-sector organizations has been the use of financial and internal controls to ensure that organizations and programs are operating within their legal, financial, and policy responsibilities and achieving the objectives set for them (see Chapter 10 for more information on internal controls). The "compliance audit" has been a key tool for judging whether a particular program was in compliance with the U.S. Code, Code of Federal Regulations, OMB regulations, state law, and so on. However, even the public sector is undergoing changes. As the Organisation for Economic Co-operation and Development pointed out in its 2005 *Policy Brief,* "In the past two decades, new forms of public sector management, privatization and new technologies have changed the way the public sector operates, but have also created a need for new ways of making both agencies and governments accountable for what they do."

Public agencies are simultaneously responsible for establishing and enforcing regulatory standards for both external and internal spheres of responsibilities. As an organizational body with employees, physical facilities, budgets, programs, and services to administer, a government organization and its agents must adhere to certain legal and ethical standards of behavior. Whether an organization is administering a correctional facility in Arizona, providing environmental services to a tribal government in Minnesota, operating a remedial education program in Vermont, or reconstructing the front steps of a federal building in Washington, D.C., issues of accountability, ethics, internal controls, compliance, and transparency in operations and administration are increasingly of paramount concern to government agencies at all levels of government. Indeed, units of local government are subject to many of the same laws and regulations as both private and nonprofit organizations. For instance, the Americans with Disabilities Act, the Fair Labor Standards Act, the Family Medical Leave Act, and Title VII of the Civil Rights Act of 1964 are applicable to all employees, regardless of sector.

The need for government agencies to assure accountable, compliant, and ethical behavior within their own organizations has fostered a network of public-sector compliance-related functions. It is not surprising to find a Department of Reporting and Regulatory Accountability in a county public school district in Maryland that focuses on compliance with federal, state, and local laws, or an Office of Compliance in Atlanta, or the maze of state auditors, attorneys general, inspectors general, and legislative bodies that investigate, enforce, and oversee federal, state, and local operations. In 1995, Congress created the Office of Compliance, which oversees the applicability of 12 civil rights, labor, and workplace safety laws to the employees of the U.S. Congress and certain congressional agencies, e.g., the Library of Congress.

Privatization and Compliance

The privatization of government operations has witnessed an enormous growth. It was reported in the February 4, 2007, *New York Times* that the U.S. government spent approximately $400 billion on federal contracts in 2006, as compared to $207 billion in 2000. Moreover, this figure does not include contract services used at the state and local levels of government. Not only are private agents and contractors setting standards for government regulation, but they are also increasingly involved in the provision of government services and assuming compliance oversight responsibilities— duties traditionally performed by government employees. For example, the U.S. Department of Health and Human Services uses private insurance companies to screen Medicare and Medicaid reimbursement claims from medical providers, and the U.S. General Services Administration employs private contractors to investigate cases of possible fraud by other federal contractors.

The growth of privatization has raised a number of concerns about compliance and accountability. For instance, concerns have been expressed about the lack of public scrutiny of contractors' actions, which are often protected by privacy laws. As the *New York Times* article just cited reported, "Members of Congress have sought unsuccessfully for two years to get the Army to explain the contracts for Blackwater USA security officers in Iraq, which involved several costly layers of subcontractors."

Summary

The complex and massive weight of legal and regulatory requirements, combined with an increased requirement that organizations assume greater responsibility for their own compliance oversight, has created an enormous compliance burden for organizations. The challenge for organizations is not only to develop the structure and resources to manage these responsibilities effectively, but, equally important, to provide an organizational culture that supports compliance and ethics.

Notes

1. An ISO 14001 environmental management system is meant to develop a systematic management approach to the environmental concerns of an organization. The goal of this approach is continual improvement in environmental management.

PART II

THE FOUNDATIONS OF COMPLIANCE

3

Compliance and Ethics: Challenges and Approaches

As we have seen, the road to compliance is often not easy. The challenges of compliance, both individually and organizationally, involve a complex set of psychological, cultural, legal, policy, economic, organizational, and ethical considerations. Compliance is a complex topic. It involves multiple layers of nuance and understanding. A 2000 report by the London School of Economics and Political Science, *Risk Regulation, Management and Compliance*, commented:

> *It is important to distinguish between the compliance of the organization and the compliance of individuals within the organization. There is no straightforward explanation of compliance. Organizations and individuals vary in their abilities and motivations to comply and they differ over time and across issues. Moreover it needs to be understood that compliance varies between organizations and also within organizations.*

The issue of individual and organizational compliance was illustrated in the case of the Washington, D.C.–based Riggs Bank. In 2005, the bank

pleaded guilty to charges of failing to report suspicious money transactions by the former Chilean president, Augusto Pinochet, among others.
Addressing the issue in the March 21, 2005, *Washington Post*, Jeffrey A.
Sonnenfeld of the Yale School of Management noted that the bank's failure "appears to be linked to a culture and environment where multiple
people dissociated their own ethics from their conduct, whether out of
fear of being perceived as not a team player or some other reason."
Sonnenfeld went on to say: "There's a deeper, darker set of issues in these
breakdowns. People know right from wrong. You don't need morals training
to know what you're doing is wrong. There's often a group-think mentality
where the notion of diffusion of responsibility sets in. . . where it becomes
impossible to consider alternatives or voice dissent."

Intertwined but Not Interchangeable Concepts

Ethics and compliance are intertwined but not interchangeable
concepts. The importance of the two concepts is reflected in the 2004
Amendments to the Federal Sentencing Guidelines for Organizations,
which restated and broadened the guidelines' standards from criteria
for "effective compliance programs" to criteria for "effective compliance
and ethics programs," recognizing the crucial role that ethics plays in
managing organizational behavior. Indeed, an organization's practices
and behaviors reflect its culture, values, ethics, and morality. Its philosophy and actions reflect how the entity responds to its compliance
responsibilities.

Compliance generally refers to the organization's adherence to the
laws, rules, regulations, standards, and codes of conduct that govern its
behavior. Ethics refers to the organization's values and moral standards.
It addresses and defines the issues of integrity, respect, diversity, and quality
in an organization. Values and ethics shape the organization's image and
reputation in the minds of its external and internal stakeholders.
Moreover, ethical failures can have a devastating impact on any organization,
ranging from loss of reputation to employee morale issues, enhanced
government oversight, impaired client relations, and, of course, potential
legal and civil sanctions.

Motivations for Compliance

Understanding the motivations for individual and organizational compliance helps to put the changes in regulatory compliance strategy into context. It also aids the organization's policy makers and decision makers in developing effective policies and strategies.

The Traditional Deterrence Approach

The deterrence approach assumes that organizations will do "the right thing" only to the extent that it is in their self-interest to do so. This has been the basis for the command-and-control regulatory approach. The Organisation for Economic Co-operation and Development (OECD) report on regulatory compliance noted that some theorists believe:

> *that since all corporations have profit-maximization as their main goal, they will always be "amoral calculators" who only ever comply with regulatory requirements when the penalties are heavy enough to ensure their calculations come up with the correct answer. . . . On the whole the assumption is that deterrence motivates via fear of punishment or rational calculations of the potential cost of penalties or sanctions.*

Given this rather rigid and pessimistic belief concerning the behavior of organizations and individuals, it is not surprising that the uncompromising command-and-control style of regulatory control would be a natural strategy for managing compliance. While the deterrence approach has had some attraction as a motivational theory, researchers have discounted it as the primary reason in favor of a more eclectic and sophisticated understanding of how deterrence and compliance work.

An Eclectic Understanding

As an alternative to the traditional deterrence theory, it is useful to examine a complex set of factors, both negative and positive, that influence organizational motivations for compliance.

The Effects of Negative Publicity. Reputation is everything. The risk of damaging or destroying an organization's reputation is a significant motivating factor. As the OECD study noted, "[A] series of studies have found that maintaining or advancing the corporate reputation and counteracting negative publicity is an important reason for enterprise interest in ensuring compliance." Jane Wexton, a noted lawyer and authority on compliance, has emphasized the crucial role that reputation plays in maintaining compliance: "The larger the 'logo,' the more valuable the reputation."

Self-Interest. Organizations want to protect themselves from the consequences (both direct and indirect) of being found in violation of regulatory requirements, e.g., government sanctions (fine, criminal sanction, imprisonment, or disbarment), private lawsuits, increased insurance premiums, and increased employee discontent.

Corporate and Individual Responsibility. The concept of organizational corporate responsibility can be viewed from a moral perspective: "doing the right thing." Organizations and individuals have moral principles and feel a sense of moral obligation to comply with the spirit as well as the letter of the law and regulation. This point was illustrated by an encounter that the author had with a clergyman years ago in rural Vermont. In his discussion with the clergyman, he described the efforts that he and his colleagues went through, even as employees of major multinational corporations, in trying to develop policy that was the "right thing." The clergyman was so shocked that he invited the author to address his congregation on the topic.

Cooperation and Trust. The concepts of cooperation and trust are critical to the relationship between regulators and those subject to regulation (the regulatees) in achieving compliance. "Trust between regulator and regulatee simultaneously builds efficiency and improves the prospect of compliance," the OECD notes. "If regulatees trust regulators as fair umpires who administer and enforce laws or regulations that have important substantive objectives, then the evidence is that compliance will be higher, and resistance and challenges to regulatory action will be low. If regulatees feel that regulators treat them as untrustworthy, then defiance and resistance build up so that inefficiency and non-compliance both increase."

Enforcement. The relationship between those who regulate and those who must comply, as noted previously, has been the subject of considerable research. Researchers have focused on the frequency of inspections, the willingness to impose sanctions, and even the style of the regulators. As to the latter, Peter May, a sociologist who has studied compliance motivations, wrote in *Law & Society Review* in 2004, "The relevant consideration is more one of the character of interactions [between the regulator and regulatee] rather than the thoroughness of inspection. That is, a thorough inspector who is friendly and facilitative will be perceived differently than a thorough inspector who is formal and gruff. As such, the enforcement style of an inspector is expected to be the more relevant consideration for influencing affirmative motivations than are the actions of the inspector."

Similarly, consistency and predictability play an important role in compliance. As May writes, "Consistent interpretations of rules and actions foster a sense of fairness in the application of regulations that contributes to the affirmative dimension of compliance motivations."

Barriers to Compliance

The noted Australian regulatory theorist John Braithwaite wrote eloquently in a 1993 paper, *Improving Regulatory Compliance*, that "regulations are the sinews of modern government, the legal instruments that connect abstract government policies with the day-to-day activities of commerce and private life." When these sinews are weakened or broken, significant problems arise.

This section examines some of the reasons why organizations and individuals do not comply with regulations. This analysis is based in part on the work undertaken by Braithwaite for the OECD. While Braithwaite's work was principally focused on government regulatory actions, its lessons transcend organizational sectors and offer significant insight into the elements that impinge upon the development of effective compliance policy and procedures. Understanding these reasons for noncompliance, along with what motivates people to comply with law and regulation, can help compliance policy makers more effectively apply practical solutions to developing compliance policies and programs. Research has shown that organizations and individuals fail to comply for various reasons: cost of regulatory compliance, insufficient resources and expertise to address compliance requirements, lack of knowledge of requirements, or even indifference. Three other factors also pose significant obstacles to compliance.

Organizational Structure and Complexity

Organizations are increasingly complex institutions that present a unique set of compliance challenges. Consider, for instance, a modern global institution, created out of multiple mergers or acquisitions, that operates in different locations with diverse product and/or service lines. Such an entity confronts varying cultures and values (e.g., something that is considered a conflict of interest in one region or country may be viewed as a traditional way of doing business in another), different histories and relationships with regulators, variations in organizational structures and patterns of decision making, and differing views about and appetites for risk. All these factors will influence an organization's values and attitudes toward compliance.

Failure to Understand the Law

In the words of the OECD, "To improve compliance with the law, the business community must first understand the law. This is a deeply underestimated source of non-compliance." People cannot comply with laws and regulations if they do not understand what is required of them or even know that such requirements exist in the first place. Even with the reduction in regulatory staff, "regulatory inflation" has become a hallmark of the U.S. system. The sheer volume and complexity of federal rules, regulations, and standards in such areas as the environment, taxes, and securities can be overwhelming. For instance, in testimony before the House Budget Committee on February 16, 2007, Chris Edwards cited the enormous complexity of the U.S. tax code. "The number of pages of federal tax law and regulations has increased from 40,500 in 1995 to 66,498 by 2006," he said. With an increase in the complexity and volume of regulation comes the risk of and the potential for compliance failures.

Collapse of Belief in Law

Compliance requires that organizations and individuals who are asked to comply with laws and regulations also believe in those laws. Compliance entails belief both in the detailed rules that constitute the laws and regulations and in the policy objectives that lie behind them. As the OECD points out, "When business actors reject the policy objectives lying behind the law but accept the rules that are intended to secure those objectives, disastrous results are likely. A truck driver who takes the rest breaks required in the law but who believes he can drive well after all-night parties is a risk."

The Organization's Cultural Framework

While issues related to the management (or lack thereof) of the rules and regulations governing organizational behavior are critical, the reality is that organizations face challenges that transcend compliance with a particular rule. The egregious corporate actions of the past decade became a siren call for action, reform, and introspection. Despite codes of conduct, compliance officers, and compliance programs, the scope and depth of organizational wrongdoing were staggering. Clearly, new directions were needed. These included not only greatly enhanced accountability and transparency in organizational behaviors, but, equally important, a focus on ethics and corporate culture as part of a compliance initiative.

The Advisory Committee's 2004 recommendations for the Federal Sentencing Guidelines for Organizations reflected this need for an

BOX 3.1   Organizational Culture and the Courts

A judge's ruling in a 1995 court case involving Con Edison, the New York City public utility for electricity, dramatically illustrates the impact that an organization's culture can have on the outcome of a court case. As reported in the 1996 *Food and Drug Law Journal,* the judge sentenced the company to the maximum fine allowable and placed it on probation for three years following its conviction for concealing for eight days the fact that a manhole explosion had released more than 200 pounds of asbestos into the air. The judge said:

> One of the things I found disturbing here was the sense that there were people at Con Edison, who testified at the trial, who clearly knew and who should have been jumping up and down saying there is asbestos there, we know it. It was obvious they didn't say it because they were intimidated from saying it, because they didn't think that was the corporate culture; and that was not the corporate culture that came across to me in this trial. It is fair to say that I was concerned about the degree of candor of some of the people who testified. I am not accusing anybody of testifying falsely, but certainly they weren't testifying openly. So I do think there was a sense here, at certain levels within this company that you had better not tell the bad news.

emphasis on organizational culture. The amended guidelines read, "To have an effective program to prevent and detect violations of law. . . an organization shall. . . promote an organizational culture that encourages a commitment to compliance with the law" (§8B21(a)). An interesting example of organizational culture and its impact on employee behavior can be seen in a judge's ruling found in Box 3.1.

What are the organization's values, beliefs, attitudes, policies, and practices that form the bases for an effective and efficient compliance and ethics program? A lawyer and compliance consultant, Rick Wolf, has called compliance "a window into the soul of the organization." It is a view into the essential spirit of the organization. For instance, do employees view compliance and ethical concerns as peripheral to the basic mission of the organization? Does senior management view compliance and ethical concerns as mere "necessary evils" to placate regulators and/or other concerned stakeholders? It is the answers to these and similar questions that form the baseline against which the board of directors and senior management can begin to address weaknesses or deficiencies in their organization's culture.

- How does the organization, and its management staff, set expectations for standards of behavior? Is there a pressure to perform that inevitably leads to ethics and compliance concerns?
- How does the organization create a work environment that supports ethical behavior and discourages unethical behavior? Is it difficult to raise ethical or compliance issues? Is there a person or unit in the organization that will listen to an employee's concerns?
- How does the organization reward (or fail to punish) employees for their behavior? What are the compensation and reward policies and practices of the organization? Do they include compliance and ethics criteria?
- Does the organization's mission, code of conduct, or ethical statements reflect the reality of the organizational norms and expectations?
- Does short-term interest prevail over long-term organizational viability and credibility?
- Has the organization established a compliance and ethics program? Where does it report to? What are its resources, scope of operations, and authority? Does it have credibility in the organization?
- Does reputation matter in the organization? Are quality and pride in the organization's products and services organizational expectations?

Rules versus Integrity

The relationship between compliance and ethics has been the source of considerable discussion and debate over the past two decades. In brief, the debate has centered around the two different philosophical approaches that compliance and ethics represent as a way of affecting organizational behavior. Compliance is perceived as a rules-based approach that focuses on preventing and punishing violations of law, while ethics or integrity-based programs seek to define organizational values and encourage employee commitment to ethical aspirations.

The genesis for this controversy was an article written by Lynn Sharp Paine in the *Harvard Business Review* (March–April 1994). In the article, Professor Paine extolled the virtues of an "ethics and integrity based" approach to achieving organizational change rather than the "rules-based" compliance program approach. Paine wrote:

> *Designed by corporate counsel, the goal of these [compliance-based] programs is to prevent, detect and punish legal violations. But organizational ethics means more than avoiding illegal practice; providing employees with a rule book will do little to address the problems underlying unlawful conduct. To foster a climate that encourages exemplary behavior, corporations need a comprehensive approach that goes beyond the often punitive legal compliance stance.*

For more than a decade, Paine's views have framed the debate over the appropriate course of action. In 2006, an article in the *Journal of Health Care Compliance* ruefully commented on the seemingly never-ending controversy, "Many people are either in the compliance or the ethics camp. Although they will often be quite civil about it, there seems to be a deep sentiment for one or the other. For some reason we seem to think it has to be either/or."

Philosophic disagreements aside, the reality is that most compliance programs combine the two different orientations (although some research has indicated that integrity-based programs may be more effective than rules-based programs in shaping employee behavior).

Corporate Codes of Conduct

A classic illustration of the intertwining of compliance and ethics is organizations' codes of conduct. Codes of conduct are essentially public commitments by organizations to certain standards of ethical conduct. Codes of conduct have been a long-standing practice in many professions: for example, doctors, attorneys, psychologists, accountants, and engineers adhere to a code of conduct. However, as a Notes commentary in *Harvard Law Review* (2003) pointed out: "Aside from the duties imposed by the corpus of doctrine known as 'corporate law,' however, no single code of behavior governs the actions of the professionals who oversee America's public companies."

Growth

The notion that an organization's code of conduct is a purely voluntary effort to demonstrate the organization's values and ethics has been transformed by the growing body of legal mandates governing the development of a code of conduct. The impetus behind the growth of corporate codes of conduct has come from several sources: the spread of organizational scandals in the United States, the increasingly accepted concept that corporate codes of conduct are an essential part of an organization's self-governance requirements, and the enactment of the Federal Sentencing Guidelines for Organizations in 1991. The contemporary emphasis on codes of conduct is the result of the passage of the Sarbanes-Oxley legislation in 2002.

Sarbanes-Oxley. Section 406 of the Sarbanes-Oxley legislation directed the Securities and Exchange Commission (SEC) to issue rules requiring public companies to disclose whether or not (and if not, the reason why not) they have "adopted a code of ethics for senior financial officers, applicable to its principal financial officer and comptroller or principal accounting officer, or persons performing similar functions."

The Securities and Exchange Commission. In promulgating the implementing regulations for Sarbanes-Oxley, the SEC describes a "code of ethics" that is designed to promote:

1. Honest and ethical conduct, including the ethical handling of actual or apparent conflicts of interest between personal and professional relationships

2. Full, fair, accurate, timely, and understandable disclosure in reports and documents
3. Compliance with applicable governmental laws, rules, and regulations
4. The prompt internal reporting of violations of the code to an appropriate person or persons
5. Accountability for adherence to the code

In reviewing the SEC code, the Advisory Group on the Federal Sentencing Guidelines for Organizations[1] noted that "the SEC standards call for an ethics oriented code, not just one aimed at achieving law compliance. . . . [L]aw compliance is apparently not even the most important type of ethical conduct to be promoted by these codes, being addressed only third in the list of types of misconduct or unethical behavior a code must address and combat." For boards of directors and the senior management of organizations, the meaning is clear: the focus must go beyond the bounds of legal compliance to the broader issues of culture, ethics, accountability, and transparency in organizational behavior.

New York Stock Exchange. As noted earlier, the governance standards of the New York Stock Exchange (NYSE) go beyond Sarbanes-Oxley and mandate that all companies listed on the exchange adopt and disclose a code of business conduct and ethics that is applicable to all employees of the organization as well as to its corporate directors and officers. The NYSE's Corporate Governance Rules recognize, "No code of business conduct and ethics can replace the thoughtful behavior of an ethical director, officer or employee. However, such a code can focus the board and management on areas of ethical risk, provide guidance to personnel to help them recognize and deal with ethical issues, provide mechanisms to report unethical conduct, and help to foster a culture of honesty and accountability."

Skepticism

Perhaps the *Harvard Law Review* article noted earlier said it best when it commented on the finely worded code of conduct of the failed Enron

Corporation, which extolled the virtues of good governance: "The Enron debacle makes clear that a corporate code of behavior is only as good as the people charged with enforcing it and those who must demonstrate the importance of compliance by their example." Despite lofty statements, proclamations of virtue, and grand ideals, the credibility of organizational codes of conduct ultimately comes down to their enforcement.

Recommendations for Developing a Code of Conduct

Despite the skepticism, codes of conduct have become established practice for many organizations. In developing an organizational code of conduct, several points should be considered:

- Effective codes transcend a simple list of prohibited behaviors or rules. They are an opportunity for an organization to encapsulate its ethical values and practices, as well as reinforce key legal and regulatory obligations.
- Notwithstanding this, extreme care should be taken in writing organizational codes of conduct. Codes are inevitably an organizational balancing act between legal and aspirational statements, reality and ideal, rules and values. Organizations will be held to the code's statements by both internal and external stakeholders.
- All persons associated with the organization must be held accountable to the code's provisions. No one, from the board of directors on down, should be immune from the code's provisions.
- Codes must be sensitive to regional, cultural, and legal differences, especially if the organization is establishing a code of conduct for a multinational population. This point was illustrated by the frustrations expressed by a compliance officer who cited the difficulties in developing a code of conduct for a multinational corporation. Non-U.S. senior managers of the organization had disparaged the document as "too American" in its tone and content.

- Well-developed codes are an opportunity to teach employees. They provide guidance and insight into problematic and risk-laden areas. They empower employees to "do the right thing."

Scope of the Code. Organizational codes of conduct are often a combination of values and rules that address corporate governance. They are an opportunity for the organization's board of directors and senior management to establish

- Broad-based ideals and values
- A standard of conduct for the organization's employees and its agents
- An ethical framework in which the organization conducts its affairs
- A mechanism for employees to report violations of the code

While the specifics of codes of conduct vary from organization to organization, they generally address such topics as

- Ethical principles
- Insider trading
- Conflicts of interest
- Workplace practices
- Government relations
- Compliance with laws and regulations
- Integrity in the marketplace
- The role of the organization's compliance and ethics programs
- Reporting mechanisms

Beyond these items, codes of conduct often provide guidance to employees in addressing specific compliance and ethical situations, applying values and ethics to the rules incorporated into the code, and determining how to behave in specific ethically ambiguous situations.

For instance, Altria Group's Code of Conduct for Compliance and Integrity reminds its employees:

> *Ask Before Acting . . .*
> - *Is it legal?*
> - *Does it follow company policy?*
> - *Is it right?*
> - *How would it look to those outside the company? For example, how would it look to our customers, the people in the communities where we work, and the general public?*

Enforcement. To obviate the skepticism surrounding codes of conduct, organizations are taking enhanced measures to enforce their codes of conduct.

- Requiring employees to read and sign their code of conduct. GE, for example, in its policy guide, *Integrity: The Spirit and the Letter of Our Commitment*, requires all hires to sign the corporation's acknowledgment, "Your Personal Commitment to Integrity."
- Making violations of the code have serious consequences for employment. SAP's *Code of Business Conduct for Employees* (March 2006) states, "Any contravention of this Code will be internally investigated. In applicable cases it will also have consequences in employment law and may lead to external investigations, action in the civil courts, or prosecution."

Training and Communication. Organizations are undertaking various training and communications activities to demonstrate their commitment to their code of conduct:

- To create a culture of openness and honesty, it is important that employees hear about the policy regularly. Senior management should make every effort to talk about the company's commitment to ethical behavior in memos, newsletters, and speeches to company staff. Publicly acknowledging and rewarding employees who pinpoint ethical issues is one way to send the message that management is serious about addressing issues before they become endemic.

- Organizations are incorporating their code of conduct into both orientation training for new employees and in-service training. Some conduct Web-based training in association with the code and self-testing on its provisions.
- Organizations are translating the code of conducting into multiple languages for their non-English-speaking populations. Codes are being published on the organization's Web sites and in annual reports.

Creating an Ethical Culture: The Linchpin

The issue of compliance/rules vs. integrity/ethics does not have to be a zero-sum game. Most organizational compliance initiatives combine elements of both compliance-based and integrity-based programs. In light of the 2004 Amendments to the Federal Sentencing Guidelines for Organizations, which focus on ethics and culture, the quest for many organizations is to effectively meld the critical aspects of both philosophic approaches into a modern compliance initiative. As Trevino et al. state in their Winter 1999 study of ethics and compliance programs in the *California Management Review*, "When it comes to creating a formal ethics/compliance program, managers need not choose between values-based and compliance-based approaches. Rather these approaches are complementary. . . . [H]owever, to be most effective, formal efforts to manage ethics and legal compliance should be oriented primarily toward values."

Key Elements

To this end, research and experience have shown that there are a number of measures that organizations can take to help to create an ethical climate or culture that sustains an effective compliance program, incorporates values, leads to a culture of compliance, and will ultimately reduce the incidence of wrongdoing in an organization. The diverse elements that contribute to this ethical climate include the following.

Leadership. The board of directors and senior management establish the values, expectations, and standards of behavior for an organization. It is this leadership team that creates and maintains the ethical framework for the organization. Trevino et al., in their study of ethics and compliance, found that leadership was a key factor in creating an effective organizational environment. The importance of the board of directors and senior management in creating a cultural and ethical framework for managing compliance risk was reiterated by the Basel Committee on Banking Supervision (see Box 3.2)

Perceived Fairness. Employees often view ethics in terms of to how they are being treated by the organization. The author recalls an incident in a company that involved a supervisor who had been accused of workplace harassment, but who nevertheless received a sizable bonus (the proverbial "workplace grapevine" works very effectively in this era of instant communication). While the allegations were ultimately dropped, employees expressed considerable bitterness about a perceived "double standard" in the treatment of the supervisor as compared to that of a lower-ranking individual who might have been involved in a similar situation.

BOX 3.2 Ethics, Compliance, and Banking: An International Perspective

Compliance risk management is most effective when a bank's culture emphasizes high standards of ethical behavior at all levels of the bank. The board of directors and senior management should promote an organizational culture which establishes through both actions and words the expectation of compliance by all employees (including senior management) with laws, rules and standards when conducting the business of the bank. A compliance function within a bank . . . should support management in building a robust compliance culture based on ethical standards of behavior, and thus contributes to effective corporate governance.

Basel Committee on Banking Supervision

> **BOX 3.3   Rationalizations, Enron, and Ethics**
>
> In an April 21, 2007, interview in the *Wall Street Journal*, Ben Gilson, Jr., the former Enron treasurer, spoke of his three-year jail sentence and the lessons he had learned from his experience:
>
> > *It is easier to get here than you would think. It's easier to wind up on the wrong side and get involved in something that you shouldn't. Then, you craft a rationalization as to why it's OK. People, me specifically, can rationalize a great deal. And at Enron there were a lot of different flavors of rationalization.*

Accountability and Responsibility. An ethical culture encourages persons to accept accountability and responsibility for their actions. It also encourages employees to question authority when something is amiss. An organization that requires employees to accept management's dictates without challenging them, even when a person knows that something is wrong, is not likely to have employees come forward when ethical issues arise. Ultimately, it is the employee's decision. As Ben Gilson, the convicted former Enron treasurer, notes, rationalizing one's wrong behavior is a dangerous practice that is fraught with risk (see Box 3.3).

Compensation and Reward. Issues of accountability, responsibility, and fairness are also reflected in the organization's compensation and reward systems. As the earlier anecdote illustrates, money and related rewards are clear signals of organizational values. To the extent that an organization rewards employees for ethical and compliance behavior, it sends a very strong message as to what it values.

Nonprofit Organizations

The nonprofit sector has similarly struggled with problems of compliance and ethics. Scandals involving United Way, the American Red Cross, private foundations, and colleges and universities have challenged the image of nonprofit organizations as taking the ethical and moral "high road." Acknowledging these lapses and foreseeing legislative actions that would lead to their operations being more closely monitored, nonprofit organizations over the past decade have started to address the issues of ethical and compliance culture.

Independent Sector, a leadership forum for nonprofit and charitable programs, for example, has developed a checklist for nonprofit accountability to help organizations in "building an organization committed to the highest ethical standards." Many of the steps advocated by Independent Sector are strikingly similar to the measures being adopted by corporations.

- Develop a culture of accountability and transparency.
- Adopt a statement of values and code of ethics.
- Develop a conflict of interest policy.
- Ensure that the board of directors understands and fulfills its financial responsibilities.
- Establish a policy and a mechanism for reporting suspected misconduct.

Similar to the Independent Sector's recommendations, in 2004 PricewaterhouseCoopers provided a series of recommendations for college and university officers and trustees dealing with expanded standards of governance and transparency. While the report, A *Foundation for Integrity*, addressed the need for codes of conduct and conflict of interest policies, it also dealt with the issue of executive compensation and the need for institutions to be more forthcoming about their compensation policies and practices.

As these checklist items have been developed, nonprofit organizations have started to take a number of steps to address their compliance and ethics culture. The 2006 *Board Governance Survey for Not-for-Profit Organizations*, undertaken by the accounting firm Grant Thornton, of 960 not-for-profit organizations showed that nonprofits are continuing to implement new policies, procedures, and controls to ensure sound governance. According to the survey, more than three-quarters (78 percent) have a conflict-of-interest policy, compared to 67 percent in 2005, and 58 percent of the organizations surveyed have a code of ethics statement, similar to the 2005 findings.

Public Sector

The issue of ethics and compliance in the public sector is an old song that has been sung many times previously, with new verses seemingly added each year. From the former World Bank head, Paul Wolfowitz, to bribery scandals involving local officials in New Orleans, stories involving ethical lapses continue to unfold. In a blistering attack on the U.S. Department of the Interior, the organization's inspector general in 2006 derided the agency's ethical behavior. In a congressional hearing reported in the September 14, 2006, *New York Times*, Earl R. Devaney said, "Simply stated, short of a crime, anything goes at the highest levels of the Department of the Interior. . . . Ethics failures on the part of senior department officials—taking the form of appearances of impropriety, favoritism and bias—have been routinely dismissed with a promise 'not to do it again.'"

In light of these issues, government officials and agencies have taken numerous steps to address the issues of ethical behavior, accountability, and transparency in government operations. In August 2007, Congress passed reform legislation to change its operations, particularly with respect to its dealings with lobbyists. At the state level, there has been a proliferation of agencies addressing ethical issues. One survey reported in *The Book of the States 2005* found 38 state boards and commissions that administer codes of ethics for state officials. Even at the local level, the issue of compliance and ethics is being addressed. In 2006, for instance, San Bernardino County, California, hired an ethics and compliance officer to develop and oversee various programs for the county administration.

Speaking at an international conference in 2001,[2] the head of the U.S. Office of Government Ethics, Amy Comstock, stated the challenge and need for ethical behavior by public officials:

> *If we are to create a democratic culture, if we are to avoid the cynical conclusion that public officials merely use their public offices for their own profit and advantage, if we are to ask people to have faith in Government and to believe that all will be*

treated fairly, we must have institutions and systems that ensure that public officials are held accountable and that Government operations are open to public scrutiny.

Summary

Albert Einstein is reported to have said, "Relativity applies to physics, not ethics." Whether Einstein's quote is apocryphal or not, the issues of ethics and compliance cannot be divorced from effective organizational behavior. The need for organizations to understand the nuances of compliance and the barriers and challenges to inculcating an ethical and compliance culture goes beyond simply being a "nice thing to do." Organizations and individuals are judged, often harshly, by the courts, the media, their customers, their employees, and other critical stakeholders on the basis of their actions and their values. It is the organization's leadership that sets the tone and framework for compliance and ethics.

Notes

1. U.S. Sentencing Commission, "Report of the Ad Hoc Advisory Group on the Organizational Sentencing Guidelines," October 7, 2003, http://www.ussc.gov/corp/advgrprpt/AG_FINAL.pdf.
2. Amy Comstock, Director, U.S. Office of Government Ethics, "Remarks to the Global Forum II Law Enforcement Workshop," The Hague, Netherlands, May 29, 2001.

4

Leadership and Culture: The Foundations of Compliance

It is axiomatic that organizational leadership establishes the values, patterns, and practices for organizational compliance. The manner in which an organization's leaders recognize and deal with risk and reward, compensate employees for their actions (or inactions), and decide when and how to deal with issues that impinge upon their vital interests sends a clear message about what is acceptable behavior—what is valued and rewarded.

As we have seen, the spate of judicial, legislative, administrative, and regulatory actions in the 1990s and the early part of the twenty-first century had a profound effect on the governance and leadership of modern organizations. And not without reason or need. Kirk Hanson, executive director of the Markulla Center for Applied Ethics at Santa Clara University in California was quoted in a Winter 2003 *Directors & Boards* article as saying about the Enron debacle, "Enron was the collapse of a large company that was touted as the company of the future! There was massive fraud, greed on an unparalleled scale, and unrestrained conflicts of interest. The board and audit committee were asleep as executives escaped with their wallets intact. And the employees—the human assets—suffered tremendously."

Given this and other similar cases of corporate malfeasance, boards of directors and senior management now have an affirmative duty, under these new governance requirements, to

- Implement compliance programs to detect and prevent criminal misconduct by the organization's employees and its agents.
- Monitor those programs to ensure that they are working properly.
- Perhaps most importantly, foster a culture of ethics and integrity within their organizations to create an atmosphere that is conducive to compliance.

Carole Stubblefield, a lawyer, commented in a 2005 article in *The Metropolitan Corporate Counsel* on this connection between organizational governance and compliance.

> *While no single definition of corporate governance has emerged over the past few years, I would suggest that it encompasses conducting business and managing the company in a manner that emphasizes ethical and honest behavior, compliance with applicable laws and regulations, effective management of the company's resources and risks, and accountability of persons within the organization.*

This requirement has been echoed in the ubiquitous phase "tone at the top," which has become the mantra for characterizing an organization's values and ethical standards. It is the credo that reverberates throughout the organization. It sets the patterns of behavior, expectations, and standards to be followed by the organization's board of directors, senior management, and employees, and also those who operate on behalf of the organization, e.g., agents, temporary employees, and contractors. As Lori A. Richards of the SEC aptly expressed in an April 23, 2003, speech, "You know it's *not* enough to have policies. It's *not* enough to have procedures. It's *not* enough to have good intentions. All these can help. But to be successful, compliance must be an embedded part of your firm's culture."

The Legal and Regulatory Underpinnings

The enhanced emphasis on compliance, ethics, accountability, and transparency by organizational leadership has been buttressed by a number of requirements mandated by government agencies, regulatory bodies, and case law. These actions have focused on the role of the board of directors and senior management in promoting a culture of compliance and integrity within the organization.

The Federal Sentencing Guidelines for Organizations

On November 1, 2004, the U.S. Sentencing Commission revised and expanded the original 1991 Federal Sentencing Guidelines for Organizations (FSGO). Among the amendments was a significant focus on the issue of organizational governance and the role of the board of directors and senior management in affecting behavior within the organization. These changes were derived in part from the passage of the Sarbanes-Oxley Act two years earlier (which mandated that the U.S. Sentencing Commission review the Federal Sentencing Guidelines for Organizations to ensure that they were "sufficient to deter and punish organizational criminal misconduct"), 13 years of experience with compliance programs since the passage of the original Federal Sentencing Guidelines for Organizations, and the *Caremark* court decision (discussed later in this chapter).

In considering revisions to the original sentencing guidelines, the Advisory Group on the Federal Sentencing Guidelines for Organizations noted the financial scandals involving Enron, Adelphia Communications, Tyco, WorldCom, Quest, and HealthSouth, among others. The advisory group observed in its October 2003 report:

> *It is obviously unrealistic to expect that the Federal Sentencing Guidelines for Organizations will deter all corporate crime. No set of sentencing incentives and penalties can, in every case, overcome the impact of corporate culture and individual greed, fear or arrogance that drives corporate malfeasance. . . . What should be troubling, however, is the fact that much of this*

misconduct was perpetuated by senior management and was only belatedly discovered despite the existence of auditing and other internal reporting systems.

Given the failures of organizational leadership, the advisory group promulgated a series of recommendations that addressed the issues of culture, ethics, and the role of senior management in creating the organizational climate necessary for an effective compliance program. A number of the amendments focused specifically on organizational leadership and its responsibilities with respect to a compliance program. For instance, the FSGO require:

- Mandatory compliance training, to include high-level company officials and board members
- Board members "to be knowledgeable about the content and operation of the compliance and . . . exercise reasonable oversight with the respect to the implementation and effectiveness of the compliance and ethics program"
- Senior management to "ensure that the organization has an effective compliance and ethics program . . . [and to assign] specific individual(s) within high-level personnel . . . overall responsibility for the compliance and ethics program"
- Corporate officials responsible for the organization's compliance and ethics program to "report periodically to high-level personnel and as appropriate, to the governing authority [i.e., the board of directors], on the effectiveness of the compliance and ethics program . . . [and have] direct access to the governing authority or an appropriate subgroup of the governing authority."

The amendments reflected a seismic change from the Federal Sentencing Guidelines for Organizations' original approach. Organizations, in the words of the advisory group, must now "promote an organizational culture that encourages ethical conduct and a commitment to compliance with the law." The message was clear: organizational leadership had to change and evolve from a passive to a proactive role. In addressing compliance and ethical issues, the credo of not knowing or being responsible was no longer acceptable.

The Caremark Case

The court case *In re Caremark International Inc. vs. Derivative Litigation* was one of the factors contributing to the Federal Sentencing Guidelines for Organizations' enhanced focus on issues of compliance by boards of directors and senior organizational leadership. The case came before the Delaware courts in 1996 and had a significant impact on the role of corporate directors in compliance programs.

Caremark, a pharmaceutical services company, and two of its employees had violated the federal Anti-Referral Payments Law, as well as other state and federal laws. The company agreed to pay $250,000,000 to settle federal and state proceedings in the case. The corporation's shareholders sued Caremark's directors to recover the corporate losses on several grounds, including the claim that the directors had breached their duty of care by failing to supervise Caremark employees adequately or to institute corrective measures.

The suit was eventually settled, and Chancellor William T. Allen of the Delaware Court of Chancery had to review and approve the agreement. Under the settlement, Caremark agreed to amend its bylaws to add committees and procedures designed to avoid a repeat of the conduct that resulted in the violations. While Chancellor Allen found the settlement fair to the shareholders and agreed to the dismissal, he also used the opportunity to define the directors' duty of oversight.

In his opinion, Chancellor Allen stated that "a director's obligation includes a duty to attempt in good faith to assure that a corporate information and reporting system, which the board concludes is adequate, exists," and that it is impossible for directors to satisfy their obligation to be "reasonably informed" about a corporation's operations without doing so.

Under *Caremark*, directors must require a corporation to adopt procedures to gather and evaluate "timely, accurate information" to permit both management and directors to "reach informed judgments concerning the corporation's compliance with law and its business performance." Directors must ensure that such procedures exist, and that they are adequate "in concept and design" to ensure that appropriate information will come to the attention of management and the directors "in a timely manner as a matter of ordinary operations."

This opinion had significant ramifications for corporations and their boards of directors. The failure to institute a meaningful program to supervise a corporation's internal monitoring and reporting systems not only placed the corporation at risk, but also placed the organization's directors at personal liability for failing to carry out their fiduciary obligations.

The Disney and Abbott Cases

Since the *Caremark* case, two additional cases of note have addressed the issue of a director's fiduciary duty to act in good faith. In the first case, *In re Walt Disney Company Derivative Litigation*, the plaintiffs challenged a compensation package and severance payment for Michael Ovitz, the former president of Disney, valued at approximately $140 million. The Delaware court found that the board had failed in its duties and did not exercise any business judgment in approving the compensation. The court said that the directors "knew that they were making material decisions without adequate information and without adequate deliberation, and that they simply did not care if the decisions caused the corporation and its stockholders to suffer injury or loss." In a federal case, *In re Abbott Laboratories Derivative Shareholders Action*, the Seventh Circuit found that the board had failed to act in good faith by failing to address the company's long history of FDA violations and not disclosing the violations in question to the SEC. The court held that the Abbott board's failure to take actions to correct knowing violations of law over a long period of time constituted a lack of good faith.

In a July 2, 2003, note ("To Our Friends and Clients"), the law firm of Fried, Frank, Harris, Shriver & Jacobson commented, somewhat humorously, on the effect of these two cases: "Good corporate governance mandates that directors proactively inform themselves about corporate developments and aggressively intervene to understand reported troublesome corporate behavior that is not voluntarily brought before the

Board by management. Accordingly, directors who knowingly put their heads in the sand to avoid taking action on corporate issues may offer plaintiffs a tempting anatomical target at which to kick."

Sarbanes-Oxley Act of 2002

The passage of the Sarbanes-Oxley Act of 2002 added another significant governance mandate for organizational leadership. As noted previously, the importance and impact of Sarbanes-Oxley cannot be underestimated. While the focus of the legislation is on publicly traded companies and the protection of investors by improving the accuracy and reliability of corporate disclosures, its scope, power, and influence reverberate throughout organizations in all sectors of the economy. The law, and the SEC regulations implementing it, has established new or enhanced standards for corporate accountability and penalties for corporate wrongdoing. It defines a higher level of responsibility, accountability, and financial reporting transparency on behalf of organizations and their senior management and boards of directors.

For boards of directors, the legislation imposed new responsibilities and obligations ranging from expanded duties of audit committees to the development of codes of conduct. Similarly, the responsibility and liability of senior management were significantly enhanced. The legislation required the organization's chief executive officer (CEO) and chief financial officer (CFO) to certify not only the completeness and accuracy of the information contained in quarterly and annual financial reports, but also the effectiveness of the underlying internal controls that generated the information. The CEO and CFO are held accountable for the development and maintenance of the organization's internal controls. They are required to alert the audit committee and the organization's auditors of any problems in the design or operation of internal controls that might affect an audit, and to report any changes in the organization's internal control processes.

In the March/April 2004 issue of *BizEd*, Ira Millstein, an authority on corporate governance, stated quite explicitly the impact of Sarbanes-Oxley on boards of directors:

> *Congress passed Sarbanes-Oxley because so few companies followed rules of best practices. . . . Sarbanes-Oxley simply turned*

what you should do into what you must do. Now, I no longer have to plead with and cajole people into following codes of governance. I can just point to the law and listing requirements. . . . It placed total responsibility for good corporate behavior and good fiscal reporting back to the board of directors. It makes it very, very clear that the board is responsible for the behavior of the corporation.

U.S. Department of Justice

Adding to the governance duties of boards of directors and senior management has been the U.S. Department of Justice's Principles of Federal Prosecution of Business Organization. In light of the Sarbanes-Oxley mandate for active director oversight of governance activities, the principles seek to identify whether directors have fulfilled their key fiduciary obligations. The principles state: "In evaluating compliance programs, prosecutors may consider whether the corporation has established corporate governance mechanisms that can effectively detect and prevent misconduct. For example, do the corporation's directors exercise independent review over proposed corporate actions rather than unquestioningly ratifying officers' recommendations; and have the directors established an information and reporting system in the organization reasonably designed to provide management and the board of directors with timely and accurate information." The opinions and guidance expressed by Chancellor Allen on the role and duties of directors in the *Caremark* case can clearly be seen in the principles.

Self-Regulatory Organizations: New York Stock Exchange

In developing its own corporate governance standards after the debacle of corporate wrongdoing, the New York Stock Exchange (NYSE) declared in its 2002 *Corporate Governance Rule Proposals:*

> *Now, in the aftermath of the "meltdown" of significant companies due to failures of diligence, ethics and controls, the NYSE has*

the opportunity—and the responsibility—once again to raise corporate governance and disclosure standards. . . . The system depends upon the competence and integrity of corporate directors, as it is their responsibility to diligently oversee management while adhering to unimpeachable ethical standards. The Exchange now seeks to strengthen checks and balances and give diligent directors better tools to empower them and encourage excellence.

Boards of Directors

Creating an organizational culture that supports an effective compliance program starts with the organization's board of directors. A well-educated, informed, and dedicated board of directors is a vital link in the organization's leadership and oversight responsibilities. Regardless of whether the organization is public, private, or nonprofit, its board members undertake a fiduciary responsibility—a duty of loyalty, a duty of care—to oversee the welfare and management of their respective organizations. As the Committee of Sponsoring Organizations of the Treadway Commission (COSO) said in its 1992 *Internal Control—Integrated Framework*, "Management is accountable to the board of directors . . . which provides governance, guidance and oversight. By selecting management, the board has a major role in defining what it expects in integrity and ethical values [and] can confirm its expectations through its oversight activities."

An Expanded Role, Vision, and Responsibilities

To manage their compliance obligations effectively within this new environment, boards of directors must adopt an expanded role, vision, and set of responsibilities. Directors must ensure that

- They adequately understand the external and internal compliance risks and requirements facing their organization.

- The organization has comprehensive policies, procedures, and resources in place to address these concerns.
- The organization has an operating philosophy and environment that encourages compliance and ethical behavior.
- Compliance and ethics are made an integral part of organizational life.

Anthony Knerr, an authority on corporate governance, expressed the need for board members to exercise their fiduciary responsibilities within the framework of the Golden Rule — "do unto others as you would have them do unto you" — put into a business context. In a 2004 article in *Directors & Boards*, Knerr said:

> *The heart of being a fiduciary is acting as you would wish another to act on your own behalf. Representing the interests of the shareholder as a director of a company means putting yourself in the position of continually asking how you would wish to be treated if you were yourself a shareholder. . . . [I]t is hard to believe that board members of Adelphia, MCI, or Tyco were truly acting as they would wish to have been treated.*

Personal Qualities of Board Members. To have a board of directors that provides the effective leadership needed to have a culture of compliance and ethics requires that individual board members bring certain qualities of integrity and competency to the function. In guidance prepared for nonprofit organizations,[1] two professional organizations identified basic qualities of a good board member that are applicable to all organizations.

- *Vision and leadership:* the ability to see the big picture and the courage to set direction to achieve the organization's mission
- *Stewardship:* the integrity to serve the interests and pursue the goals of the organization, as well as the interests of the public and the organization's intended beneficiaries

- *Knowledge:* knowledge of the organization's constituents and operations and its organizational and managerial acumen
- *Diligence:* dedication and commitment to fulfilling the organization's goals
- *Collegiality:* having a sincere and respectful attitude toward colleagues and their views

A veteran board member, who has served on numerous boards, suggested that in addition to these qualities, an effective board member must be able to

- Understand the difference between the role of the board (policy) and the role of the staff (management). As he said, "In all organizations and nonprofits in particular, members of boards often have a hard time staying out of the management function."
- Keep confidentiality. For board members, especially in relatively small communities, it is sometimes very hard to keep from talking about an organization's issues and problems in a social context where non-board members are present. The duty of confidentiality is extremely important.

Board Structure

Boards of directors have taken several approaches to address their compliance and ethics mandates. Principally, the actions have involved an expanded role for the board's audit committee and, to a lesser extent, the creation of a compliance committee.

Expanded Compliance Role for the Audit Committee. Of all the traditional committees of boards of directors, it is the audit committee, whose lapses in oversight led to many instances of accounting and financial wrongdoing in organizations such as Enron and WorldCom, that has faced the greatest challenges in both its composition and its scope of responsibilities. Under the new regulatory strictures, audit committees for publicly traded companies have become the focal point for enhanced corporate governance activities, including, for many organizations, enhanced oversight of the organization's compliance framework and emerging compliance risk issues. Even the titles of many audit committees have changed to reflect their new duties, e.g., audit and compliance committee (RadioShack and Novartis), audit and risk management committee (Citigroup), or audit, corporate responsibility, and compliance committee (Health Care Service Corp.).

The enhanced role of the audit committee has become a challenge for many organizations: the requirement that it be composed only of independent members, the need for at least one "financial expert," the expanded audit and accounting mandates, and the new and expanded fiduciary duties related to compliance and ethics. Under section 301(4) of Sarbanes-Oxley, the audit committee must establish procedures for

- The receipt of complaints received by the company regarding the organization's accounting, internal accounting controls, or auditing concerns
- Handling confidential, anonymous information submitted by organization employees about concerns regarding questionable accounting or auditing matters

While technically limited to accounting-related matters, these requirements have opened the floodgates for the audit committee to receive a wide range of allegations regarding organizational behavior. With respect to the latter, PricewaterhouseCoopers noted in a white paper, *The Sarbanes-Oxley Act of 2002*, that these new regulatory and reporting obligations impose an extra requirement on the audit committees: "Importantly, the audit committee should also determine that the company's operating culture—including its own and management leadership—encourages and supports open communication about any employee concerns."

Compliance Committees. As an alternative to the audit committee, some organizations have added a compliance committee to the board of directors to address compliance and ethics matters. These committees have often developed as a result of a settlement between the organization and government regulators and/or prosecutors. For instance, a 2005 regulatory settlement agreement between Marsh & McLennan and various chief state insurance regulators specifically called for the establishment of a compliance committee of the board of directors. Similarly, in 2005, Aon Corporation, a financial services corporation, settled its regulatory violations by creating a compliance committee of its board of directors to monitor the corporation's conduct.

Separate from the board's audit committee, the compliance committee, which is made up of independent board members, ensures that the organization and its employees are acting in accordance with applicable laws, regulations, and codes of conduct.

Advocates for the compliance committee structure maintain that its sole focus on regulatory, ethical, and compliance concerns makes it a more effective mechanism for dealing with compliance and ethical issues, unlike audit committees, which are burdened with myriad accounting and audit responsibilities. However, compliance committees are not without their detractors. Specifically, it is claimed that a compliance committee usurps one of the responsibilities of an organization's audit committee. Joseph Grundfast, a law professor at Stanford University who sits on the audit committee of Oracle Corporation, said in the April 2006 issue of *Bank Accounting & Finance* that compliance committees "could be the sign of bad governance" because "you're duplicating information and creating the risk of somebody missing information."

Key Questions for the Board of Directors

Given the enormous responsibilities placed on organizational boards, the following questions are designed to help boards of directors address their legal, ethical, and compliance obligations. (Specific questions concerning the operation of the organization's compliance program are addressed in Chapter 5.)

How independent is the board?
Effective boards demonstrate their ability to be independent from management: to be able to say no when the situation warrants it, to ask hard questions, and to be willing and able to reject plans and strategies that are risky or not well developed.

How confident are the board and its committees that they are receiving all relevant management information?
Effective boards want and expect more information from management to enable them to exercise their independent judgment. As the audit chair of a major corporation explained in a 2005 survey, *The Global 50: Perspectives of Leading Audit Chairs*, by Spencer Stuart, "Before [Sarbanes-Oxley] management simply presented the answer [to a disagreement], now, directors want to know what the sensitivities were and the give-and-take that helped determine the resolution."

Does the board fully understand the compliance risks facing the organization? Who oversees these risks? How often, and in what manner, are these issues brought to the board's attention? How is the organization managed to address these risks effectively?
Directors must understand the strategic goals of the organization and the management steps needed to achieve those objectives. They should inquire about and understand the key drivers of those strategies, and the risks and vulnerabilities that can affect those goals. Especially for organizations in highly regulated industries such as finance, health care, and environmental services, it is critical that board members be particularly aware of the regulatory challenges that the organization faces.

How attentive is the board to the affairs of the organization and its supervision of these activities?
Regulators are quite clear on the roles and responsibilities of boards of directors. The Federal Deposit Insurance Corporation,

which regulates banks, states in its *Risk Management Manual of Examination Policies* that "the quality of management is probably the single most important element in the successful operation of a bank." It goes on to say about the organization's board of directors, "Perhaps the most common dereliction of duty by bank directors is the failure to maintain reasonable supervision over the activities and affairs of the bank, its officers and employees."

Do the organization's reward and compensation policies and practices include compliance- and ethics-related criteria?

Boards should review the organization's compensation and reward policies and practices to determine what criteria are used to award bonuses, stock options, salary increases, and other forms of reward. Working with the director of human resources, the board should review the organization's compensation philosophy and practices to encourage transparency and should tie compensation to a performance evaluation that rewards ethical behavior and/or motivates others in the organization to act ethically. According to the March 25, 2007, *New York Times*, boards of large organizations are using "clawbacks of pay" to force senior managers to compensate shareholders for misdeeds. As one compensation expert wryly stated about the advantages of a "clawback" policy, "What we tell people is, the only thing worse than having the bad news hit about a financial misstatement or wrongdoing is having news hit the press seven days later that the executive left with $100 million."

How does the organization manage ethical issues? Where can people go to report ethical issues and concerns?

Board members must understand how issues of ethics and integrity are raised within the organization, what types of issues arise, who manages these concerns, and how they have been addressed. There should be an effective reporting mechanism in place and a process by which the board can respond to issues that arise from any level or area within the organization.

How effective are the organization's audit and internal control polices and procedures?

A key component of an effective organizational compliance program is a comprehensive audit and internal control program that can identify and manage compliance risks. The board should ascertain the degree to which the organization has established an effective internal control program to monitor and mitigate key compliance risk exposures.

Nonprofit Organizations

Boards of directors and senior management of nonprofit organizations ranging from health-care organizations and foundations to educational institutions are facing a similar need to demonstrate leadership in the areas of compliance, accountability, ethics, trust, and transparency. Like their business counterparts, boards of directors or trustees for nonprofit organization have a critical role to play in defining and overseeing the organization's goals and mission, its management team and operations, and its governance. Also like their corporate counterparts, directors of nonprofit corporations have the basic fiduciary duties of loyalty and care to their organizations.

State attorneys general, the U.S. Department of the Treasury, state governments, and the IRS have been aggressively seeking to extend corporate governance reforms to nonprofit organizations. Even credit rating services, such as Fitch Ratings,[2] state that the principles in Sarbanes-Oxley are applicable to nonprofit hospitals seeking public financing.

Many of the larger nonprofit organizations and their boards of directors have accepted the spirit and best practices of the legislation and started to incorporate many enhancements into their corporate governance policies and practices. A November 2005 report by the Center for Effective Philanthropy, *Beyond Compliance: The Trustee Viewpoint on Effective Foundation Governance*, surveyed 53 large U.S. foundations and found that 42 of the 53 CEOs (79 percent) had voluntarily made changes of the type mandated by Sarbanes-Oxley, including the addition of a separate

BOX 4.1

An example of the impact of Sarbanes-Oxley on nonprofit organization governance is the Philadelphia Zoo. As reported by J. Stephen McNally and Joseph T. Steuer in the Winter 2006 *Pennsylvania CPA Journal,* the zoo, which is America's oldest (chartered in 1859), is visited each year by 1.2 million persons and has an annual budget of over $32 million. Overseen by a board of directors and spurred by the passage of Sarbanes-Oxley, the organization took a number of steps to improve its governance and compliance capabilities, including

- Adding a chief governance officer to the board of directors.
- To ensure that board members understand the mission and goal of the organization, requiring each board member to periodically attend "Zoo School," a full-day workshop that provides information on the zoo's day-to-day operations.
- Adopting a statement on operational risk management and the board's oversight responsibilities.
- Creating a separate audit committee of the board (previously it had been a sub-committee of the finance committee) and expanding its duties to include the monitoring of operational risk and financial risk. The committee's name was changed to the audit and compliance committee, and it was given a published charter, an annual work plan, and four prescheduled meetings per year.

Reprinted with permission from the *Pennsylvania CPA Journal,* a publication of the Pennsylvania Institute of Certified Public Accountants.

audit committee. However, for smaller nonprofit organizations, limited resources and other issues pose significant barriers to introducing governance reform. An interesting example of one nonprofit organization, the Philadelphia Zoo, and its corporate governance improvements is illustrated in Box 4.1.

Expanded Audit Committee Functions

For many nonprofit organizations, especially the larger ones, the passage of Sarbanes-Oxley has meant the creation of a separate audit committee where none previously existed (or where this was subsumed under another committee function). For instance, a January 2004 PricewaterhouseCoopers survey, *Sarbanes-Oxley: Relevance and Implications of Certain Provisions for Non-Public Healthcare Organizations,* reported that only 25 percent of health system trustees who responded to a poll in 2002 said that their board had a formal audit committee, and 5 percent said that an audit sub-committee of the board's finance committee had an audit responsibility.

The new and/or expanded audit committee is responsible for hiring or firing the organization's outside auditors, preapproving all related services, taking on a financial expert, and assuming a compliance oversight role similar to that of its corporate counterparts. California's Nonprofit Integrity Act of 2004 requires charities registered with the attorney general and having annual gross revenues of $2 million to have an audit committee.

Board Oversight

While the points discussed in this chapter regarding board oversight have applicability to nonprofit organizations, these organizations have additional compliance and accountability issues that boards of directors or trustees should address:

- The board should engage in an active, informed, independent oversight of the organization's management and operations. Has it considered establishing an independent audit committee, with at least one financial expert on it? As a matter of best practices, the organization's CEO and CFO (or its equivalent) should sign off on all financial statements, including Form 990 tax returns.
- The board should review the organization's audit practices. Both BoardSource and Independent Sector, two influential organizations involved in nonprofit governance, recommend in *The Sarbanes-Oxley Act and Implications for Nonprofit Organizations* (January 2006) that nonprofit organizations "with $1 million or more in total annual revenues (excluding houses of worship or other organizations that are exempt from filing Form 990) should have an audit conducted of their financial statements and consider attaching a copy to their Form 990 or 990PF. Smaller charities with revenues of at least $250,000 should choose a review or at least have their financial statements compiled by a professional accountant. The boards

of nonprofit organizations that forgo an audit should evaluate that decision periodically."

- The board should review whether the organization has, as a matter of good corporate practice, adopted a code of conduct or ethics that sets forth the basic values and standards of behavior for all persons associated with the organization. The code should address such issues as conflicts of interest, loans to insiders, destruction of records, and so on.
- The board should ensure that the organization has established policies and procedures, such as whistle-blowing programs or hotlines, that encourage individuals to come forward as soon as possible with credible information on illegal practices or violations of adopted policies. Employees and volunteers who identify misbehavior must feel safe to report it without fear of retaliation.

Note of Caution. Despite this movement toward governance and compliance reform, the leadership of many nonprofit organizations, especially smaller ones, continues to face a number of challenges, both financial and philosophical:

- Many small nonprofit organizations do not have the financial resources to comply with governance reforms. For instance, a national survey by the Urban Institute in 2005, *Nonprofit Governance and the Sarbanes-Oxley Act*, found that among nonprofit organizations with less than $100,000 in expenses, 28 percent reported that it would be "very difficult" to comply with a requirement for a separate audit committee.
- Governance reform requires time devoted to administrative tasks, additional administrative structure, and additional staff. While laudatory (and often mandatory), this focus on administration touches a very sensitive nerve for many nonprofit organizations. As one nonprofit administrator stated, the thought of her organization "going corporate"—i.e., creating a bureaucracy and introducing controls, policies, and procedures—was for many of her employees anathema in terms of their very reason for joining the organization.

The issue of mission vs. administration is an ongoing struggle that boards of directors and senior management of nonprofits, especially smaller one, will have to continuously address.

Senior Management

The linkage between organizational leadership and compliance is unequivocal. While boards of directors play a critical leadership role in fostering and maintaining a culture of compliance within their respective organizations, they are only a part of the leadership team. The actions and decisions taken by the organization's senior management send an equally clear message as to what is considered acceptable and nonacceptable behavior (see Box 4.2 for a classic example of senior leadership mismanagement). So what can organizations, and their senior managers, do to address these concerns and establish a culture that fosters integrity, compliance, accountability, and ethical behavior? There are a number of actions that senior managers, both personally and organizationally, can take to foster a climate of compliance and integrity.

BOX 4.2   An Example of What *Not* to Do

In 2004, the board of directors of the Federal National Mortgage Association (Fannie Mae) engaged an outside law firm and a former U.S. senator to investigate issues of mismanagement within the organization. The findings, *A Report to the Special Review Committee of the Board of Directors of Fannie Mae (Executive Summary)*, present a startling picture of mismanagement by the organization's senior leadership:

> *Through the end of 2004, management did not fully inform the Board of the Company's accounting issues, internal control deficiencies, or the inadequacies of its internal systems. Further, although management paid lip service to a culture of openness, intellectual honesty, and transparency, the actual corporate culture suffered from an attitude of arrogance (both internally and externally) and an absence of cross-enterprise teamwork (with a "siloing" of information), and discouraged dissenting views, criticism, and bad news. Finally, the Company lacked appropriate structure and personnel for adequate risk management across risk areas (with an extremely broad collection of functions and authorities residing in the CFO), and lacked a genuine cross-enterprise approach to operational risk management.*

Compliance Leadership

An effective organization's senior management demonstrates a clear and unequivocal commitment to compliance, ethics, and integrity in its actions and words. It assumes that people are neither naïve nor fools. We live in an era in which, all too frequently, an organization's employees, volunteers, agents, regulators, clients, and other stakeholders listen, watch, and look for signs of hypocrisy and cynicism by the organization's leaders. It is the actions, big and small, taken by the organization's leaders that send the clearest message concerning what is acceptable and valued behavior within the organization.

To create an organizational culture that is ethical and compliance-oriented, senior organizational leaders should

- Be clear about their message and their expectations in terms of ethics, integrity, and compliance. There should be no misunderstandings concerning what the expected standards of behavior are and the consequences for failing to live up to these expectations and requirements.
- Be credible. They keep their commitments. If the senior leaders espouse certain principles of ethics, integrity, and accountability, they must translate those sentiments into action. If people do not comply with these standards, is the organization willing to take action against them? What values count most in the organization: the ability to generate income and funds, or integrity and ethics? As Joan Helpern, the founder of the Joan and David luxury fashion organization, commented, "It is critical that leadership create a culture that allows employees to be more than a cog in a machine. Senior management allows employees to maintain their humanism and dignity; it sets a tone of mutual respect."
- Be consistent in their message. Compliance and integrity must be viewed as a significant business priority, not merely a by-product of a one-time incident or a passing fad in organizational management. Creating a culture of compliance

and integrity requires management discipline, focus, and attention. It is not an afterthought.

- Understand that their actions reverberate throughout the organization. In an era of intranets, Web sites, and blogs, there are few "dirty little secrets" in organizations.
- Recognize the importance that mid- and lower-level managers play in conveying a message of compliance within their organizations. Leaders at all levels of the organization can and should serve as ethical and compliance role models for others.
- Know how to assign responsibility and hold people accountable for their actions. This is central to creating an effective organizational culture in which people understand their duties and responsibilities, and are accountable for their actions.
- Dedicate the resources needed to address the compliance requirements of the organization. Words are often easy—it's the commitment of people, time, and funds that demonstrates organizational priorities.
- Be aware that they are sending a clear message as to what is important by the management staff they appoint, the qualities that these individuals present, and their expectations for those who work for them.
- Recognize that they do not operate in a vacuum, but are part of a greater community. Effective senior leaders understand the importance of corporate social responsibility and the role it plays in fostering a climate of public trust in the organization.
- Recognize that their organization's operations involve not only the organization's employees but also a chain of other actors: suppliers, distributors, vendors, consultants, and temporary employment agencies. These other players become a de facto part of the organization, and who they are and what they do sends a clear message concerning what is important and valued. The author, while conducting a compliance audit of a business, remembers an encounter with a woman manager who told him that she was scared to death to stay at the facility after 7 p.m.

because of the unsavory nature of the contractors who serviced the office's technology systems.

- Institute a compensation system that rewards employees and managers for demonstrating and encouraging ethical behavior, and for taking measures to make compliance and integrity an integral part of their organizations.

Public-Sector Organizations

While this chapter has focused on private- and nonprofit-sector organizations, the mandate for leadership in public-sector organizations is rooted in elected officials, their appointees to senior administrative positions, and the cadre of full-time professional civil servants who administer governmental and quasi-public-sector organizations.

As in organizations in the private and nonprofit sectors, the issues of fostering compliance, ethics, accountability, and transparency in agencies and institutions at the federal, state, and local levels have been widely expressed. The Treasury Board of Canada, in a 2005 public management document, stated quite succinctly that effective public-sector management requires "sound judgment that is well grounded in ethics, values, and principles and a desire to uphold the rule of law and pursue the public interest."

At all levels, from members of Congress to administrators of city government, the need for accountability and ethical leadership in government administration has been a rallying cry for public-sector leadership.

- The International City/County Management Association (IMCA), a local government leadership and management organization, has established a vigorous ethics training program for its members. Its mission is to create excellence in local governance.
- On the state level, as of 2007, the governors of Ohio, Florida, and New York had ethics reform on their program agendas.

- In 2007, Congress passed significant legislation that overhauled its rules governing ethics and lobbying.

Enhanced accountability for the use of public funds has been reflected in the Office of Management and Budget's Circular A-123, which requires public agencies to adopt internal control procedures analogous to those mandated for publicly traded companies in the private sector by the Sarbanes-Oxley Act. The federal government, as part of President George W. Bush's President's Management Agenda, seeks management reforms in five areas (expanded electronic government, budget and performance integration, competitive sourcing, improved financial performance, and strategic management of human capital) and requires executive-branch government agencies to cite their progress in improving management practices by posting them on a White House Web site.

This reform movement could not come at a better time for public-sector officials. A 2006 public opinion poll of America's political leaders conducted by Harvard's Kennedy School of Government found that while high ethical and moral standards are seen as the most important attribute of the country's leaders, only 38 percent believe that most leaders have high ethical standards.

In our complex government structure, even the leaders of quasi-municipal corporations, such as school districts, water boards, parking authorities, and transportation authorities, have started to take steps to address the issues of compliance and ethics within their own organizations. An interesting example is the Louisville (Kentucky) Water Company, a quasi-municipal corporation that supplies water to more than 800,000 residents in the Louisville metropolitan region and parts of Oldham and Bullitt Counties. The company, overseen by a board of water works, took a number of steps to address the corporate governance requirements cited by Sarbanes-Oxley, including the adoption of a code of ethics for the company, the introduction of a whistle-blower policy, and an enhanced focus on internal controls.

Summary

In discussing the issue of corporate leadership, perhaps Alan Greenspan, former chairman of the Federal Reserve Board, stated it best. In a 2005 commencement address to a future generation of organizational leaders at the University of Pennsylvania's Wharton School, Greenspan said:

> It seems clear that, if the CEO chooses, he or she can, by example and through oversight, induce corporate colleagues and outside auditors to behave ethically. Companies run by people with high ethical standards arguably do not need detailed rules on how to act in the long-run interest of shareholders and, presumably, themselves. But, regrettably, human beings come as we are— some with enviable standards, and others who continually seek to cut corners. Rules exist to govern behavior, but rules cannot substitute for character. In the years going forward, it will be your reputation—for integrity, judgment, and other qualities of character—that will determine your success in life and in business.

Notes

1. The Society of Corporate Secretaries and Governance Professionals and the National Center for Nonprofit Boards, "Governance for Nonprofits."
2. Fitch Ratings, "Sarbanes-Oxley and Not-for-Profit Hospitals," August 9, 2005.

PART III

THE MODERN COMPLIANCE ORGANIZATION

5

Managing Compliance: Goals and Structure

The compliance function has gone through an evolutionary change. This development, however, has not been consistent or uniform. The manner in which organizations approach their compliance obligations varies considerably. This chapter examines the different approaches to developing and managing a compliance program that organizations have taken.

Variations in organizational compliance programs are attributed to numerous factors: the degree and type of regulatory oversight, an organization's resources and risks and the skills and experience of its staff, the organization's relationship with its stakeholders, and the organization's history. Legislative, regulatory, and judicial opinions do not specifically identify the types of structure and organization that an organization must adopt. They do, however, provide a critical framework for what is considered an effective and appropriate compliance structure for a particular type of organization or industry.

In creating a compliance program, the organization needs to consider a number of issues related to compliance's role and reporting structure, and how it is going to adapt and accommodate to the organization's resources, needs, size, and structure. To be effective, a compliance program must reflect and be integrated, as the National Center for Preventive Law's *Corporate Compliance Principles* noted, "into the organization's culture, ethos, and corporate objectives."

Designing the Compliance Program

Creating an effective compliance program involves multiple steps. The first phase is to understand the environment in which the organization operates, including the legal and regulatory requirements that govern the organization's compliance obligations.

The Organizational Context

No organization functions in a vacuum. An organization is the creation and reflection of history, personalities, need, and opportunity. Organizations are subject to the cyclonic forces of law and regulation, as well as to external and internal stakeholder expectations. An effective organization compliance program needs to understand and manage within these dynamics.

The Risk Environment

Each organization has its own unique legal, regulatory, operational, and reputational risks. The organization's strategic objectives, its risk tolerance, and its ability to manage risk will help determine the need for a compliance program and the scope of that program.

Organizational History

Each organization has its own particular history. Was it created by a merger, an acquisition, a divestiture, or a consolidation of different organizations? Was it the brainchild of an inspired leader or of a faceless investment entity? Was it created a hundred years ago or yesterday? Was it born of need, greed, or happenstance? These conditions will determine the organization's values, ethics, image, brand, and public reputation, which contribute to the need for and extent of a compliance program.

Organizational Structure

A key variable in creating the compliance program is the organization's structure. Is it decentralized or centralized? What is the decision-making structure? Are operations concentrated in one country or geographic region, or are they dispersed internationally? How is the organization staffed: does it have full-time or part-time employees, independent contractors, or temporary employees? Is it Web-based? What functions of the organization are outsourced? What person(s) in the organization is currently responsible for the audit, legal, risk management, compliance, human resources, and internal controls functions? Each of these factors will help to determine the scope and nature of the compliance program.

Key Players and Stakeholders

Who are the principal decision makers in the organization, and what are their attitudes, experience, skills, and knowledge with respect to compliance and a compliance program? What are the views of the board of directors, senior management, risk management, legal and accounting staff, human resources, and internal control staff? One comment that is often made by senior managers or board members has been, "Why do we need a compliance program when compliance should be everyone's business?" What is the attitude of the general employee base? What has been the history of the organization's relationship with its regulators, the media, nongovernmental organizations (NGOs), customers, and suppliers?

The Organization's Values and Culture

The organization's values and culture will have a significant impact on the development of an effective compliance program. A major contributory factor to this success will be the extent to which the organization's board of directors and senior management

- Support and endorse compliance and ethics
- Are willing to provide the necessary resources and commitment of time and effort to the compliance initiative
- Publicly reinforce the ethos of the organization

Government and Regulators' Guidance

There are few specific directives on how organizational compliance programs should be structured. Regulators, understanding the variations in size, resources, and structure of different organizations, have been reluctant to give specific requirements, relying instead upon general guidance. Here are some examples, both general and industry-specific, of regulators' guidance concerning the construction of organizational compliance programs.

General

The 2004 Amendments to the Federal Sentencing Guidelines for Organizations (FSGO) and the U.S. Department of Justice's Principles of Federal Prosecution of Business Organizations, both of which have been described in previous chapters, provide broad outlines of what they consider to be effective organizational compliance and/or ethics programs.

Industry-Specific

In addition to the general guidance cited earlier, regulators and self-regulatory organizations (SROs) have issued specific guidance for their respective industries.

Health Care. The Office of the Inspector General (OIG) of the Department of Health and Human Services (DHHS) has issued extensive compliance guidance, modeled after the Federal Sentencing Guidelines for Organizations, for various sectors of the health-care industry, including pharmaceutical manufacturers, ambulance suppliers, nursing facilities, hospitals, "Medicare + choice" organizations, clinical laboratories, and home health agencies.

In addition, the U.S. Deficit Reduction Act of 2005 requires health-care providers that receive $5 million or more annually in Medicaid reimbursement or payments to update their compliance policies and employee handbooks concerning health-care fraud and abuse and whistle-blower protections by January 2007.

Financial Services. In the heavily regulated and fragmented U.S. financial services industry, there are myriad compliance requirements. In the banking sector, multiple regulators (e.g., the Federal Reserve Bank and the Office of Comptroller of the Currency) have issued various directives and guidance delineating the structure of compliance programs in the organizations they regulate. In addition,

- The Securities and Exchange Commission (SEC) requires all registered investment companies and registered investment advisors to adopt and implement internal compliance programs that are reasonably designed to prevent the violation of federal securities laws.
- The USA Patriot Act of 2001 requires certain financial institutions to develop formal anti-money-laundering programs, which must include, at a minimum, reasonable detection and reporting procedures, the designation of a compliance officer, ongoing employee training programs, and independent auditing and testing of the program.
- The New York Stock Exchange (NYSE) and the Financial Industry Regulatory Authority (FINRA) require each member to designate a chief compliance officer (CCO). Additionally, each member's chief executive officer (CEO) and CCO are required each year to certify that they have a process in place to establish, maintain, review, modify, and test policies and procedures that are reasonably designed to achieve compliance with applicable rules and regulations.

Defense Industry. The Defense Federal Acquisition Regulations Supplement (DFARS) for contractors identifies criteria that should be part of an organization's compliance program. Like the Defense Industry Initiative on Business Ethics and Conduct (DII), discussed previously, these include a written code of business ethics and conduct and an ethics training program for all employees; periodic reviews of company business practices, procedures, policies, and internal controls for compliance with standards of conduct and the special requirements of government contracting; and the creation of a hotline program.

Environmental Services. The Environmental Protection Agency's National Environmental Investigations Center (NEIC) has issued guidance for compliance programs in its "Compliance-Focused Environmental Management System—Enforcement Agreement Guidance" (CFEMS). Modeled after the Federal Sentencing Guidelines for Organizations, the CFEMS identifies 12 criteria (e.g., management policies, oversight of the organization's environmental management system, controls, evaluations, training, and communication) that enhance and ensure an organization's compliance with applicable environmental law and regulation.

The Compliance Program Charter

Consistent with its evolution in significance, the role and duties of the organizational compliance function have grown commensurately. It is the obligation of the organization's board of directors and senior management to define the duties and powers of the compliance program and its management.

Prerequisites

In making this determination, there are a number of important considerations, based on both law and sound management practices, that define an effective organizational compliance program.

- The board of directors and senior management must clearly and unequivocally endorse the role, function, and administrative powers of the compliance program and the chief compliance officer.
- The organization should make every effort, where possible, to maintain the compliance program's independence, impartiality, and objectivity. For instance, the compliance program should not report to a revenue-generating business unit.
- To ensure the compliance program's access to senior management, it is critical that the program not be administratively "buried" within the organization's bureaucracy. Some organizations, for example, follow a rule that the chief compliance officer cannot be more than two staff levels down from the senior business manager.
- The organization must recognize and acknowledge that compliance and ethics are not the sole responsibility of one unit. The National Center for Preventive Law's *Corporate Compliance Principles* point out that the board of directors and senior management leadership "must establish mechanisms that hold all organizational directors, officers, employees and agents accountable for compliance in the course of activities that they initiate or oversee." While the organization's compliance program can bring attention to the issue of compliance and provide the tools and insight necessary to address compliance risks, effective compliance is ultimately the responsibility of the organization's line managers.
- There should be no gaps in the organization's oversight and control of its key compliance risks. Each organizational function that has a control or oversight responsibility—e.g., legal, audit, internal control, financial control, risk, line management, human resources, and security—must clearly understand their roles and their areas of responsibility.

Key Questions

What are the goals for the organization's compliance program?
The board should have a clear and realistic understanding of the goals, policies, programs, standards, and processes that the organization has established. It should be prepared to hold management accountable to these standards, while recognizing the reality that no compliance program, no matter how well designed and executed, can completely protect an organization against wrongdoing.

Is there a clearly defined individual in the organization who has ultimate responsibility for the organization's compliance program? Is there is a clearly defined compliance structure in place, with lines of accountability clearly articulated and communicated?
The organization's directors and senior managers must ensure that the organization has established an effective compliance program that, at a minimum, addresses the elements outlined in the Federal Sentencing Guidelines for Organizations. An effective compliance program requires that an organization assign high-level individuals who will have direct, overall responsibility for the compliance program and give them adequate resources and authority to ensure the program's implementation and effectiveness.

What is the role of the compliance program?
For many organizations, the role of the compliance program has been primarily advisory or counseling. However, over the past decade, compliance programs have evolved and have taken on a number of operational responsibilities, or, as one senior compliance officer termed them, "assurance" activities, such as monitoring and testing business operations. For example, the Securities Industry and Financial Markets Association's *White Paper on the Role of Compliance* (July 2005) says that a compliance program "performs an advisory, monitoring and education role to support management's supervisory responsibility and its efforts to achieve compliance with government and self-regulatory organization ("SRO") rules and regulations and firms policies."

What are the issues that the organization's compliance program will address?
A critical and often vexing question concerns the scope of the issues that the compliance program will address. Will it be involved in all legal, ethical, operational, financial control, and regulatory compliance-related issues? What are the jurisdictional boundaries between the compliance program and organizational units such as audit, legal, and risk? Given the nascent nature of the compliance program, defining its boundaries has been a major issue. One industry professional characterized compliance as "ill-defined." Another veteran compliance officer said, "Compliance has to define for itself what are its boundaries. . . . [E]veryone struggles with these issues. There are no role models."

What are the powers and authority of the chief compliance officer?
The organization should clearly define the powers and authority of the CCO and the compliance program. The person designated as the CCO should have the appropriate level of power and authority to make the compliance program effective. The role and duties of chief compliance officers are discussed further later in this chapter.

Has the organization committed an adequate level of resources to the compliance program?
The board of directors must ensure that management provides sufficient resources (funds, staff, and time) to maintain an effective compliance program.

Features of a Modern Compliance Program

While specific compliance duties may vary depending on the industry, organization, or regulatory requirements, there are certain functions that are increasingly common to all compliance organizations and programs. These functions, based on the recommendations of the Federal Sentencing Guidelines for Organizations and related regulatory guidance, include the following.

Advisory/Counseling

The traditional primary function of modern compliance has been advisory. Working with the organization's board of directors, senior management, and senior managers of individual units, the compliance program offers advice and guidance on matters ranging from relationships with regulators and establishing training protocols to advising on ethical matters. One of the critical advisory functions of compliance units is their involvement in the development of new products and services to identify potential risks and problems and to provide solutions that allow the organization to avoid legal or regulatory situations.

Compliance Policies and Procedures

As the Federal Sentencing Guidelines for Organizations indicate, establishing compliance policies and procedures is a cornerstone of an effective compliance program. The organization's compliance policies and procedures articulate the organization's rules and standards of behavior, organizational processes, oversight responsibilities, and consequences of noncompliance.

Communication

The compliance program develops a comprehensive communication program that provides for the flow of critical compliance- and ethics-related information throughout the organization. It routinely communicates to the organization's employees, contractors, business partners, and other key stakeholders its compliance and ethics policies and practices, developments in law and regulation, and other issues that are of major concern to the organization. Equally important, an effective organizational communication program provides for a mechanism through which employees, volunteers, agents, customers, and other persons can provide information to the organization's senior management, board of directors, or compliance program about any instances of suspected wrongdoing or unethical behavior.

Ethical Issues

The compliance program is actively involved in developing the organization's code of conduct and policies involving standards of behavior (e.g., conflicts of interest), as well as investigating and/or providing advice and guidance involving issues of unethical behavior.

Training and Education

The compliance program implements a comprehensive training and education program that informs and educates employees, including the senior management and directors of the organization, on key issues related to compliance and ethical matters.

Monitoring

Compliance monitoring is another important function of the compliance program. Working with the organization's control and operating units, the compliance program ensures that monitoring or self-testing of key activities, programs, or processes is integrated into business operations. The compliance program reviews monitoring results and works with organizational units to address issues and information that arise from monitoring activities.

Risk Assessment and Internal Controls

The compliance organization undertakes a proactive program to identify critical compliance risk areas (regulatory, reputational, compliance, and ethical) and to determine the effectiveness of the organization's internal control policies and procedures in managing these risks.

Regulatory Relationships

The compliance program plays an important role in maintaining relationships with the organization's regulators to ensure that there is an effective flow of communication between the two parties, ensure that regulatory inquiries are swiftly and appropriately handled, and ensure that the organization is aware of the regulators' current views on compliance requirements and priorities.

Investigations

In conjunction with the organization's legal and audit departments (or outside counsel), the compliance program undertakes investigations into alleged violations of legal and regulatory requirements, compliance policies and practices, or ethical conduct.

The Compliance Structure

The structures of compliance programs are as diverse and unique as their parent organizations. They may be centralized or decentralized, functional (i.e., focusing on a specific risk area, such as equal employment opportunity or anti-money-laundering), attached to a business unit, or stand-alone. They may report to different units in the organization from the CEO or board of directors down through the organizational hierarchy. One interesting example of a compliance program in the public sector is described in Box 5.1

Key Questions

In establishing an organization's compliance structure, the board of directors and senior management will have to address a number of important questions:

- Will the compliance program be a separate unit? If it is a separate unit, where will it operate, and to whom in the organization will it report (administratively or operationally)?
- Will the compliance program be part of another unit? If so, which unit(s) should take on these responsibilities?

> **BOX 5.1   Example of a Public-Sector Compliance Organization**
>
> **The City of Atlanta**
> Public-sector compliance programs have traditionally centered on myriad oversight organs such as autonomous regulatory bodies, executive regulatory bodies, and specialist regulatory bodies and inspectorates (e.g., water compliance specialist, police board, or equal employment opportunity specialist).
>
> However, the city of Atlanta is an exception. It established within its Law Department a compliance unit that is responsible for proactively evaluating, reviewing, and enhancing compliance standards and processes within the city of Atlanta, with a centralized focus on eliminating or reducing the potential for municipal liability with regard to the city of Atlanta's compliance with federal, state, and local laws and regulations.

- What are the views and recommendations of the organization's primary regulator?
- How will the compliance structure fit within the organization's overall administrative and decision-making structure and processes?
- What compliance-related duties and responsibilities will remain at the corporate level? What will be delegated to the other businesses to manage?
- Is the scope of the compliance program's charter consistent with the compliance structure?
- How will the organization coordinate its preexisting control and oversight organizations (e.g., legal, audit, financial, and internal control) with the proposed compliance organization?

Compliance Structures

Given the breadth of the different structures and styles of organizational compliance programs, it is difficult, if not impossible, to typecast any one particular compliance program as a "representative" model. One senior compliance officer for a major corporation noted that in setting up his organization's compliance program, the organization "picked the best features" of numerous compliance programs it had surveyed. The following discussion illustrates some of the designs and structures that organizations frequently use in creating their compliance programs.

The Independent Structure. With an independent structure, the compliance program is a separate and distinct operating unit. It is administratively separate from other organizational units such as legal, audit, and financial control. The chief compliance officer reports directly to the organization's chief executive officer or chief operating officer, with a matrix reporting relationship to the board of directors or one of its committees.

This structure has been lauded by regulators as a preferred method for ensuring the compliance program's independence. In particular, the Office of the Inspector General of the U.S. Department of Health and Human Services has been a strong advocate of this compliance structure. The OIG's views can be seen in the *9th Annual Survey—2007 Profile of Health Care Compliance Officers* by the Health Care Compliance Association. It reported that two-thirds (67 percent) of the compliance offices were stand-alone departments with budgetary responsibilities and staff, and that 64 percent reported directly to the CEO or president of their organization. In contrast to this survey of the health-care industry, surveys of other industries indicate that the independent structure is not widely employed. A November 2005 Ernst & Young survey, *Corporate Regulatory Compliance Practices*, found that only 9 percent of the compliance programs reported directly to the CEO.

The Semiautonomous Structure. With the semiautonomous structure, the compliance program is a separate and distinct operating unit; however, it is administratively a component of another organizational function, most frequently the organization's legal organization and less often risk management (principally in financial services), audit, or financial control (principally for colleges and universities). In this configuration, the chief compliance officer does not report directly to the organization's chief executive officer or the board of directors. However, it is not uncommon for the CCO to have routine access to senior managers within the organization and to report to the board of directors periodically.

The Ernst & Young survey found that more than half of the companies surveyed (52 percent) indicated that the compliance program reported directly to the general counsel, followed by 12 percent that reported to risk management. In contrast, the 2007 survey of health-care compliance officers found that only 12 percent of the compliance officers in that industry reported directly to the organization's general counsel.

The Centralized Compliance Structure. In the centralized compliance structure, the organization's corporate compliance unit establishes and manages the compliance program and mission for the entire organization. All employees of the organization's compliance program, regardless of where they are located geographically or what business function they are assigned to, report through a central compliance organizational structure. They are compensated by the compliance program, not the business unit they may be assigned to.

Under the centralized compliance structure, the organization's compliance officers have a matrix (or "dotted-line") relationship with their business head counterparts, but do not functionally report to those businesses. In this fashion, the compliance program, like a centralized audit function, keeps its own separate identity and sense of independence from the business units that it serves and monitors.

Proponents of the centralized compliance structure cite its standardization of reporting and compliance activities across the organization, as well as the economies of scale that it creates with respect to training, communication, systems, and technology.

The Decentralized Compliance Structure. In the decentralized compliance structure, a corporate-level compliance program establishes the overall compliance program and mission for the entire organization. Unlike the situation in a centralized compliance structure, however, each individual business and compliance unit has the freedom, authority, and resources to develop a compliance organization and program that meets its own particular business needs and requirements.

In this model, there is often a relatively small corporate-level compliance program that coordinates the compliance activities of the organization:

- Establishing minimum standards (a "floor") for business compliance programs
- Developing organization-wide training programs
- Running hotline programs
- Coordinating the flow of information up and across business lines
- Serving as the compliance liaison to the organization's senior management and board of directors

For instance, Altria Group created 11 compliance standards that its operating companies must adhere to in implementing their respective compliance programs. (Box 5.2 shows a sample of some of the Altria Group standards.)

Proponents of the decentralized model cite the flexibility it offers each local operating business to structure a compliance organization program that meets its own particular needs and requirements, and yet keep within the parameters set by the corporation.

The Great Debate: Where Should Compliance Report?

In considering the organization's compliance program and structure (such as the independent and semiautonomous structures described earlier), considerable discussion has raged as to whether compliance should be a separate and distinct function reporting directly to the head of the organization, or whether it should report to another function, most often the organization's general counsel (although in many financial services organizations, it is the chief risk officer) or the audit[1], finance, security, or human resources function. As we have seen, for a majority of non-health-related organizations, the compliance program is a component of the organization's legal unit. The following discussion summarizes the differing points of view.

BOX 5.2   Standards for Compliance and Integrity Programs

Altria Group, Inc.

These Standards have been established to guide our operating companies and corporate functions in carrying out their Compliance and Integrity responsibilities. Each operating company and corporate function will be expected to meet these Standards, and their performance against the Standards will be regularly evaluated.

1. Each operating company and corporate function must have a specific management structure for carrying out its Compliance and Integrity activities.

2. Each operating company and corporate function will define appropriate Compliance and Integrity accountabilities with appropriate business and individual objectives.

3. Each operating company and corporate function will develop an annual Compliance and Integrity plan outlining the concrete steps it will take during the year to meet these Standards.

4. The annual Compliance and Integrity plans will be based on a systematic risk assessment process that identifies potential legal, policy and reputational risks relevant to the business or function. The risk assessment process must incorporate internal and external inputs and link to the strategy, budget and planning cycle of the operating company or corporate function.

5. The senior management of each operating company and corporate function will regularly communicate the importance of Compliance and Integrity. Strong Compliance and Integrity messages will be a part of employee orientation and business training programs at every level.

6. Each operating company and corporate function will develop and implement Compliance and Integrity training and communications programs to educate employees on both their overall obligations and on specific risk areas related to their jobs. These training and communications programs will be reviewed periodically for coverage and effectiveness.

Reporting to the General Counsel. The principal argument made for this reporting relationship is that compliance, with its focus on legal and regulatory matters, is a natural subset of the organization's legal unit. Having the organization's general counsel direct the compliance program ensures that legal expertise is being applied to shape and manage the operations of the program. The general counsel, Dov Seidman explained in the February 2005 issue of *Optimize*, offers several other advantages. He or she is "familiar with critical compliance areas, likely has established relationship with relevant regulatory bodies, and enjoys access to senior management and the board."

Not surprisingly, the American Bar Association has endorsed this position. Its Task Force on Corporate Governance wrote, "Counsel. . . should have primary responsibility for assuring the implementation of an effective legal compliance system under the oversight of the board."

Other advocates for this approach cite the following issues:

- The advantages of attorney-client privilege that the compliance program enjoys when it is part of the organization's legal unit.
- The prestige and power of being associated with the organization's chief legal officer (CLO). As a former senior lawyer for a major investment corporation noted, "CLOs have a lot of clout in the organization."
- Finally, there are the views of a former head of a major global corporation who favored having the compliance program report to his chief legal officer, not directly to him. He preferred that the company's CLO use his or her judgment to screen which compliance issues would be brought his attention.

Reporting to the CEO and the Board. Advocates of having the compliance program report directly to the organization's CEO and board of directors offer the following reasons:

- Many of the core responsibilities of an effective compliance and ethics program are functions and duties that are generally not part of the responsibilities of the chief legal officer's organization. They include training, communication, risk assessment, and auditing and monitoring programs—functions that attorneys generally have neither the training, the experience, nor the interest to oversee.
- By having a compliance program report to the general counsel's office, there is a fear that it will become a "second-rate" issue.

Steve Ortquist, a compliance officer (and attorney) noted this concern in the *Journal of Health Care Compliance* (May/ June 2004):

> *I have talked to many compliance professionals who are at the end of their rope precisely because they report to a general counsel or other organizational leader, with no outlet to the organization's chief executive or board, and the general counsel is too busy with other things to give [the] compliance program's operation the attention that it needs.*

Even a U.S. senator has had a view on this matter. In 2003, the Senate was investigating the Tenet Healthcare Corporate regarding its use of federal tax monies. In a September 5, 2003, letter to Tenet, U.S. Senator Charles Grassley of Iowa said, "Apparently, neither Tenet (nor its General Counsel) saw any conflict in her wearing two hats as Tenet's General Counsel and Chief Compliance Officer. . . . It doesn't take a pig farmer from Iowa to smell the stench of conflict in that arrangement."

The Regulators' View. Not surprisingly, regulators in various industries, such as finance and health care, have voiced their opinions on this matter and expressed support for a direct reporting relationship between the chief compliance officer and the CEO and the board. In the health-care industry, for instance, the OIG of the U.S. Department of Health and Human Services has expressed concern about possible conflict between the compliance program and other functions in the organization, including the general counsel. In its guidance to the pharmaceutical industry, it said the following:[2]

> *The OIG believes it is generally not advisable for the compliance program to be subordinate to the pharmaceutical manufacturer's general counsel, or comptroller or similar financial officer. Separation of the compliance function helps to ensure independent and objective legal reviews and financial analysis of the company's compliance efforts and activities.*

Outsourcing Compliance

The outsourcing of organizational compliance is not a new phenomenon. For many organizations, it is a long-standing practice. The use of external accountants to assist with tax and reporting requirements, outside counsel to address legal issues, and temporary employment agencies to manage staffing responsibilities is common practice. What has changed, however, is that for many organizations, the range and weight of legal and regulatory requirements and the lack of resources (e.g. funds, systems, or in-house technical expertise) have opened a new avenue for dealing with compliance matters: outsourcing all or part of the organization's compliance program to a third party.

Recognizing the financial opportunities, a virtual industry of vendors, consultants, and service providers has arisen over the past decade. These entities will undertake any number of compliance-related functions for client organizations, ranging from risk assessment and regulatory reporting to training and communication, development of policies and procedures, and even organizational climate surveys. It is common practice for organizations to outsource the management of their hotline programs.

Advantages and Disadvantages of Outsourcing Compliance

Given the growth of the outsourcing industry and its impact on organizational compliance programs, it is important to examine the arguments that have been advanced for and against this practice.

Advantages. Organizations view the outsourcing of their compliance from several perspectives.

- A third-party vendor offers a wealth of experience and knowledge; its sole focus is on compliance. It knows the industry, regulatory requirements, "best practices," systems, and technology. The vendor can evaluate an organization's operations and controls to assess their effectiveness and provide a range of services that the client organization could not afford to provide with its own internal staff or resources.

- Financially, outsourcing reduces organizational costs. Ruth Evans, writing in the *Journal of Investment Compliance* (2005), said, "[T]he purpose of outsourcing is to achieve a permanent reduction in costs but it can also offer flexibility in a shorter timeframe. Capital outlay can be shared or even avoided. Functions that do not bring the firm competitive advantage or which are high in labor costs can be shed discreetly to a supplier who can spread the costs efficiently over several customers."

Disadvantages. Outsourcing a compliance program or a component of that program does not absolve the client organization of responsibility for meeting regulatory requirements. By outsourcing this function, the client organization loses control over the compliance operation to some extent, and outsourcing also increases the potential for significant problems if the outsourcing vendors do not have adequate safeguards in place to manage the client organization's resources (e.g., client data) effectively and safely. Finally, by outsourcing a compliance program, the client organization loses or fails to develop an internal capability to ultimately manage this responsibility (especially if it decides to take back the outsourced compliance program).

When Considering the Outsourcing of Compliance

There are a number of issues that an organization should consider if it decides to outsource its compliance operations.

Which components will be outsourced?
An organization needs to determine whether it will outsource its entire compliance operation or a compliance-related component. For instance, would it outsource transaction monitoring, training, communications, hotline operations, or a combination of all of these?

What is the quality of the vendor?
It is incumbent upon the client organization to thoroughly evaluate the potential service provider:

- What are the qualifications of the service provider (e.g., principal staff, equipment, and systems)?
- Does the service provider have the appropriate licenses, and is it familiar with the policies, rules, and examination procedures of the client organization's regulator(s)?
- Is the service provider financially stable?
- How well does the service provider know the client organization and its industry?
- Can the service provider effectively customize its systems and services to make them applicable to the client organization?

What are the views of the organization's regulators?
The views of the organization's regulators concerning the outsourcing of compliance functions may have a significant bearing on whether the client organization proceeds with outsourcing. In recent years, for example, a number of regulators in the financial services sector (the Basel Committee on Banking Supervision, the International Association of Insurance Supervisors, and the International Organization of Securities Commissions) have issued guidance on the outsourcing of compliance. In the United States, the Securities and Exchange Commission has strong views regarding the outsourcing of compliance. In a 2004 speech, Lori Richards, director of the SEC's Office of Compliance Inspections and Examinations, said:

> *I also understand that many fund firms are thinking about "outsourcing" the Chief Compliance Officer function. . . . [L]et me caution you that the Chief Compliance Officer is responsible for administering the fund's compliance program, which includes both adopting and implementing the policies and procedures. She has to have intimate knowledge of the firm's operations in order to administer an effective compliance program. . . . I am wary about whether compliance "rent a cop" could really be up to the task.*

What are the legal liabilities?

You need to clearly understand the client organization's and the service provider's legal liabilities. Who is responsible for mistakes or failures? Does the consulting agreement include guarantees of confidentiality and protection of the client's intellectual property? What are the limits on the consultant's liability?

Managing an Outsourced Compliance Program

To manage an outsourced compliance program effectively, the client organization, at a minimum, should

- Ensure that any agreement between the client organization and the service provider is in writing, and that the duties and responsibilities of the service provider are clearly delineated.
- Monitor the service provider on an ongoing basis. Ask to see a copy of its SAS 70 report. Visit the service provider. If it is handling organizational data, understand the provisions it has put in place to protect the privacy of the information, backup facilities, restoration of data, background checks on people handling the data, and other such information. If it is sending the data to other countries to handle, what are the provisions in those countries for handling client and other critical data adequately and safely?
- Never forget about the outsourced program. Understand that the client organization never loses the ultimate responsibility for the compliance obligation.

Coordinating the Compliance Program

A hallmark of an effective organizational compliance program is its ability to work closely with others, to seek advice and guidance, and to gain trust, cooperation, and credibility in carrying out its mission and functions.

The Board of Directors and Senior Management

One of the major responsibilities of the chief compliance officer is working with the board of directors and senior management of the organization. See Box 5.3. This is an integral component of the compliance program. Access to the board and senior management is required under the provisions of the Federal Sentencing Guidelines for Organizations as well as specific industry regulatory requirements (e.g., FINRA and OIG-DHHS).

Key Issues

How often will the CCO report to the CEO and the board of directors?
The frequency of CCO reporting ranges from intermittent reporting on an "as-needed" basis to monthly reporting sessions. A 2006 report by the Conference Board, *Universal Conduct: An Ethics and Compliance Benchmarking Survey*, found that 39 percent of chief compliance officers reported quarterly to the board of directors.

Will the CCO have direct access to the board and/or its key committees, and what will he or she report on?
Under the provisions of the Federal Sentencing Guidelines for Organizations, the chief compliance officer is obligated to "report periodically to the Board on the status of the compliance program, the resources required to maintain its viability, and the organization's response to identified compliance deficiencies." The SEC, in its rule on compliance programs of investment companies and investment advisors, states:

> *We are requiring that the chief compliance officer meet in executive session with the independent directors at least once each year, without anyone else (such as fund management or interested directors) present. The executive session creates an opportunity for the chief compliance officer and the independent directors to speak freely about any sensitive compliance*

BOX 5.3   Delivering Bad News. . . and Surviving

One of the more challenging duties of a compliance officer is having to deliver "bad" news to the organization's board of directors and senior management. Based on discussions with senior compliance, human resources, legal, and business managers, the following advice is offered:

- Be confident in your discussion of the situation.
- Make sure that your facts are accurate in the following areas:
    The incident
    The people involved (employees, third parties, or someone else)
    The time sequence
    The initial response and subsequent actions
- Keep the discussion objective, not personal.
- Know why it is important that a presentation is being made to this person or group.
- Know the audience (the senior management team or the audit committee).
- Understand the possible consequences of the reported misbehavior for the organization or other employees: reputation damage, fines, penalties, criminal or civil actions, disbarment, or even termination of employment.
- Be prepared for a range of responses from shock, disbelief, and anger to no reaction at all and "whose fault is it?"
- Be prepared to discuss possible next steps to address the situation.

issues of concern to any of them, including any reservations about the cooperativeness or compliance practices of fund management.

Compliance Committees and Councils

A popular mechanism for coordinating the flow of information and compliance activities across diverse aspects of an organization has been the formation of compliance committees or councils. Both the Office of the Inspector General of the Department of Health and Human Services and the Federal Deposit Insurance Corporation (FDIC) advocate the creation of a compliance committee. These committees are known by a variety of names: compliance and integrity council, business conduct committee, or compliance coordinating council. Organizations have established these committees at various levels of their organizations: corporate, regional, country, or local.

While their titles and their location in the organizational hierarchy may vary, these committees generally share some common characteristics, functions, and responsibilities:

- These committees often include representatives from the key business or operating units and the legal, compliance, audit, risk, human resources, and finance functions.
- They provide guidance on organizational policies and practices, training, and communication.
- They address gaps in compliance areas or identify conflicts or overlapping areas of responsibility.
- They review the effectiveness of existing compliance programs.
- They identify and discuss forthcoming legal and regulatory developments in their areas of responsibility and discuss the potential impact of those developments on the organization.

Compliance committees can be a valuable tool. Having representatives from the organization's key operating groups participate demonstrates the importance of compliance and the reality that compliance transcends more than only one person or function. A compliance committee can also assist the organization's compliance officer in difficult strategic or conflict situations. As one compliance officer said, "It takes the load off when issues get sticky." The FDIC, however, has cautioned that a compliance committee has its limitations. In its 2003 publication *Compliance Management Systems*, the FDIC said, "The ultimate responsibility of overall compliance with all statutes and regulations resides with the board."

Major Organizational Units

A major responsibility of and challenge for the nascent compliance function is its interaction with other organizational units. Without careful planning and a clear understanding of unit prerogatives and responsibilities, there is a strong possibility of confusion over the roles and duties of the compliance program vis-à-vis other organizational units, e.g., legal, audit, risk, and business line management. A veteran senior compliance officer for a major financial institution emphasized the importance of establishing an effective working relationship with peer organizational units. Without careful coordination, these units run the risk of not only stepping on each other's toes but, perhaps more importantly, antagonizing the business head with conflicting organizational units addressing the same issues. This view was confirmed in the 2005 Ernst & Young report *Corporate Regulatory Compliance Practices*. It reported that "less than half of the respondents [said] that the roles and responsibilities of the compliance function were clearly differentiated from other groups such as Legal, Audit, Operational Risk Management, and the Business Units. Overlapping roles and responsibilities, both actual and perceived, is prevalent."

Business or Operating Units. An effective relationship between line managers and compliance is crucial. The reality is that within organizations, the relationship between managers and the compliance program runs the gamut from acceptance as an important corporate function to enmity as a corporate nuisance, impediment, or worse. The author vividly remembers an encounter with a senior manager in his organization who described the author's role as a compliance officer as a "necessary evil."

Perhaps the veteran senior compliance officer cited earlier summed it up best when he said that inherently "it will always be a struggle" between the compliance function and a business manager. The compliance officer is in a conflicting role as a consultant and an auditor, as well as a member of the organization's management team. The compliance officer has to be able to give independent advice and go above the business manager to senior management or the board of directors if something is amiss.

Staffing the Compliance Program

A critical decision point for the organization involves the management personnel for the compliance program. The knowledge, skills, and attitudes of the organizational compliance staff are critical determinants of the program's ultimate success or failure. This is especially important because most compliance programs have a relatively small number of full-time employees. For example, the Conference Board's report found that a majority of the 225 companies surveyed (58 percent) said that "their company's compliance and ethics programs have less than three full-time equivalents (FTE's) dedicated to carrying out the compliance and ethics functions. Almost one out of every three companies has only one person (or less) dedicated to the compliance and ethics function." Only 3 percent of the organizations surveyed had 21 to 30 full-time employees dedicated to the compliance function. There are several choices, each with its own strengths and weaknesses, that an organization can consider in staffing its compliance program.

A Typology of Compliance Officers

The skills and experiences of an organization's chief compliance officer and his or her staff need to mesh with the compliance program. In broad terms, the roles and duties of compliance officers can be categorized into three major groupings, although there may be some overlapping of roles and duties, especially in smaller organization, where compliance officers frequently assume multiple tasks.

The Compleat Compliance Officer. The compleat compliance officer focuses on the broad issues of organizational compliance: culture, ethics, integrity, training, communications, investigations, and broad risk assessment. His or her focus is less on specific compliance with particular laws and regulations (which is the responsibility of specialized units) and more on the major issues of governance, ethics, and integrity.

The Technical Compliance Officer. In contrast to the compleat compliance officer, the technical compliance officer, as the name implies, focuses principally on compliance with technical rules and regulations. Such an officer's principal duties revolve around issues related to self-assessment, controls, monitoring, risk assessment, surveillance, and testing to ensure compliance.

The Ad Hoc Compliance Officer. The ad hoc compliance officer generally has other principal control and oversight functions and responsibilities, such as financial control, audit, or risk management, but is utilized "as needed" when the situation arises, e.g., in the case of a regulatory audit or a special training program.

Skills and Experience

Staffing the compliance program depends on the scope of the anticipated compliance program and the skills, knowledge, and experience that the staff will have to bring to the anticipated function. Organizations have a variety of choices: lawyers, business specialists, auditors, professional compliance staff, technologists, and communications and educational specialists. A popular choice has been former industry regulators who have extensive knowledge of regulatory issues, philosophy, examination practices, and personnel.

The need for experience may also dictate whether the organization will promote someone from inside the organization, who knows its inner workings, or hire an individual from outside the organization who brings new experience and insight. Another factor in deciding whether to use a new hire or a current employee is whether the organization is facing a regulatory examination. There may not be adequate time for a new employee to learn the organization before the forthcoming examination.

Chief Compliance Officer—a Lawyer or Not?. Similar to the controversy over whether the chief compliance officer should report to the organization's general counsel, there has been considerable discussion about whether or not the chief compliance officer should be a lawyer. In many respects, the issues involved in this discussion mirror the arguments in the earlier controversy.

Proponents of having the organization's chief compliance officer be a lawyer cite the immediacy and importance of the legal and regulatory issues that the compliance program must address. Jose Tabuena and Jennifer Smith, writing in the *Journal of Health Care Compliance* (July/August 2006), observed, "An attorney provides legal advice on how the organization can comply with applicable laws while attaining its business objectives. It is this 'legal advice' that is subject to licensure, regulation, and professional standards."

The alternative perspective is that an effective organizational compliance and ethics program transcends legal and regulatory issues. Citing the Federal Sentencing Guidelines for Organizations, it views an effective compliance and ethics program as involving education, training, communication, risk assessment, internal controls, and policy-making activities. Many of these activities are not traditionally part of the corporate attorney's experience or training.

Beyond the issue of skills or experience, there is the subtle issue of the role and attitudes of a lawyer in performing a compliance function. It has been argued that lawyers have a "narrow legalistic view," while a chief compliance officer often needs a "broader vision" of issues, or, in the words of one CCO, has to be someone who has "a big picture vision." Tabuena and Smith frame the issue in a slightly different fashion:

> *Being general counsel and being CCO are very different things, a lawyer, ethically, has a duty to give sound legal advice and to represent the client's interests "zealously." The compliance officer's mission is substantially different: it is to do whatever it takes to prevent and detect misconduct. While the lawyer may give legal advice, the compliance professional translates that advice into management action.*

Finally, from a pragmatic standpoint, being a lawyer may give the CCO a degree of prestige and respectability in the eyes of his or her peers and superiors that a nonlawyer might not enjoy. One CCO, who happens to be a lawyer, succinctly called it "an optics thing."

The Role of the Chief Compliance Officer[3]

What are the appropriate role, power, and authority for the organization's chief compliance officer? Each organization has its own unique circumstances, and the board of directors and senior management will have to determine the scope and limits of their chief compliance officer's realm. Following are some of the issues that will have to be addressed.

Will the chief compliance officer have the power, prestige, and authority necessary to make the compliance program effective?
The CCO, in the words of the National Center for Preventive Law's *Corporate Compliance Principles,* must have the "authority and access to the organization's governance authorities in order to ensure both that the officer is able to exert effective control over compliance-related matters and that compliance management is perceived as an important activity by other organization members."

The reality, however, is that compliance officers often have restricted powers and authority. Their powers are those that have been expressly granted to them by the CEO or the board of directors. In most organizations, they cannot fire employees for misbehavior, compel organizational managers to cooperate in an initiative, or unilaterally stop a new product or service that potentially represents a compliance risk. Their authority and prestige come from their "nexus of power" with the organization's board of directors, CEO, or executive committee and their ability to be a "moral persuader," in the words of one CCO.

Will the chief compliance officer have the required access to the organization's resources, documentation, and employees?
The chief compliance officer should be able to

- Draw upon the expertise available in the organization (e.g., legal, accounting, system, communication, or human resources expertise) to accomplish his or her mission.
- Have unfettered access to the records, systems, and personnel of other organizational units to pursue investigations or other areas of inquiry.
- Have the authority and ability to communicate throughout the organization on key compliance-related issues.

Is there someone on the board or one of its committees that the chief compliance officer can speak with directly when the situation requires that organization's CEO or some other senior management official be excluded because that individual is the subject of serious allegations of wrongdoing? Provision should be made for the chief compliance office or his or her equivalent to meet directly with the board or the committee head responsible for compliance to address special situations involving senior management.

What is the CCO's role and accountability in the compliance process? Questions have arisen as to the role and accountability of the CCO in overseeing an organization's policies. Is the CCO's role oversight or enforcement? In a 2005 article in *National Underwriter*, a CCO for a major investment company saw his role as being an overseer of policies, not an enforcer of those policies. He said, "It's about internal control. . . . I'm not taking accountability [to mean] day-to-day control of the processes, but [to mean] I have accountability for monitoring those processes," to ensure that they are operating appropriately.

Qualities of an Effective Compliance Officer

A paramount concern for an organization is the qualities and personal characteristics of the individual who will be leading and promoting the organization's compliance and ethics program. Given the generally small number of full-time compliance officers in most organizations, this is a critical organizational decision. The CCO becomes the embodiment of the organization's attitudes toward compliance, ethics, and integrity.

- In the words of the National Center for Preventive Law's *Corporate Compliance Principles*, the chief compliance officer's "reputation for integrity, ability to forge relationships of trust, and personal credibility ethics are of paramount importance for a successful program." The compliance officer not only must have a personal reputation that is above reproach, but must be able to make unpopular decisions and stand by his or her views.
- An effective compliance officer has the critical skill to relate to different personalities in the organization to manage conflicting demands and requirements, and to successfully present his or her ideas and suggestions (see Box 5.4). One veteran compliance officer,

BOX 5.4   A Word of Caution

Presenting compliance-related findings and recommendations to senior management and the board of directors requires skill, understanding, and expertise. Organizational managers look for the value of proposed changes. Does the proposed policy or process save money or represent concrete value and worth to the organization? However, one veteran compliance officer cautioned, "Never use 'compliance' in any proposed policy; it is the kiss of death."

Steve Ortquist, commented in the *Journal of Health Care Compliance* (March/April 2005), "Most compliance officers I am acquainted with have the ability to grasp complex situations quickly and can resolve and explain them clearly. They are able to multitask. They can negotiate successfully—even with difficult people.

- In the view of one senior attorney and former compliance officer for a major investment company, the compliance officer must be seen as "being independent" and "having a healthy degree of skepticism that only comes from experience."
- Functional expertise and experience are critical. Dov Seidman, writing in the February 2005 issue of *Optimize*, said of this quality, "When selecting a CCO, the company should target an individual with a deep, nuanced understanding of the compliance issues and regulatory requirements germane to the company and industry."

Protections for the Compliance Officer

It is evident that the position of compliance officer has risks and carries with it the potential for termination of employment, whether voluntary or involuntary. See Box 5.5. While no compliance officer is ever guaranteed immunity from having his or her employment terminated, there are actions that the organization's board of directors and senior management can take to assure some degree of protection for the compliance staff:

- Establish in the charter of the compliance program criteria for protection of the compliance officer. One option is to require the

> **BOX 5.5   Falling on One's Sword**
>
> There comes a moment in all employees' careers, including that of the organization's chief compliance officer, when a decision as to whether they can continue to be employed in their function has to be made. The particular decision point is unique to each person. For people in the compliance function, the circumstances may include
>
> - The CCO has no ability to influence senior management or the board.
> - The CCO has no access to senior management or to the board.
> - People stop listening to the CCO and his or her staff.
> - The CCO is unable to prevent or stop illegal or unethical actions.
> - Documentation to the board or senior management is censored or so edited that it does not reflect the CCO's findings and judgments.
> - There is a radical reduction in resources, making it impossible to maintain an effective compliance organization and program.

    approval of the board of directors before the chief compliance officer can be dismissed, demoted, or transferred to a new position.

- Give the compliance officer an employment contract that provides him or her with some protection. Although this is not a common employment practice in the United States, except for the most senior positions in organizations, it is an opportunity to articulate the specific criteria for dismissal for its chief compliance officer and any compensation or benefits that he or she may be entitled to.
- Establish mandatory reporting to the board of directors, one of its committees, or the chair of the board when management is ignoring the chief compliance officer's advice and guidance.
- Give the CCO the ability to acquire his or her own lawyer at the organization's expense. According to the 2007 *Profile of Health Care Compliance Officers*, 41 percent of the respondents had this opportunity.
- Ensure that the chief compliance officer is included under the company's directors and officers (D&O) insurance coverage. This provides some protection to the CCO and allows him or her to undertake investigations or inquiries, or make decisions that may be problematic.

Full-Time or Part-Time Staff

Depending on the scope of the organizational compliance program and the resources available to the organization, a decision will have to be made regarding the need for full-time or part-time staff, or a combination of both. As discussed previously, except in a small minority of large, heavily regulated businesses, most organizational compliance and ethics programs are relatively small. The goal for many organizations is to maximize the resources it can provide to the compliance program within budgetary limits.

Part-Time Staff. The use of alternative staff configurations has its virtues as well as its downside. Companies frequently utilize part-time compliance staff who have a matrix (or dotted-line) reporting relationship with the corporate compliance program. These staff members have various titles—business practices officers, compliance champions, or compliance liaisons—but they all share the same goal: representing the corporation's compliance program and providing a compliance presence in their various businesses. Their duties are often the same as those of their full-time peers: training, policy interpretation, advice on ethics issues, self-assessment, communication, and risk assessment.

A study by Joshua Joseph in *Business and Society Review* (2002), which focused on ethics officers but is equally applicable to compliance officers, explored these staffing arrangements.

Pros:

- Part-time employees can bring important operational knowledge and experience to the function and can increase "program credibility among employees."
- Using part-time staff "can help to increase program ownership among employees and reduce potential isolation of the [compliance] and ethics function."

Cons:

- The compliance and ethics knowledge of part-time ethics staff may not be on a par with that of full-time employees.

- Full-time employees have greater continuity in their positions than part-time staffers. The "timeliness in [compliance and] ethics-related work can be a problem for part-time ethics staff because their other responsibilities may sometimes take precedence."

One of the key issues associated with part-time compliance officers involves their independence and their primary relationship to the business organizations in which they work. Various strategies have been used to maintain a degree of compliance control with respect to these positions:

- The matrix compliance manager should approve all persons named to part-time compliance positions. Part-time compliance staff should have the same skills and personal qualities of ethics and integrity as full-time compliance employees.
- The matrix compliance manager should review the performance appraisal and compensation for the part-time compliance officers.

Certifications and Licensing

There are few governmental or regulatory requirements mandating that organizational compliance officers be certified or licensed (the securities industry is an exception). The certification of compliance officers is primarily driven by industry standards and practices, and the breadth of certification programs can be staggering:

- Certification programs in health-care corporate compliance
- Certification programs for compliance professionals in the pharmaceutical and medical device industries
- Certification programs for specialized bank compliance functions (e.g., Bank Secrecy Act, Anti-Money Laundering, or USA Patriot Act certification)
- Even a certification program for a compliance and ethics professional

There is also debate within the compliance community as to the merits of certification for compliance professionals. As discussed in a 2007 report, *Leading Corporate Integrity: Defining the Role of Chief Ethics and Compliance Officer*, proponents cite the professional enhancement that certification offers, while others point to the difficulty of defining the precise scope of the compliance professional's role or even developing a test to measure competency. On the latter point, the report said, "[K]nowledge of ethics, personal character, familiarity with process, and legislation are all broad areas, some of which are difficult to quantify."

Budgeting for the Compliance Program

Compliance is a two-edged sword: while it offers protection, it comes at a cost. There is no evading that reality. The head of a small financial resources organization calls it "a non-income-producing event." For many organizations, this is an era of tight budgets and limited resources. Compliance entails costs in terms of staff, time, and resources, e.g., training, systems, consulting, travel, and communications expenses. Yet these are costs that most organizations feel they have no choice but to absorb (or pass along to their customers). The passage of Sarbanes-Oxley has focused attention on the costs of compliance. This has been especially the case for small and medium-sized public organizations, which have expressed grave concerns over the accounting cost incurred to comply with the legislation.

An effective compliance program's budget and staff must be commensurate with the size and activities of the organization. The National Center for Preventive Law cautioned, "Appointment of a compliance manager without any resources to allow the manager to effectively carry out the compliance program may be seen by judges as an effort to mislead the court. That can have a worse effect on criminal sentencing than having no program at all." However, the CCO of a global corporation had some sobering words of caution. A compliance program "cannot look like we are fat. . . . [We have] got to be lean."

Depending on the scope, size, and mandate of the compliance program, the organization will have to address several budgetary issues:

Who controls the budget for the compliance organization?
Ideally, the compliance program should able be to operate without undue or improper influence from other segments of the organization. To achieve this measure of independence, the compensation of the compliance staff should not be tied to the financial performance or revenues produced by a specific business or product. As a result, the budget for the compliance program should be set by the highest authority in the organization.

How is compensation (salary, increases, bonus, and stock options) for compliance employees determined?

- *Salary.* There are various professional publications and trade associations that publish annual surveys of compliance officers' salaries; for example, the Ethics & Compliance Officer Association publishes an annual salary survey of compliance officer compensation across industries. Similarly, the Heath Care Compliance Association and America's Community Bankers publish compensation surveys for their respective industries.
- *Bonus.* A key issue is whether to tie the compliance officer's bonus to financial criteria (i.e., the financial performance of the organization) or nonfinancial criteria. Tying the compliance officer's bonus to financial performance can be problematic insofar as it gives the appearance of undue influence over compliance performance. Nonfinancial criteria that can be used include the CCO's effectiveness in meeting his or her annual management objectives or the CCO's performance in detecting and responding to problems, working with colleagues and regulators, installing compliance programs in the organization, and developing education, training, and communication initiatives.

What are the criteria for promotions?
As for any other managerial-level position, the evaluation of the compliance officer's performance and opportunities for advancement should

measure such factors as individual performance evaluations, achievement(s), and effectiveness of unit goals.

How can the organization take advantage of existing resources to offset the cost of compliance programs?

For organizations with limited financial resources, it may be prudent to determine whether some of the compliance program activities can be accomplished using existing organizational resources. For instance, employee communications can use the same resources that the organization uses for communicating with managers and employees on other matters, or the organization's technology staff can help to design online reporting and training programs.

Compliance Costs

In general, the cost elements for an organizational compliance program fall into three major categories:

Headcount. By far the largest cost item for a compliance program is for staff. This expense item includes salaries and benefit costs for full-time and/or part-time compliance staff. The 2007 Annual Profile of Health Care Compliance Officers reported that 63 percent of the organization's compliance budget was spent on salaries. A February 2006 report by the Securities Industry and Financial Markets Association (SIFMA), *The Costs of Compliance,* noted that staff expenses accounted for more than 90 percent of an organization's compliance costs.

Administrative. This expense item includes office space, office equipment and supplies, and travel.

Program Expenses. These expenses include such items as consultants, communication costs, technology, subscriptions, conferences (vital for information and benchmarking purposes), training and education, staff training, and professional dues.

Small and Medium-Sized Organizations

The vast majority of businesses and nonprofit organizations in the United Stares are small or medium-sized organizations.[4] Their relationship to compliance is complex, combining elements of resignation, pro forma compliance, financial burdens, limited resources, and often reliance on third parties to meet their compliance obligations. As a museum official artfully explained, compliance is in the "natural language" of how they have to conduct their operations. There is no real choice. The challenge is how to meet these diverse and time-consuming obligations with limited staff, money, and expertise. The president of a small college echoed this concern. With a limited budget and constant pressure for limited resources, he said, "You can't dot all the 'i's,' and cross all the 't's.'"

The struggle of small and medium-sized organizations to manage their regulatory burdens is well documented. Like their counterparts in the non-profit world, they struggle to keep their organizations flexible and cost-efficient without having to establish bureaucratic structures and systems, and yet, at the same time, to satisfy the compliance requirements of their respective regulators. The director of a small investment company expressed frustration at the ongoing requirements of satisfying regulators' demands for systemic internal controls and reports in a business that serviced only a relatively small handful of select clients. How does an enterprise remain small and entrepreneurial and avoid having to institutionalize the type of processes and internal controls required of organizations a thousand times its size? This investment company director's frustrations were echoed by the head of a small financial services organization, who for the first time had to hire a full-time internal auditor to satisfy the firm's burgeoning regulatory requirements.

At a 1999 conference[5] hosted by the Office of the Inspector General of the Department of Health and Human Services and the Health Care Compliance Association, the concerns of small and rural health-care providers about undertaking a comprehensive compliance program were vividly summarized:

> *Many cannot afford the cost of extensive employee screening, training and hotline services. Some providers that have made significant investments into human resources functions cannot*

maintain both offices at full capacity, nor can they meet all the requirements of the OIG's compliance program guidance. Cost is a major factor in implementing a compliance program and as one attendee stated: "the more compliance you do, the more you have to do."

The head of the small financial services organization mentioned previously summarized the issue succinctly: "If you cannot comply [with regulations] don't do the business." It is like insurance, the person said. You can function without it, but at great risk to the organization.

Regulatory and Compliance Responsibilities

While small and medium-sized organizations are required to meet the same compliance obligations as their larger organizational counterparts, regulators and self-regulatory organizations have recognized the challenges posed by the need for compliance programs and have started to address these concerns in their regulatory guidance.

- The Federal Sentencing Guidelines for Organizations specifically address small organizations. They state, "Small organizations shall demonstrate the same degree of commitment to ethical conduct and compliance with the law as large organizations. However, a small organization may meet the requirements of this guideline with less formality and fewer resources than would be expected of large organizations. In appropriate circumstances, reliance on existing resources and simple systems can demonstrate a degree of commitment that, for a large organization, would only be demonstrated through more formally planned and implemented systems."
- In 2000, the Department of Health and Human Services' Office of the Inspector General issued its "Compliance Program Guidance for Individual and Small Group Physician Practices." The guidance is important for two reasons: it recognizes that small entities do not have the resources that larger organizations possess, and, equally important, its suggestions can serve as a

model that other small organizations can use to address their compliance obligations.

- The EPA's Small Business Compliance Policy offers special incentives to small businesses that promote environmental compliance. The agency will eliminate civil penalties for small businesses that "voluntarily discover, promptly disclose, and correct violations in a timely manner." Conditions for participation in the program require the small business to (1) have a "good" compliance record, (2) voluntarily discover the violation (e.g., through on-site compliance assistance or a voluntary environmental audit), (3) disclose the violation in writing within 21 days of discovery, and (4) correct the violation and remedy any associated harm within 180 days of its discovery (360 days if correction will involve using pollution prevention technologies).

Strategies, Practices, and Resources

The reality for small and medium-sized organizations is that the resources needed to create a separate, formal compliance program are often prohibitive (and disproportionate to their size and needs). As the FDIC has noted in its *Compliance Management System*, "The formality of the compliance program is not as important as its effectiveness. This is especially true for small institutions where the program may not be in writing but an effective monitoring system has been established that ensures overall compliance."

In the absence of a formal compliance program, these organizations employ a number of strategies and techniques to address their compliance obligations while managing costs. Many organizations have adopted an "externalization of compliance" strategy in which they rely on the advice and guidance of vendors, service providers, and others to provide critical information and assistance to address their compliance obligations.

For example, the head of human resources for a small Midwestern company uses her insurance broker to help her keep up-to-date on issues related to employee benefits and overtime laws. In the health-care industry, small organizations similarly rely on external resources. A small physical therapy practice in New York State uses a network of external resources to help manage its compliance requirements: for tax compliance, it calls upon its accountant; for patient reimbursement issues under Medicare, it consults with the Department of Health and Human Services' third-party payment contractor; to ensure that its equipment meets government standards, it relies on its equipment maintenance company; and for advice on practice and legal issues, it relies on its professional association for the latest updates on legal developments and advice.

Key Points

For small and medium-sized organizations, a realistic compliance goal and strategy is incremental organizational change to address key compliance vulnerabilities, not a radical introduction of a new compliance program and structure. As a first step in addressing their compliance obligations effectively, these organizations should ascertain the following:

- What are their compliance risks, where are their greatest vulnerabilities, and where do they need to place their resources?
- Do their existing programs meet their regulatory requirements?
- What additional resources may be needed to address their vulnerabilities and fill any gaps? Are the organization's existing resources sufficient to deal with these vulnerabilities, or will changes have to be postponed until additional resources are available?

Other strategies include the following:

- The 2004 Amendments to the Federal Sentencing Guidelines for Organizations provide examples of what are acceptable practices for smaller organizations:
  - The [organization's] governing authority directly managing the organization's compliance and ethics efforts

- Training employees through informal staff meetings and monitoring them through regular "walk-arounds" or continuous observation while managing the organization
- Using available personnel, rather than employing separate staff, to carry out the compliance and ethics program
- Modeling the organization's compliance and ethics program on existing, well-regarded compliance and ethics programs and best practices of other similar organizations
- A crucial element for managing compliance in small and medium-sized enterprises is experienced and knowledgeable staff members who know when to ask questions and raise concerns to senior managers.
- As noted, organizations are using outsourcing strategies to address their compliance obligations. From anti-money-laundering information systems to e-mail archiving systems, organizations are using vendors to address their compliance requirements.
- Organizations are increasingly using compliance-based information Web sites established by government agencies and other organizations. These Web sites convey critical information on laws, regulations, voluntary compliance programs, and technical assistance opportunities. The Defense Industry Initiative on Business Ethics and Conduct has a Web site for its subcontractors, many of which are small companies, in which it offers a "tool kit" on organizational compliance for these organizations to use.
- As discussed earlier, small and medium-sized organization often rely on employees wearing multiple hats to manage the organization's compliance responsibilities. Kirk Ruddell, a compliance officer for a small rural hospital, offered some guidance for compliance officers in similar circumstances. In an interview in the March/April 2006 *Journal of Health Care Compliance*, he said:

For the part-time compliance officer with no dedicated staff in a small facility, the first thing I would say is, "Don't bite

*off more than you can chew."... Concentrate on a few things
one quarter, a few more the next, and don't hesitate to let
some wait until next year if possible. Second, I would say,
"Don't try to do it all by yourself." Cultivate collaborative
relationships with the experts in your organization.*

Summary

Establishing an effective organizational compliance and ethics program can be a daunting task. The process of establishing boundaries, developing effective working relationships with both senior management and peers, understanding the nuances of the compliance professional's role, and finding resources is never easy. Yet the absence of such a program can be even more devastating. An effective compliance and ethics program is an organization's safeguard. In the next several chapters, we explore some of the key activities undertaken by an organization's compliance program to address and reduce compliance risks.

Notes

1. Many colleges and universities have established compliance programs within their audit or finance department. This is not surprising given their focus on compliance with federal regulations and contracts for research, teaching, and provision of services.
2. Department of Health and Human Services Office of the Inspector General, "OIG Compliance Program Guidance for Pharmaceutical Manufacturers," *Federal Register* 68, no. 86 (May 5, 2003).
3. The issue of nomenclature is a continuing source of contention in the compliance profession. A group of industry professionals is advocating the title "chief ethics and compliance officer" to reflect the importance of ethics, value, and culture as part of the compliance function.

4. In 2005, small and medium-sized entrepreneurial organizations (SMEs), which the federal government defines as having fewer than 500 employees, represented 99.9 percent of the approximately 25.8 million businesses in the United States! Only 17,000 businesses had 500 or more employees.

5. "Building a Partnership for Effective Compliance," a report by the Government-Industry Roundtable, April 2, 1999.

6

Policies, Communication, and Training

An effective organizational compliance program has a number of important components—specifically, policies, communication, and training. All three are inexorably linked. Organizations need to establish standards of behavior in response to legal and regulatory obligations, to communicate these requirements effectively, and to provide employees and others with the means to understand and learn these policies and standards.

Policies and Procedures

Policy development is central to many compliance organizations. Whether what is developed are strategic policies that set forth broad organizational mandates or tactical policies that focus on narrower compliance issues, the need to develop and articulate the organization's compliance policies effectively is paramount for an effective compliance function.

Federal Sentencing Guidelines for Organizations

The first requirement under the Federal Sentencing Guidelines for Organizations (FSGO) states, "The organization shall establish standards and procedures to prevent and detect criminal conduct." As Melinda Burrows, a lawyer writing in *Practical Lawyer* (Fall 2006), recommends:

> *The first step is the most basic: Companies must establish standards and procedures to prevent and detect unethical conduct. . . . The standards should be incorporated into a written code of conduct, and provide for audit systems and other procedures that have a reasonable chance of preventing and detecting wrongdoing.*

Specific Regulatory Requirements

In addition to the general requirements set forth by the FSGO, organizations must also understand the requirements established by their respective regulators. The following are two examples from the financial services and health-care industries.

Financial Services. The Federal Deposit Insurance Corporation (FDIC), in its June 2003 *Overview of the Compliance Examination*, defines the role of banks' policies and procedures:

> *Compliance policies and procedures generally should be described in a document and reviewed and updated as the financial institution's business and regulatory environment changes. Policies should be established that include goals and objectives and appropriate procedures for meeting those goals and objectives. Generally, the degree of detail or specificity of procedures will vary in accordance with the complexity of the issue or transactions addressed.*

Health Care. The U.S. Department of Health and Human Services, Office of the Inspector General's *Compliance Program Guidance for Pharmaceutical Manufacturers* calls for:

> *The development and distribution of written standards of conduct, as well as written policies, procedures and protocols that verbalize the company's commitment to compliance (e.g., by including adherence to the compliance program as an element in evaluating management and employees) and address specific areas of potential fraud and abuse, such as the reporting of pricing and rebate information to the federal health care programs, and sales and marketing practices.*

Drafting Compliance Policies and Procedures

Simply writing a compliance policy and assuming that it will be adhered to is naïve. Effective compliance policies must be carefully developed, designed, and communicated if they are to achieve their stated goals. This process entails a number of important steps and issues.

What Criteria Should Be Considered When Developing the Compliance Policy? In keeping with the points noted earlier, organizational compliance policy makers must develop a sophisticated view of their target audience. This includes such key factors as

- The characteristics of the target audience
- How the organization is structured and how it makes decisions
- The incentives that are likely to motivate both the affected individuals and the organization to comply with the regulation
- The obstacles to compliance

Organizational compliance policies can never be effectively developed in a vacuum. Policy makers must understand the context of the policy and the market at which it is targeted.

Policy formulation must involve key organizational units (e.g., legal, systems, human resources, audit, internal control, financial control, systems and technology, business managers) in the preparation and implementation of the policy. Without the effective coordination of these organizational resources, a policy will not succeed. William Rundorff, writing on compliance policy in the May/June 2006 issue of ABA *Bank Compliance*, emphasized this need for coordination:

> *The complexity of compliance activity requires the involvement of many individuals and departments . . . so the opportunity for overlap between different departments is ever-present. Costly mistakes and errors are likely to happen, and for that reason it is imperative that all be acutely and accurately aware of their responsibilities. Compliance management is a genuine team effort and there is no room for confusion.*

Effective compliance policy requires not only consultation and coordination with key organizational units and persons, but, equally important, buy-in and approval from senior management and the board of directors. Draft policies should be reviewed and approved by the organization's senior management and the affected business units, and ultimately by the organization's board of directors (depending on the scope and impact of the proposed compliance policy).

The policy should clearly identify the target audience for the policy, whether it is all employees or specific functions of the organization (e.g., billing, procurement, or hiring practices).

The policy must clearly identify responsibilities and accountabilities. For instance, if an organization decides to implement a drug testing program, it must identify who is responsible for oversight of the program, for the collection process, for the testing and reviewing of results, for the notification of the employee, and so on. For each step in the policy, there should be a clear delineation of responsibilities.

The policy should be written in plain language. Avoid jargon, legalese, obtuse language, or obscure references whenever possible. There should there be no misunderstanding on the part of either management or employees as to what is needed or expected. If the organization has a large non-English-speaking population, make provision for the translation of the policy into the appropriate language.

If there are exceptions to the policy, they must be, in Rundorff's words, "identified, catalogued, and reported to the appropriate management and Board committees."

Is It Acceptable to Use Someone Else's Policy and Substitute One Name for Another? The compliance policy must be specific to the organization, not borrowed from another. The organization's policies and procedures should reflect its actual policies and practices. While it is tempting to use a generic policy guide or to borrow someone else's policies and practices (substituting the organization's name for another), this can be a dangerous practice. Remember, an organization is held accountable by regulators for its actual policies and practices. If they are not the same as the written policies, the organization will have difficulty explaining the conflicts.

Who Should Issue the Policy? The decision as to who issues the policy will depend on the nature and scope of the policy and on the structure of the organization (e.g., whether it is decentralized or centralized). There are several options:

- If the policy has broad strategic applicability across the entire organization, it should be issued by the most senior executive of the organization.
- If the policy has broad strategic applicability but needs to be customized to meet local business or legal needs, a frequent practice is to have a local business manager issue a companion policy.
- If the policy addresses a narrow technical point, it may be appropriately issued by the compliance program or another organizational unit with a compliance responsibility (e.g., audit, financial control, or human resources).

Are There Any Other Issues That an Organization Should Be Aware of as It Plans to Disseminate the Policy? If the organization issues its policy statements as both written and Web-based documents, it should ensure that the two sets of statements are consistent with each other. It is not unusual to find discrepancies between the two documents.

If the organization requires the employees to sign policies and procedures documents, make sure that it can easily locate and retrieve the signed statements. If the organization plans to distribute the policy electronically, consider the use of augmented e-mails that require employees to acknowledge receipt of the policy and to agree to abide by the terms and conditions of the policy by clicking either an "accept" or a "decline" button.

What Are the Characteristics of an Effective Compliance Policy? An effective compliance policy meets five basic criteria:

- The involvement and endorsement of the organization's senior management
- Consistency with the organization's goals, mission, and values
- Relevance to the organization's needs and priorities
- Clearly defined responsibilities and accountabilities
- An effective implementation plan

Implementing Compliance Policies and Procedures

Well-written, thoughtful, thorough, and inclusive policies and procedures are a critical element of an organizational compliance program. They are useless, however, if they are never properly implemented. The Canadian Centre for Occupational Health and Safety's *Guide to Writing an OHS Policy Statement* (2000) makes this point succinctly:

> No matter how well written, a policy is no more than empty words if a plan does not exist to put the policy into effect

throughout the organization. The policy can only be put into effect where:

- *responsibilities are clearly defined and assigned,*
- *methods of accountability are established,*
- *proper procedures and program activities are implemented,*
- *adequate provision of financial and other resources are provided, and*
- *responsibilities for carrying out the policy objectives are clearly communicated and understood within the workplace.*

Reviewing Existing Compliance Policies

As important as developing new policies is, the organization must also review its existing policies and procedures periodically to ensure that they remain compliant with current laws, regulations, and organizational standards. According to Ernst & Young's *Corporate Regulatory Compliance Practices,* 58 percent of the companies in its survey reviewed their compliance policies on an "as needed/ad hoc" basis, 27 percent did it annually, and 8 percent did it on a semiannual basis or more often. In reviewing their current policies, organizations should consider the following:

- Do the duties and responsibilities of the functions cited in the existing policy statement reflect organizational reality? Organizations change, people move, new positions are created, and functions are transferred to new areas. These changes should be reflected in the organization's policies and procedures.
- Do the policies reflect the current views of the board of directors and senior management? If not, they must be updated to reflect the views of the organization's senior policy makers.

- Do organizational policies reflect current law and regulation? When was the last time the organization's policies and procedures were reviewed by legal counsel?
- Do the organization's policies reflect the new technology and systems that the organization uses? Do the organization's policies address issues regarding privacy, e-mail usage, Internet or intranet protocols, and laptops?

Communication

Communication is intrinsic to an effective compliance function. The swift and unimpeded flow of compliance-related information, internally and externally, is critical to the organization. Even government regulators recognize the critical role that communication plays in a compliance function. The Federal Reserve Bank of Kansas City, in its guide to maintaining an effective compliance program in banking institutions, said that "effective communications is a critical part of almost all business success. Compliance is no exception." Communication transcends words in a policy statement or bits of electronic data. Communication reflects the culture and tenor of the organization.

Communication Strategies

There are myriad ways in which organizations and their compliance function can facilitate the flow of compliance-related information, both internally and externally. An effective compliance function knows that information can be disseminated by and received from many different sources, from postings on bulletin boards and memorandums to the latest Web-based technologies. The following illustrate some of the methods used by organizations.

Training and Orientation. Training, whether on the first day of employment, through periodic updates, or in staff meetings, is an excellent method for keeping employees informed about key organizational compliance policies and programs.

Policy and Procedures Manuals. For many organizations, policy and procedures manuals have been, and continue to be, the primary source of information on compliance-related matters. They can be effective tools if the information in them is current, easily accessible, and in a format that is easy to use.

Guides. As an adjunct to policy and procedures manuals, organizations often create practical "guides" to address employee conduct in specific compliance areas. For instance, in the pharmaceutical industry, it is not uncommon to find guides dealing with specific practices under the U.S. Foreign Corrupt Practices Act (FCPA), such as permissible foreign payments or how to deal with minor foreign officials.

Newsletters. Organizational newsletters, whether print or electronic, can be an effective tool for disseminating compliance-related information. Examples abound, from the Indiana University Athletic Department, whose compliance newsletter features articles on such issues as recruiting information for coaches, to the U.S. Environmental Protection Agency's (EPA) "FedFacs," an environmental bulletin that highlights news and developments of particular interest to federal facilities. Newsletters can be used to describe information about and trends in compliance matters, recent regulatory developments, new systems and technology programs, and training opportunities.

Web Sites (Internet and Intranet). Over the past decade, organizational Web sites have become a key communication mechanism used by organizations to convey information on compliance-related matters. Internet Web sites are increasingly being used to display the organization's standards of conduct, ethical policies, and business practices, often on the organization's main or home page.

Organizations are increasingly using their intranet Web sites for communicating ethical and compliance-related information to their employees. Using a combination of technologies, intranet sites can provide not only text (e.g., the organization's code of conduct), but links to specific corporate policies and practices that further elaborate elements of the code. Companies are using their intranet capabilities to provide compliance- and ethics-related material (in text or video form) for use in understanding ethical issues, managing employee conflicts, or holding staff training sessions.

For public-sector organizations, the use of the Internet to convey regulatory and compliance matters has become an effective and efficient tool for communicating critical legal and regulatory information and updating it when necessary.

Conferencing Technologies. Three conferencing technologies (audio, video, and Web-only) offer organizations the ability to reach wide audiences swiftly and inexpensively. Web conferencing in particular is growing in popularity as a means of compliance communication. Some Web conferencing vendors even offer customers an option that allows them to automatically store saved conferencing sessions and transfer them to archiving systems to document them for potential compliance purposes.

Video/Webcasting. Organizations are using their intranet capabilities to broadcast presentations on ethics and compliance and to offer training programs.

Hotline Programs. The availability of a hotline mechanism that allows employees to communicate issues, concerns, and problems is a key component of an effective compliance program.

Exit Interviews. An often-overlooked source of information for organizations is employee exit interviews. If the compliance function is working in conjunction with the organization's human resources department, exit interviews can be a useful source of information on organizational practices, especially if those practices include unethical or illegal activities that are potentially damaging to the organization.

Customer Complaints. The FDIC says that "complaints may be indicative of compliance weaknesses in a particular function or department. Therefore a compliance officer should be aware of the complaints received and act to ensure a timely resolution. A compliance officer should determine the cause of the compliant and take action to improve the institution's business practices, as appropriate."

Training

Training and education are no longer simply nice things to do. They are an integral component of a modern compliance program. Surveys have shown that compliance and ethics training programs have become standard practice for many organizations. The Conference Board's 2006 report, *Universal Conduct: An Ethics and Compliance Benchmarking Survey*, found that "70 percent of the companies with [ethics training] programs said that they included at least 91 percent of their workers. . . . [T]hese figures contrast with the findings of the 1987 study (which preceded the sentencing Guidelines) in which only 44 percent of participating companies provided employees with any kind of ethics training at all."

Under the Federal Sentencing Guidelines for Organizations, organizations are required to undertake training programs for their employees, including senior management and directors.

The scope of compliance training has expanded enormously; it now includes traditional instructor-led classroom teaching, seminars and conferences, one-on-one instruction, Web-based training programs individually geared to specific organizations, government-sponsored training academies, industry-specific organizations, and university courses specializing in compliance topics.

Assessing Training Needs and Requirements

As a prerequisite to introducing an education and training program, an organization has to address the fundamental questions concerning its key compliance educational needs and risks.

Will the education and training program adequately address the organization's key compliance risks?

An effective education and training program addresses critical organizational compliance needs and risks. Does the organization synchronize its risk assessments with its training efforts? Has the organization had significant audit problems, had a high turnover of staff and supervisors, added new project lines or services, or expanded into new geographic areas? All these changes will affect the organization's training needs and priorities.

Are there any legal or regulatory requirements for compliance training and education programs?

Depending on the location of the organization and the industry involved, it might have a legal or regulatory obligation to provide compliance-related training. For instance, businesses in California, Maine, and Connecticut are required to have supervisory staff attend two hours of sexual harassment training (specific requirements vary from state to state). In the area of hazardous materials requirements, the Occupational Safety and Health Administration (OSHA) requires employers to provide employees with effective information and training on hazardous chemicals in their work area at the time of their initial assignment and whenever a new physical or health hazard is introduced into the area.

Regulatory examinations often include a review of the organization's training programs. For instance, the U.S. Office of the Controller of the Currency specifically reviews a bank's training program covering the Bank Secrecy Act. Similarly, the U.S. Food and Drug Administration (FDA) evaluates company training as part of its audit program

How knowledgeable and effective is the organization's current compliance instruction in meeting its compliance needs?

Compliance education programs must be able to provide expert instruction that addresses the organization's compliance risk requirements. This instruction should not only be substantively knowledgeable but, equally important, able to impart information in a way that encourages learning and understanding.

How will the organization's compliance training program reach its employees, volunteers, and others effectively?

A major challenge for large organizations that are widely dispersed or have round-the-clock operations is providing timely and accessible compliance information and instruction.

What pedagogical techniques would work best for the organization (e.g., e-learning, instructor-led programs, small group, or individual instruction)? The answer to this question will depend on a number of factors, including the number and distribution of the organization's employees, the level and type of training required, the resources and facilities available, evaluations of previous training efforts, and the immediacy of training (e.g., a new law or regulation).

What are the organization's resources for education and training? In an era of tight budgets and limited resources, organizations need to constantly assess the resources they have available for education and training. Recognizing that both funds and staff time available for training purposes may be limited, organizations should be creative, as well as realistic, in addressing their education and training requirements. For instance, an organization can concentrate on high-risk areas that require immediate training, explore combining education and training with that of other similar organizations to take advantage of economies of scale, or partner with local institutions of higher learning.

Is the size of the organization factored into the requirement for a training and education program? In its commentary on the 2004 Amendments to the Federal Sentencing Guidelines for Organizations, the advisory group took a rather sensible approach to the training requirements. It said:

> *The Advisory Group believes that organizations should have the flexibility to determine the types of compliance training and information dissemination that are appropriate given the size of their workforces, the types of misconduct that are of concern given the organizations' operations and fields of activity, and other factors such as the job responsibilities of the persons being trained.*

Key Elements of the Education and Training Program

An effective education and training program has a number of important components and considerations.

Administration
Who is going to be responsible for the conception, design, production, and delivery of the training program?
A decision must be made as to which organizational unit will be responsible for the training program: the compliance function, the organization's training unit, the business unit, legal, or some other unit. If the training program is to be a collaborative venture, what responsibilities will each party have?

Who pays for the training program?
This is always a sensitive issue. The perennial question is from whose budget the training program will be paid. The 2007 *Profile of Health Care Compliance Officers* found that 67 percent did not have a budgeted line item for training (33 percent did have funds for training). Of the 67 percent who did not have a budgeted line item for training, 66 percent reported that compliance training was paid for by departmental budgets.

Does the organization pay employees to take training? Does it reimburse them for travel or food expenses?
If training is to be given outside of working hours, organizations should check with their human resources department or employment counsel to determine whether there are any federal or state laws that address payment for training under certain circumstances. Also, if training is being delivered off-site, the organization will have to decide if it will reimburse employees for travel or food expenses associated with attending the training program.

The Design
Who will be receiving the training?
All employees, including senior managers and board members, should be adequately trained and should understand the regulatory requirements

governing their job functions. The Federal Sentencing Guidelines for Organizations (Section 8B2.1(b)(4)) provide some guidance. They specify that compliance training must be provided to "the members of the governing authority, high-level personnel, substantial authority personnel, the organizations employees, and, as appropriate, the organization's agents."

Organizations should be careful not to overlook regulatory training for people in staff functions that support the organization's primary mission. Those in the human resources, financial control, internal control, and information technology functions need to understand not only the compliance and regulatory requirements associated with their own particular area, but also the broader regulatory and compliance context that governs the organization's operations. An issue, for instance, that is brought to the attention of the organization's human resources function might appear to be limited to a particular issue (e.g., disciplinary action for violation of expense account reporting), but might have potentially broader compliance ramifications (e.g., violations of the Foreign Corrupt Practices Act) if the HR person is not adequately trained to understand and report the incident.

How much time can staff members devote to training and education without impairing their ability to carry out their primary organizational responsibilities?

This is a decision that the business manager must make in collaboration with the organization's training coordinator and compliance officer. Based on survey results, however, this should not be a major problem for many organizations. According to the 2007 *Profile of Health Care Compliance Officers*, 51 percent of the employees spend one to three hours each year in updated compliance training, 12 percent spend three to six hours, and 3 percent spend six hours or more. An interesting finding was that 33 percent of employees spent less than one hour a year on compliance training.

Will the organization make education and training programs a requirement for all managers and supervisory staff?

Many organizations (and some state laws) require that management and supervisory staff receive periodic training in employment and labor matters (e.g., equal employment opportunity, sexual harassment, the Americans with Disabilities Act, the Family and Medical Leave Act, and workers' compensation), ethics, and updates on regulatory matters specific to their job functions.

Will the organization's compliance training program be included as part of its orientation training? Will it have an ongoing compliance training program? Will it have both?
Many organizations provide compliance and ethics training both during an employee's orientation to the organization and periodically during the course of his or her employment.

Orientation training. Orientation for new employees, for people who transfer into the organization from another function or country, or for volunteers frequently focuses on some of the key laws and regulations applicable to the organization, an overview of the organization's compliance program, and a discussion on ethics and integrity in the organization. Orientation can be presented to small groups, individually, or a combination of the two. For instance, a large regional medical center in New England conducts half-hour compliance briefing sessions for all new employees as part of the organization's new-hire orientation process. Organizations should establish a time limit by which orientation training must have been conducted, e.g., no later than 30 or 60 days from the date of the person's entering the organization.

Ongoing training programs. Semiannual or annual compliance training programs provide an opportunity for an organization to remind and update all employees and volunteers on key developments in compliance-related topics. The 2007 survey of health-care compliance officers reported that 86 percent of the organizations provide annual update compliance training.

What are the training requirements for the organization's board of directors and senior managers?
Boards of directors and senior management have an expansive and proactive role in compliance. The Federal Sentencing Guidelines for Organizations,

as noted earlier, specifically require that directors and senior management receive compliance training. Despite the guideline requirements, training for board members is not extensive. The Conference Board's survey found that 58 percent of the companies' board members received training in compliance pursuant to the FSGO. Of those that did provide training, the length of the training was minimal: 31 percent received less than one hour of training per year, and 38 percent received from one to two hours annually. Only 8 percent reported that their board members received more than five hours of compliance training per year.

What about the organization's compliance personnel?
Unlike the proverbial shoemaker's children, compliance officers should not be forgotten. It is important that they undergo periodic training to update their knowledge of laws and regulations, industry trends, self-regulatory organization (SRO) developments, and best practices in peer organizations.

Who will conduct the training?
It is critical that the organization have qualified instructors for its training programs. Inexperienced, unqualified instructors will often do more harm than good in conveying critical compliance information. "Train-the-trainers" programs have their virtues, as they provide an inexpensive method for expediting the flow of information, but organizations using them run the risk of ineffective instruction.

Curriculum
What topics will the training program address, general issues or specific course material?
A fundamental question that all training programs wrestle with is the type of training needed. A credit union executive noted in the May 2006 issue of *Credit Union Magazine*, "We used to think everyone should know everything, so we provided the same training for everyone. That was a mistake. Now we do more specialized training so employees are more proficient in their own areas."

In general, compliance-related curricula can be divided into four basic categories:

- "Generic training" courses that focus on laws and regulations that affect all employees in the organization regardless of function, e.g., e-mail usage, sexual harassment, workplace harassment, information security, or insider trading.
- "Regulatory-specific" courses that focus on key specific industry regulations, e.g., those of the FDA, OSHA, Department of Defense (DOD), EPA, and Internal Revenue Service (IRS), that all organizational employees should be aware of. These courses provide a greater understanding of the industry and the consequences for failing to comply with federal or state regulations.
- "Examination-specific" courses that focus on specific regulatory examination practices. These courses identify areas of regulatory focus, the role and powers of the regulators, how to handle regulatory inquiries, and other such material.
- Code of conduct and ethics training that focuses on standards of business conduct and addresses ethical conflicts and situations, such as conflicts of interest, gifts, bribery, and financial integrity.

The Conference Board's survey cited earlier found that "the three most common 2005 formal and mandatory training topics were employment law related topics: sexual harassment (71 percent), workplace harassment (60 percent), and ethical sales (59 percent)." Information protection and security was another topic of concern. The survey found that 49 percent of the companies had "formal and mandatory employee training programs in 'Confidential Information/Information Security.'"

How well does the organization know its audience?
Training should be targeted to the specific needs and characteristics of the audience. The *FDA Enforcement Manual* (February 2005) reported that at a conference on compliance in the pharmaceutical industry, one of the participants cited the need for focused compliance training: "compliance training can be very unpopular among a sales force merely because the trainers tend to 'use really big words.'"

Compliance training material should be specific to the employee's needs and requirements. Training should be focussed on how the regulation affects the employee and how it is applicable to his or her job. It should avoid extraneous information. Effective compliance training is not simply a matter of memorizing specific laws or regulations. Rather, the training should relate the laws or regulations to the employee's job function. Case studies (good and bad experiences, potential fines and penalties) are very useful educational tools. A banking compliance officer, Meg Sczyrba, who specializes in training, said in the July 18, 2006, ABA *Bankers News*, "What we do is . . . train by job process rather than regulation. I think when you train regulation by regulation you bog people down in a lot of details that don't necessarily concern them."

Finally, a compliance-related training program has to acknowledge the reality that the topic of compliance can be rather staid or uninspiring at times. The goal is to hold people's attention. As Sczyrba said, "Compliance has a little bit of a bad rap. It tends to be a little dry. I believe [you should] acknowledge that and understand . . . [that] you've got to work a little bit harder to get people's attention [for compliance] than you do [for] some other topics."

Instructional Techniques

There are a number of different methods that organizations can use to deliver compliance-related education and training programs. In practice, organizations tend to use a mixture of the classroom, video, and e-learning training formats. According to the 2007 *Profile of Health Care Compliance Officers*, the most common compliance training methods were

- Computer-based or Web-based training (used by 71 percent)
- Instructor-led classroom training with the compliance officer as instructor (used by 68 percent)
- Instructor-led classroom training with someone other than the compliance officer as instructor (used by 47 percent)
- Video training (used by 32 percent)

Lecture/Classroom Training. The traditional technique of presenting information in a lecture format is still widely used. Whether it is used during scheduled classroom training sessions or during meetings of the organization's employees, a well-developed lecture format that is expertly presented offers an excellent opportunity to discuss the importance of compliance, review specific compliance issues, and provide advice and guidance on addressing compliance risks. This technique has both advantages and disadvantages. On the positive side, it offers an opportunity to discuss and review compliance issues, elicit information on possible compliance issues during the course of discussion, and get immediate feedback on the training and the topic. The downside, however, is that delivering personalized training for a large and/or decentralized organization is often not feasible, either logistically or financially. Organizing staff time, locating or reserving classroom space, and preparing class materials can be laborious, expensive, and time-consuming.

Videos. The use of videos has become a staple in compliance-related training. Videos offer a variety of training opportunities: realistic scenarios, interactive quizzes, expert advice, and links to reference material such as organizational policies and practices and Web sites. The Defense Industry Initiative on Business Ethics and Conduct (DII), for instance, offers a video program called "Cases for Ethics Training" that combines the case-study model with video to "stimulate discussion and debate of ethics and compliance issues relevant to defense contractors." Another interesting use of video and interactive learning for compliance training was developed by the global media organization Bertelsmann (see Box 6.1).

E-Learning. Commensurate with the growth of the Internet, e-learning has grown enormously over the past decade. It offers a number of significant advantages for organizations:

- It eliminates the need for individual instructors.
- It makes the scheduling of training courses considerably easier, as it allows employees to access the course material at their convenience.

BOX 6.1   The Bertelsmann Family Feud Ethics Game

The quest to develop new, informative, and stimulating techniques to educate employees on ethics and compliance issues is a perpetual mission. In an innovative effort, Bertelsmann, the global media organization, has used its hit game show, *Family Feud,* and turned it into an ethics game. Created by the corporation's ethics and compliance officer, Andrea Bonime-Blanc, the "Family Feud Ethics Game" pits competing company teams against each other to provide answers to a host of ethical questions tied into the corporation's Codes of Business Conduct. Employees watching the game also participate through an interactive learning program. There are four episodes:

- "The Anti-Harassment Episode"
- "The Anti-Discrimination Episode"
- "The Use of Electronic Communications Episode"
- "The Workplace Health, Safety & Security Episode"

- It allows organizations to reach vast numbers of employees in diverse locations quickly with a consistent message and training curriculum. It aids in standardizing training.
- It allows organizations to track employees' compliance with training.
- It allows employees to go through the material at their own pace and revisit the material when necessary.
- It allows organizations to assess how effectively employees are mastering the material.

Considerations in Using E-Learning

While the utilization of an e-learning format offers a number of significant advantages, an organization should consider certain elements.

Instructional Design. A basic consideration is how the instructional program is going to effectively integrate technology into the learning experience to facilitate compliance education. E-learning materials come in many different formats, and there are numerous examples, styles, and designs available on the Internet. How effectively, for instance, does the program use graphics and animation? What is the level of interactivity?

Technology. What is the quality and effectiveness of the technology that is delivering the e-learning program? Is the program accessible to all employees?

Curriculum and Instruction. Who is going to prepare the material? Will it be a "canned" presentation that has already been prepared by a vendor, or will it be customized to your organization's needs and requirements? If the latter, is preparing it something that the organization can do with its own resources, or will it require consulting services? In all cases, the material must be consistent with the needs of the employees and the requirements of the law and regulators.

Security. If the organization is using an outside vendor for the e-learning program, ensure that adequate security provisions are in place, such as encryption of user information, firewall protection, and adequate server infrastructure.

E-Learning Caveats. There are some caveats with respect to e-learning:

- E-learning does not replace printed documents (e.g., instructional manuals), which are portable and easy to read. Each has its own value and utility in the learning process.
- E-learning does not eliminate the need for live training programs and instructors. Human instructors add a valuable element to the instructional experience in providing insight into and explanations of the material offered.
- E-learning requires sound instructional design. While graphics, animations, and interactive features of Web-based programs can be intriguing and appealing, do not forget the basics of learning. Does the material have measurable learning objectives, and is it meeting those objectives with the content?

Documentation (Testing and Tracking)

The organization's e-learning program should be designed to track employee training and assess the effectiveness of the learning experience. It should be able to produce the learning records of people who have gone through the training program. To manage these requirements, organizations are frequently using learning management systems.

Learning Management Systems. With the growth of e-learning, the past several years have seen the advent of learning management systems (LMSs). An LMS is essentially a sophisticated software program that can manage a variety of e-learning components: determine which employees need to attend training, measure the skill and knowledge levels achieved by individual employees, track the time and frequency of employee training, and inform managers of employees' training activities.

LMSs have wide application in satisfying regulatory requirements for training. For instance, organizations under the requirements of the Good Manufacturing Practices (GMP) regulations that are administered by the U.S. Food and Drug Administration frequently use an LMS to track and document employee training in specific compliance areas.

External Training Programs

A wealth of universities, independent training institutes, and professional associations offer an enormous variety of compliance-related training programs. From pharmaceuticals to financial services to health care, the range of instructional opportunities is staggering.

Summary

The need for an organization's compliance function to develop and communicate effective compliance policies, and then train employees on the importance of those policies to the organization, cannot be underestimated. These programs convey the essence and spirit of the organization's commitment to compliance, ethics, and values. But embarking upon such an endeavor without adequate insight and planning is doomed to failure. In an era of incredible communication capabilities, an organizational compliance program that understands its audience and utilizes the legion of resources available can provide an invaluable service to its organization.

7

Hotlines, Whistle-Blowers, and Investigations

The wise person who said that compliance is a window into the soul of an organization must have had whistle-blowing, hotlines, and investigations in mind. The ability and willingness of an organization's members, volunteers, agents, and the public to report incidents of ethical or legal violations up through the ranks of the organization to its most senior members, without fear of retaliation, is a telling statement indicating that there is an effective organizational culture and compliance program. Equally important, the prompt and decisive response of an organization's compliance program and senior management to allegations of wrongdoing reflects its commitment to ethical and compliant behavior. This chapter examines the issues of hotlines, whistle-blowers, and internal investigations.

Whistle-Blowing Programs

What specifically is meant by the term *whistle-blowing*? A commonly used definition was cited in a study by Terry Morehead Dworkin in the

March 2002 *Vanderbilt Journal of Transnational Law*. Whistle-blowing is "the disclosure by organization members (former or current) of illegal, immoral or illegitimate practices under the control of their employers, to persons or organizations that may be able to effect action." It is this need for disclosure that is reflected in the testimony by Stuart Gilman of the Ethics Resource Center to the Advisory Group on Federal Sentencing Guidelines for Organizations in 2002. In his testimony, Dr. Gilman spoke of the importance of organizational whistle-blowing programs:

> *For many organizations, an essential element of an effective ethics and compliance program is the creation of systems to encourage employees to report observed misconduct and to appropriately raise and voice their ethics concerns. It is well documented that employees are often unwilling to take such actions. Research on whistle blowing suggests that the top two reasons employees fail to raise ethics concerns and/or report misconduct are: (1) a belief that nothing will be done and (2) fear of retaliation. These reasons have as much to do with organizational culture as with formal mechanisms such as anonymous reporting lines.*

Dr. Gilman's testimony was buttressed by a report conducted by the Ethics Resource Center (ERC) in 2005 that showed that employees are still hesitant to report illegal or unethical actions. According to the June 4, 2007, *EthicsWorld*, the National Business Ethics Survey of 3,015 employees found that 55 percent of employees who observed misconduct at work were likely to report such incidents; however, this was down from 65 percent of employees surveyed in 2003. The most frequent reasons for not reporting misconduct were fear of retaliation (46 percent), fear of their identity not being kept anonymous (39 percent), and the belief that someone else would report the situation (24 percent). Senior managers (77 percent) and middle managers (67 percent) were more likely to report misconduct than nonmanagement staff (48 percent).

Background

The concept of whistle-blowing programs is not new. The requirement that individuals be able to report incidents of organizational wrongdoing without fear of retaliation has been codified in numerous government laws ranging from equal employment opportunity and the National Labor Relations Act (union-related activities) to miners protected under the Federal Mine Health and Safety Act.

Federal Sentencing Guidelines for Organizations. The Vanderbilt study found that "as public policy supporting whistle-blowing has matured, there has been a shift toward encouraging internal whistle-blowing and away from the almost exclusive legislative emphasis on reporting outside the organization." This trend toward supporting and encouraging internal whistle-blowing is reflected in the 1991 Federal Sentencing Guidelines for Organizations, which had an enormous impact on the growth of organizational whistle-blowing programs. They are "the most important direct cause of organizational establishment of internal whistle-blowing procedures," the Vanderbilt study concluded.

The 2004 Amendments to the Federal Sentencing Guidelines for Organizations reiterated this importance. Under the amendments, an organization must "have and publicize a system, which may include mechanisms that allow for anonymity or confidentiality, whereby the organization's employees and agents may report or seek guidance regarding potential or actual criminal conduct without fear of retaliation."

False Claims Act. Another spur to whistle-blowing was the 1989 revisions to the U.S. False Claims Act (FCA), in which the federal government extended whistle-blowing protection to nongovernmental employees. The FCA allows individuals to sue government contractors on behalf of the U.S. government if they believe that the government is being defrauded. The impact has been dramatic, as the Vanderbilt study reported:

> *The extraordinarily large whistleblowers' awards, fines, and recoveries paid to the federal government, and the dramatic*

increase in FCA whistleblowing, have led many organizations, especially those in the defense and healthcare industries, to self-police. Under the FCA, whistleblowers who successfully prosecute FCA claims against those who have fraudulently claimed federal funds receive up to thirty percent of recovered monies. Because of the amount of fraud, treble damages, and fines as high as ten thousand dollars per false claim, the average recovery for a successful FCA whistleblower is over one million dollars.

The Sarbanes-Oxley Act of 2002. Under the Sarbanes-Oxley Act of 2002, whistle-blower protection was extended to all employees in publicly traded companies for the first time. Three provisions of the legislation address whistle-blowers:

- Under section 301(4) of Sarbanes-Oxley, the organization's audit committee must establish procedures for
  - The receipt by the company of complaints or concerns involving the organization's accounting, internal accounting controls, or auditing
  - Handling confidential, anonymous information submitted by organization employees on concerns involving questionable accounting or auditing matters
- Section 806 provides whistle-blower protection to employees of publicly traded companies. It is illegal for a company to "discharge, demote, suspend, threaten, harass or in any manner discriminate against" whistle-blowers in its employment because of any lawful act that those employees may have carried out to provide information involving violations of federal law relating to fraud against shareholders. A person who believes that he or she has been treated in violation of this section can file a complaint with the secretary of labor, bring a lawsuit in federal district court, and recover compensation.

- Section 11.07 makes it unlawful to knowingly take any harmful action against a person who is providing to a law enforcement officer any truthful information that relates to the commission or possible commission of any federal offense.

The law established criminal penalties of up to 10 years in prison for retaliation against whistle-blowers.

Proliferation of Hotline Programs

As government whistle-blowing laws have become ubiquitous, organizational hotline programs have also proliferated. The 2006 Conference Board study of compliance programs found that 91 percent of the companies it surveyed had "anonymous reporting systems," up from 52 percent in a similar survey conducted in 1998. What was particularly striking in the Conference Board study was the number of organizations surveyed that had instituted whistle-blowing programs that were not covered under the provisions of Sarbanes-Oxley (which has been a prime motivating factor for many organizations). It reported that 78 percent of the companies not subject to Sarbanes-Oxley had instituted anonymous reporting systems. One possible explanation is that the whistle-blower provisions of the Federal Sentencing Guidelines for Organizations apply to a broader range of organizations than Sarbanes-Oxley does.

Instituting a Whistle-Blowing Program

Instituting a whistle-blowing program, along with a hotline mechanism and the subsequent procedures for the receipt and investigation of information, requires careful planning. This section examines the strategies, techniques, and critical elements for instituting an effective organizational whistle-blowing program, including a hotline mechanism. An effective whistle-blowing and hotline program can be an extremely valuable tool for organizations to use to evaluate their governance practices.

As noted by the consulting firm EthicsPoint in its 2005 report, *It's Not Your Father's Hotline*:

> Today, many organizations have reinforced their hotline system, and the processes they wrap around it, to move beyond the prescribed minimums. They realize that the data available from their hotline reporting system can be used as an indicator of the health of the organizational culture and are using the whistleblower hotline as a catalyst to strengthen their cultural underpinnings.

The Organizational Climate

As witnessed by the ERC's National Business Ethics Survey, it is critical that organizations create an ethical climate in which employees, agents, suppliers, and others can come forward with reports of alleged wrongdoing without fear of retaliation (see Box 7.1 for an example of one company's actions in a whistle-blowing incident). The need for organizations and their senior management to create and maintain a climate that supports ethical behavior and loyalty is essential. For whistle-blowers, the decision to come forward with information is never easy. The fear of retaliation, as Dr. Gilman stated in his testimony, possible retribution by coworkers and supervisors (both crass and subtle), and being labeled a "troublemaker" if the informant's identity is revealed make coming forward an extraordinary decision for an individual.

BOX 7.1   The Whistle-Blowers and Ocean Dumping

A 2007 case illustrates the power and the potential expenses associated with whistle-blowing. A March 22, 2007, Associated Press story reported that "a federal court had awarded $37 million to 12 whistle-blowing crew members in a case of deliberate ocean pollution from ships owned by one of the world's largest publicly traded oil tanker companies. The settlement was called the largest ever in such a case. . . . The whistleblowers were outraged by the systematic dumping, prosecutors said. In one case, a fitter allegedly was threatened with firing if he did not make a bypass pipe to facilitate the polluting. He responded by keeping a secret record of the dates of oil discharges."

Establishing the Policy

To encourage employees to report ethical and legal violations to the organization, it is critical that the organization's senior management and board of directors establish a clear and unequivocal policy that

- Encourages people who have such information to report it through the organization's internal process so that the problems can be dealt with appropriately.
- Protects people who report alleged organizational misconduct.
- Provides various points of contact within the organization for reporting alleged organizational misconduct.

Communicating the Policy

To achieve its goals, an organization's whistle-blowing policy should be issued by the most senior management of the organization, starting with the board of directors, the CEO, and the senior management staff. The organization's senior management must clearly endorse the policy and show both a strong commitment to ethics and integrity and a willingness to listen to and act on legitimate reports of organizational or individual wrongdoing. To emphasize the importance of this policy, it should not be issued by the organization's human resources organization, legal function, or compliance office. To reinforce its importance, it should also be communicated and endorsed by all managers within the organization, regardless of level.

Organizations should use various communication mechanisms, such as posters, newsletters, intranets, and employee training, to ensure that employees are reminded of the policy and the multiple points of contact available for reporting incidents.

Points of Contact

An effective whistle-blowing policy must clearly identify the process and venues for people to report their information and concerns (especially if the individual is uncomfortable speaking with his or her supervisor about the issue or the supervisor is the subject of the issue). This process may either indicate a specific chain of command for reporting such issues or identify a specific person(s) in the organization who can be reached for assistance. Such people may include

- The organization's compliance officer
- The audit staff
- The legal staff
- An ombudsperson
- Quality assurance
- A senior business manager
- The chief responsibility officer
- Human resources
- Senior management or the board of directors

It is important to remember that in an effective whistle-blowing program, a hotline mechanism is only one source of information. Other diverse sources of information include exit interviews, organizational ombudspersons, audit reviews (internal or external), and reports sent to an organization's external regulators. Equally important, it is critical that organizations train their managers and supervisory staff to inform the appropriate organizational units (e.g., compliance, audit, legal, or security) immediately when they receive any reports of corporate or individual misbehavior.

The Hotline Operation

The hotline mechanism has become one of the critical reporting components of an organization's whistle-blowing program. Institution of a hotline program requires a number of considerations.

Administering the Hotline. An issue that frequently arises is whether the organization should manage the hotline program itself or outsource the function to a vendor. The organization needs to determine

- Whether it has the resources (staff, time, expertise, and funds) to manage this function internally
- The reliability and effectiveness of a potential contractor

The Conference Board study found that 44 percent of the companies outsourced the hotline function to a third party, 31 percent handled inquiries internally, and 25 percent used a combination of the two elements.

Contracting for Services. If the decision is to outsource the hotline program, a number of decisions have to be addressed in choosing the appropriate vendor. For example,

- What is the cost for the service? Is the cost based on the number of employees the organization has or on some other factor? What are all the fees and charges that the organization will be responsible for?
- What are the qualifications of the service? How long has it been in operation? Who are its other clients? What are the background, expertise, and experience of the organization's management and its service personnel?
- What are the vendor's operating protocols? Is the vendor willing to adjust its operating procedures to meet your organization's needs and requirements?
- What communications techniques are used (telephone, e-mail)? What is the availability of the service (time and geographic locations)? Does the vendor have multiple language capability?
- How is the confidentiality of the information received maintained? How are records of all calls or other inquiries maintained? What is the vendor's records retention policy and capability?
- What training is provided to the vendor's service personnel?
- How often does the vendor report to the client on calls received? What protocols are used to alert the client organization to urgent or priority calls that require immediate attention?

Utilization of the Hotline. An important factor in establishing a hotline program is the anticipated frequency and type of calls to the organization's hotline.

- Estimates of usage vary. In general, the volume of reports to hotlines is not substantial. According to the Conference Board's survey, 63 percent of the companies surveyed had fewer than 50 reports to their anonymous hotlines annually. In the same survey, another organization had employee usage of 5 reports per 1,000 employees. Other organizations estimated a utilization range of between 2 and 7 percent. Still another organization cited an average of 1 call a month per 1,000 employees.

- A rule of thumb commonly used by compliance officers in various organizations is that the majority of calls to the organization's hotline are human resources–related. A detailed 2006 survey, *Corporate Governance and Compliance Hotline Benchmarking Report*, which looked at 200,000 reports filed by 500 companies, confirmed this opinion. It found that 51 percent of the reported incidents involved "personnel management," with issues including wage and hour complaints, supervisor behavior, working conditions, and performance appraisals. The next category of calls, violations of company policies and/or professional violations, accounted for 16 percent of the calls, and fraud incidents accounted for 11 percent.

The Primary Unit. The organization has to determine which organizational function will have primary responsibility for the hotline's operation and oversight. In many organizations, the compliance program has this responsibility. In other organizations, financial control, audit, or security may have primary responsibility. The primary unit must establish the appropriate internal protocols for distributing reports to the appropriate organizational units for investigation, for following up on reports, for bringing issues to senior management or the board of directors, and for seeking counsel when necessary.

Key Features of a Hotline Program

Regardless of whether of an organization decides to administer the hotline program internally or to outsource the function, an effective hotline system has a number of important features that must be built into the program.

Confidentiality and Anonymity. The hotline system must be able to provide confidentiality and anonymity to callers. The people calling must be reassured that the information they provide will be kept confidential and their identities protected, if they wish. Employees are often fearful of retaliation and the possible consequences if their managers find out that they reported an issue without the manager's knowledge. The *Corporate Governance and Compliance Hotline Benchmarking Report* found that 54 percent of all people who reported incidents wanted to remain anonymous. The program should also give the anonymous caller the ability to call back at a later date with more information or to answer any questions that might be helpful in understanding the issue.

Multiple Points of Access. An effective hotline program provides multiple mechanisms for reporting violations, such as toll-free telephone numbers, fax numbers, or postal mailboxes. A growing practice is using secure Web-based reporting or e-mail (although the latter is often not as secure as other methods of communication).

Availability. An effective hotline program is availability 24 hours a day, 7 days a week. It also has multiple language and translation capabilities to handle calls from a diverse population.

System Security. Given the sensitivity of the information received through a hotline mechanism, it is critical that the organization establish a means of encrypting and protecting all data and records.

Handling Inquiries. An effective hotline has experienced and knowledgeable staff who are able to understand and relate to the persons who are furnishing the information. Staff members must be able to manage often stressful or complex situations involving callers who may be under great pressure or anxiety, and yet at the same time ascertain all the key information needed to follow up on the incident.

Ombudspersons

Organizational ombudspersons are another important and growing mechanism for reporting information on organizational behavior, including issues involving legal or ethical violations. The term comes from a Swedish word meaning "agent" or "representative," and it has come to be used to refer to an independent voice in an organization that will confidentially listen to, and follow up on, employees' concerns. Ombudspersons' offices generally report to senior management in the organization. Ombudspersons are expected to be independent in their work. "Acting as an informal channel through which employees can report problems," as Arlene Redmond and Randy Williams noted in the September 2004 issue of *Risk Management*, "An ombuds program offers the neutrality, independence, informality and unqualified confidentiality needed in order to provide a safe place for employees to raise issues early and without fear of retaliation."

There are several interesting corporate examples of ombudsperson programs:

- BP retained the services of a former U.S. district judge, Stanley Sporkin, to be its U.S. ombudsman. With a staff of two, he operates a 24-hour call center to hear workers' concerns. In a 2005 letter to BP employees, the September 5, 2006, *Wall Street Journal* reported, the ombudsman said, "My mandate is to do whatever is necessary to ascertain the facts about and identify solutions for problems that exist today as well as those likely to become issues in the future."
- American Express's ombudsperson program reported that 20 percent of its 2,000 annual cases deal with potential legal issues, including Sarbanes-Oxley issues and EEO issues. As the corporate ombudsperson for American Express said in *HR Focus* (October 2005), "Things get surfaced that wouldn't get surfaced any other way."

- GE has a network of 700 ombudspersons around the world. It stated in its 2006 *Compliance and Governance* report that the program received more than 1,500 "integrity concerns" in 2006. Issues ranged from fair employment practices (which represented the largest single category of issues), conflicts of interest, and health and safety issues to petty theft.

Reflecting the growing use of ombudsperson programs, the American Bar Association in 2004 issued its *Standards for the Establishment and Operations of Ombuds Offices*, which clarifies the legal authority of the function.

Managing Information

Regardless of the source of the information (e.g., a hotline, an ombudsperson, or external reports), an effective organizational whistle-blowing program must establish a protocol for the appropriate handling and distribution of information:

Determining the Distribution

For the developers of the whistle-blower and hotline programs, working with the person(s) who will administer the programs, a critical decision involves the flow of information into the organization:

- Who in the organization will receive the initial report?
- Who, if anyone, is copied on the information?
- What constitutes a priority report?
- How quickly must reports be disseminated to the appropriate units for investigation?

Organizations manage these requirements in different ways. Depending on the nature of a report, it may be routed to a local business to manage, or, if it affects the corporation as a whole, it might be handled at a corporate level. Reports on personnel-related matters, for example, may be automatically routed to the human resources department with a requirement that the department report back to the whistle-blower administrator on the status of the investigation and any subsequent resolution of the issue.

Coordinating Body

One mechanism that organizations have employed to oversee the receipt of information effectively is a coordinating body made up of representatives from key organizational units, such as legal, compliance, human resources, security, and audit. These groups are available to review the information received and decide on an appropriate course of action. For instance, does the reported incident represent a violation of law or policy? Is there sufficient information to warrant an investigation? If so, who should conduct the investigation?

Investigations and Follow-Up

The organization must establish a policy and practice of investigating all allegations promptly and thoroughly (investigations are discussed further later in this chapter). Inaction is the best way to create cynicism about the seriousness of an organization's ethics and compliance policy, and also to create potential legal liabilities for laxness in responding promptly to complaints. According to the *Corporate Governance and Compliance Hotline Benchmarking Report*, 65 percent of the reports warranted investigation, and of those, nearly 47 percent resulted in some form of corrective action being taken. One interesting result in the survey was the fact that anonymous cases led to slightly more investigations that warranted corrective action than reports where people gave their name.

Tracking Inquiries

The volume and type of calls to the whistle-blowing and hotline programs are potentially invaluable sources of information on organizational behavior. The organization should routinely analyze the hotline's usage to discern any possible trends in reports by business, region, supervisor, or type of product or service and to identify any disruptions in the organization's internal controls or the need for additional training or for a reassessment of organizational policies and practices.

Usage (or the lack thereof) of the organization's hotline can be telling. Robert Kusserow, writing in the *Journal of Health Care Compliance* (March/April 2007), cautioned, "As the compliance officer, do you feel a little bit like the memorable Maytag repairman whose phone never rang because everything was going great? Watch out! A lack of hot line calls could mean just the opposite. You could have serious problems, but people just aren't letting you know." Organizations should examine their training and communications programs periodically to ensure that employees are aware of the hotline's existence and purpose, and that the hotline program is performing up to its expectations and performance standards.

International Operations

Whistle-blowing programs present a particular challenge for multinational organizations. Both legal and cultural barriers often prevent organizations from using these programs effectively in certain countries, especially in Western Europe. For example, Germany and France both restrict, for different reasons, the use of whistle-blowing hotlines.

Related Issues

Administering whistle-blowing and hotline programs often presents some difficult or vexing situations for the organization.

Anonymous Complaints. One of the difficulties in administering a hotline program is dealing with a person who wishes to remain anonymous. Anonymous callers pose difficulties for hotline programs for two major reasons: the inability of the organization to get additional information, if necessary, to substantiate an allegation of wrongdoing, and the inability of the organization to respond to the person to let him or her know the status of the investigation and its findings.

Malicious Complaints. While hotlines and whistle-blower programs may be a source for good in the organization, they may also be exploited by people whose motivations are less salubrious. For instance, how will the organization handle the situation if the whistle-blower is found to be using the hotline to harass or retaliate against a supervisor or coworker with false accusations?

Organizational policy has to explicitly warn employees that making allegations that are malicious, reckless, or patently false will lead to serious disciplinary action, up to and including dismissal from the organization and a possible civil lawsuit.

Handling Whistle-Blowers. A sensitive issue for organizations is managing whistle-blowers. Keeping in mind the legal protections afforded to whistle-blowers, organizations should consider a number of options ranging from counseling to time off to working with the organization's human resources and legal units to determine whether keeping (or reinstating) the person in the same job or work unit is the most appropriate course of action given the circumstances, or whether he or she should be transferred to an equivalent position in another unit.

Reports to the Board of Directors. Under both Sarbanes-Oxley and New York Stock Exchange (NYSE) regulations, the audit committee of the board is required to establish procedures for receiving complaints regarding accounting, internal controls, or auditing matters. In reality, the board and its audit committee may serve as a contact point for a variety of issues beyond accounting and audit issues. In the event that the board does receive such reports, it should ensure that each matter is appropriately addressed. It has several options:

- Refer the issue to the organization's legal or compliance office to investigate, and require that that office report back to the board on the findings of its investigation.

- Decide to investigate the matter itself. If the board chooses the latter option, it should heed the advice of Bill Kleinman, an expert on corporate governance. Writing in the November 2003 issue of *Directorship*, Kleinman says that the board should form "a committee of independent directors with authority to investigate the issues and to hire advisors. Directors who may be affected by the allegations should not be on the committee." The committee should, Kleinman advises, "Act quickly. Retain experienced counsel to conduct the investigation . . . require interviews of all employees and agents with knowledge of the matter . . . report the committee's findings and recommendations to the board . . . act to prevent retaliation against the whistleblower or other personnel participating in the investigation."

Conducting Investigations

An organization has a legal and ethical obligation to investigate reported issues of alleged wrongdoing promptly and effectively. Regardless of whether the information has been generated through internal or external channels, an effective compliance program should establish a policy and practice that ensures that reports of potential wrongdoing are responded to appropriately. Failure to respond promptly, decisively, and effectively can have a devastating impact on an organization. As John N. Joseph said in the *Journal of Health Care Compliance* (November/December 2006),

> As the government seeks to guard the public fisc and protect public welfare, health care organizations must be sensitive and responsive to complaints or allegations about misconduct in their business practices. Merely mentioning phrases like False Claims Act (FCA), qui tam action, corporate integrity agreement (CIA), and federal health care program exclusion drives home the point that allegations of misconduct cannot be ignored. Indeed, choosing to ignore such problems may be the equivalent of "betting the farm."

The Investigation Process

When allegations of wrongdoing have been raised, organizations need to determine the veracity, extent, and/or repercussions of the alleged actions, and also determine what remedies are appropriate to correct the situation. Clearly, for the organization and its compliance program, these actions should be taken immediately, in consultation with either internal or external counsel.

Key Questions. Several of the issues that need to be considered include the following:

- Does the nature of the suspected incident warrant a special investigation?
- Is there a legal issue present? Are the allegations true?
- Who should conduct the investigation (internal or external)? (See Box 7.2.)
- Who should oversee the investigatory relationship (if external) in-house?
- What should be the goal of the investigation? Clarify the facts and have a neutral party conduct the investigation, especially if it involves a senior manager in the organization.
- Who in the organization should be briefed on the investigation?
- When and how should an organization involve external parties, such as regulators and law enforcement officials?

BOX 7.2   Internal versus External Investigators

Depending on the nature and scope of the incident, a decision that organizations will have to address is whether to use internal or external resources to conduct an investigation. The use of external investigators offers several advantages: a demonstration of independence to critical stakeholders (regulators, the media, and customers), an objective review of the facts and circumstances, and a perception of "fairness" in investigating the situation. However, the use of external investigators also has liabilities. For instance, there is diminished control over the investigation and, of course, greater cost than when internal resources are used.

Assigning Investigatory Responsibility

Once a report of a possible violation of a legal or ethical policy or practice has been made to the organization, it is critical that this report be brought to the attention of the appropriate individuals. Depending on the scope and size of the issue, the nature of the report, and the structure of the organization, this may include the compliance program or the legal, financial control, audit, human resources, or security function. The decision, however, as to which organizational function(s) will have the ultimate responsibility for conducting the investigation will depend on several factors:

- The organization's resources. Does the organization and its staff have the experience and expertise to conduct an effective investigation?
- The scope and nature of the reported offense. Is it limited to only one business, or does it involve multiple businesses? Who are the individuals involved in the allegations, and what is the specific nature of the incident?
- Whether the incident has already been reported to external parties, such as regulators, the media, or outside counsel.

Independence and Qualifications of Investigators. Whoever conducts the investigation must be independent from those who are the subject of the investigation. As the National Center for Preventive Law states,

> [A]n independent investigation requires that investigative resources be under the control of an individual or group that is free of influence from those persons who may be investigated. In circumstances where high-level personnel are alleged to have acted improperly and real independence is virtually impossible in view of [the] role of the alleged perpetrator, the person in charge of compliance must have the authority to call on outside resources and to delegate the investigation to outside resources. This type of

outside attention will sometimes be necessary to ensure the inde-pendence necessary for a compliance program to be effective.

In addition to being independent, the investigator should be some-one who is fair and impartial, respected, and knowledgeable about orga-nizational policy and the appropriate area of law involved in the investigation.

Conducting the Investigation

The person(s) assigned to conduct the investigation must be provided with adequate resources and the authority to undertake an effective inves-tigation. This may include the ability to use either internal or external experts to assist in the investigation, access to all pertinent personnel and records, systems and technology support, administrative support, or other services or equipment as needed.

In conducting an internal investigation, several points should be noted.

- All aspects of the investigation (reports, interviews, and documentation collected) should be kept confidential to prevent unauthorized disclosures of information.
- All persons who are not associated with the investigation must be notified that they are not to discuss or speculate on any aspects of the investigation.
- The investigation should be conducted in an objective fashion.
- Employees are expected to cooperate fully in all aspects of the investigation (and may be subject to disciplinary actions if they fail to cooperate).
- All document destruction must cease immediately, and all records must be made available as requested by the investigators.
- Depending on the seriousness of the allegation, it may be necessary to suspend an employee from active employment pending the outcome of the investigation.

- Any communication with a government agency during the course of the investigation should be documented and kept as part of the investigatory file.

Attorney-Client/Work-Product Privilege. An issue that may arise during an internal investigation involves the discovery of incriminating evidence that could potentially be used against the organization. Depending on the nature of the investigation and the type of incident involved, an organization may wish to have an attorney oversee the investigation to protect the attorney-client and/or work-product privilege. Establishing attorney-client and work-product privileges preserves the organization's future options of either invoking the privileges or waiving them and making disclosures to the government. The organization must work with counsel to establish the appropriate procedures with respect to investigatory notes, work papers, and other internal documents to maintain these privileges.

Reporting on the Investigation

Following the investigation of the incident, the organization has to make a decision as to what it will reveal and to whom concerning its findings.

The Complainant. As noted earlier, efforts should be made to keep the complainant informed of the investigation's status and any subsequent outcomes. The National Center for Preventive Law recounted one organization's approach to this situation: "If the complainant wished to remain anonymous, but still wanted to know the status of the case, he or she was assigned a fictitious name or ID number and asked to call back at a given time."

The Board of Directors. Depending the scope and nature of the incident, the organization's chief compliance officer or general counsel may brief the board or its audit committee on the status of the investigation and any subsequent resolution or required next actions.

External Agencies. In conducting its investigation, the organization must be cognizant of any mandatory reporting requirements. To ensure timely reporting to the applicable government agencies, the organization should work with its general counsel and with unit specialists who have regulatory reporting duties. Of particular concern to the organization is the issue of voluntary self-reporting of the alleged misconduct and the outcome of its investigatory efforts. All decisions regarding the extent and process for disclosure of information must be made in consultation with counsel, senior management, and—if needed—the board of directors.

Follow-up to Investigation

As the Federal Sentencing Guidelines for Organizations state, "If criminal conduct is discovered, the organization must undertake whatever changes in its structure and procedures are necessary to foreclose a reoccurrence of that misconduct." To prevent the situation from recurring, the organization should review the facts and circumstances that led to the incident to ascertain the lessons to be learned and the remedies to be applied. For instance:

- Was it systemic failures that led to the problem? Did the incident come about as a result of inadequate supervision of employees, failure of internal controls, weakness in auditing procedures, insufficient training, or outdated systems and technology? How effective is the organization's background screening of employees? Did the compliance function perform its duties effectively?
- Was it a cultural and/or ethics issue? Were the pressures to succeed at all costs far greater than the value placed on ethical and legal behavior? What was the role of the board and senior management in setting an ethical tone?

Summary

An effective whistle-blowing and hotline program, and the subsequent investigation of allegations of wrongdoing, transcend legal or regulatory requirements. They are symbolic and lasting measures of an organization's commitment to ethical values and legal behavior.

In an August 2004 article for the Conference Board's publication *Executive Action*, Howard Anderson and Edwin Stier wrote, "How an organization responds to a crisis of confidence will define its values far more convincingly than any code of conduct—after 20 years, the responsible manner with which Johnson & Johnson handled the Tylenol crisis still lends credit to its name, while Enron's response has become a metaphor for scandal." Reputation, trust, values, and credibility define highly regarded organizations. These are the elements that organizations should be remembered for as they manage their whistle-blowing and investigatory programs.

8

Information and Technology: Challenges and Tools for Compliance

We live in an era of ever-changing means of collecting, archiving, and transmitting information. This development has had a profound effect on organizational compliance. Compliance and information technology (IT) are, in many respects, a natural marriage of need and convenience. This relationship can be viewed in two perspectives:

- The role that information technology plays in supporting the organization's compliance functions.
- The obligations to manage and safeguard organizational data that have been placed upon information technology. The Security Compliance Council states in its report, *The Struggle to Manage Security Compliance for Multiple Regulations*, "The growing importance of information technology and the transition of personal records into digital formats have made privacy and information security critical issues."

Federal Regulatory Requirements

Given the enormous breadth of federal regulation, it is not possible to catalogue the full range of U.S. law pertaining to data, privacy, and records. From the Health Insurance Portability and Accountability Act of 1996 (HIPAA) to Gramm-Leach-Bliley (GLB) in the financial services industry, the scope of the regulations governing information security and technology is staggering. Illustrative of the broad-based application of federal information and technology-related regulations is Sarbanes-Oxley.

Sarbanes-Oxley's focus on internal controls and governance has had a profound effect on information technology. Section 302, which requires quarterly certification of the accuracy and completeness of the organization's financial reports (and of the underlying internal controls) by the CEO and CFO, and Section 404, which requires an annual report by management regarding the organization's internal controls for financial reports, have spurred organizations to assess their risks and the role that information technology plays in addressing these concerns. For instance, what IT security measures are in place to prevent unauthorized access or damage to the organization's data and systems?

In addition to these requirements, the law also makes it a criminal offense for organizations to knowingly alter, destroy, mutilate, conceal, or falsify records with the intent to impair the use of these records in a governmental investigation or proceeding (Section 802). Thus, records management and retention have become critical organizational issues.

Chris Capdevila, a computer specialist, emphasized the impact that Sarbanes-Oxley has had on information technology and governance. Speaking in *Business Trends Quarterly* (March 2006), he said, "Just as Y2K caused a massive evaluation, redesign, and redeployment of ERP [enterprise resource planning] systems across corporate America, Sarbanes-Oxley is having the same effect today. It has become a catalyst for reassessing business processes in the areas of security, integrity, efficiency."

State Regulatory Requirements

In July 2003, California passed SB1386, the California Data Protection Act. It requires organizations housing sensitive personal information—including government agencies, businesses, and persons engaged in business activities—to notify California residents when data has been, or may have been, accessed without authorization. Since the passage of this act, more than 30 states, including New York, Florida, Utah, and Wisconsin, have passed legislation governing data protection and privacy. Noting the wide variety of state laws, the law firm of Cooley, Godward and Kronish commented in its *Cooley Alerts* (February 28, 2007) on the compliance implications that these diverse state regulations pose for organizations. "This variety creates the proverbial 'patchwork of laws' and makes compliance a challenge since companies that maintain personal information tend to have customers in numerous states."

International Requirements

In addition to the U.S. requirements, there is a growing volume of international law and regulation that affects all organizations doing work outside of the United States. Two of the most prominent legal developments are

- The European Union's data protection directive regarding the privacy of personal information. Of particular note are the limitations that the directive places on sharing personal information concerning EU citizens in countries that are deemed to have inadequate data security standards, such as the United States.
- In Canada, the Personal Information Protection and Electronic Documents Act (PIPEDA) protects personal information in the hands of private-sector organizations and provides guidelines for the collection, use, and disclosure of that information in the course of commercial activity.

Technology Standards

The laws and regulations just described often refer to standards, assessment processes, and risk management tools that have been promulgated by industry standards-setting groups.

ISO 17799

The International Organization for Standardization (ISO) and the International Electrotechnical Commission (IEC) have established best practices recommendations for information security management, covering electronic files, recordings, and paper documents.

Control Objectives for Information Technology (COBIT)

COBIT was developed in 1996 by the Information Systems, Audit and Control Association and the IT Governance Institute. Based in part on the Committee of Sponsoring Organizations of the Treadway Commission's (COSO's) control framework, it provides a comprehensive structure for managing risk and for the control of information technology. Like its COSO control counterpart, it is the standard framework for the management of information technology processes.

The Challenge of Multiple Regulations

While regulatory compliance obligations for information technology and security have had positive effects, the sheer volume of the laws and regulations governing information technology and security has also become a significant compliance challenge for organizations. For instance, a publicly traded U.S. company that provides international health management services is required to comply, at a minimum, with HIPAA, Sarbanes-Oxley, Securities and Exchange Commission (SEC), and EU regulations governing information technology. This multiplicity of regulations raises several important issues for regulatory compliance.

- Each new law, regulation, or compliance mandate brings with it a new set of requirements in such areas as records management, data security, and privacy that may duplicate or conflict with other compliance requirements.
- Organizations frequently address each new regulation or compliance mandate as a separate and discrete project. As a result, there is a growing tendency to create technology "silos," rather than addressing disparate information technology and security compliance mandates in a holistic fashion.
- Moreover, with each separate law or regulation comes the need for audit and control requirements that may overlap with the requirements of similar compliance obligations.

The challenge for organizations is to address these regulatory obligations in a coordinated and cost-effective fashion. A 2005 survey of more than 300 companies by the Security Compliance Council found that the multiplicity of regulations has placed a significant burden on organizations. For instance, 75 percent of the organizations had two or more sets of regulations (and corresponding audits), and 43 percent had three or more sets of regulations. The resources devoted to meeting these requirements are staggering. The report found that "organizations spend an average of 34 percent of their IT resources on activities devoted to satisfying security compliance for multiple regulations." In response to this regulatory challenge, a number of organizations are focusing on the concept of "governance, risk, and compliance (GRC)" to address this issue (see Box 8.1).

BOX 8.1 Governance, Risk, and Compliance

During the past several years, a number of consulting and software organizations have extolled the virtues of "governance, risk, and compliance (GRC)" as an effective approach or framework for addressing an organization's diverse regulatory compliance demands. Technology is used to link diverse, and often fragmented, compliance-related activities and information systems within a unified "enterprise-wide" framework. Although the concept has interesting potential, it is too early to determine whether GRC will become a focal point of compliance management or an invaluable technology tool.

Creating a Multidimensional Compliance Framework

Using information technology to address an organization's regulatory compliance obligations (as well as compliance issues associated with information technology) requires a combination of strategic and tactical elements: risk assessments, internal controls, communication and training, staff, policies and procedures, appropriate use of technology, and a commitment by the organization's board of directors and senior management to address the issues of information technology and regulatory compliance.

Governance

An effective compliance framework starts with the active and committed involvement of the organization's board of directors and senior management to determine the appropriate role and use of information technology. The Institute of Internal Auditors (IIA) examined this issue as part of a project initiated by former President William J. Clinton in 2000. The project examined the critical concerns associated with information security. In its report, *Information Security Governance: What Directors Need to Know*, the IIA speaks specifically to the issue of the board's legal and regulatory oversight obligations (and its liabilities if it fails to act appropriately).

> *Standards for the compliance, review, monitoring, and oversight functions must be built into the overall security architecture to ensure that responses meet any legal requirements or other applicable guidelines. There is potential liability to directors who fail to act.*

To be effective, an organization needs a proactive, independent board of directors that asks the right questions and assesses the effectiveness of the organization's policies and practices. It is the board's duty and responsibility to ensure

- That the organization has the appropriate resources to identify and address its information security risks and vulnerabilities, and to comply with its regulatory obligations.
- That the organization has established the appropriate structures and controls to manage these risks and obligations.
- That accountability and responsibility have been assigned to the appropriate persons and units to manage these duties.

Compliance Responsibilities

Under the leadership of the board of directors and senior management, organizations need to develop a comprehensive and coordinated compliance program to address the myriad aspects of information security: systems and technology, policies and procedures, internal controls and risk assessment, education, and communication.

Responsibility and accountability for information technology and security are often divided among different organizational units (e.g., information security, audit, internal control, line management, and risk management). Generally, the information technology function is not part of the organization's compliance function, although it is not uncommon for information technology units to have someone designated as a "compliance" specialist (or some similar nomenclature) to focus on regulatory risks and requirements.

Compliance functions and their information technology counterparts have developed various strategies for working together. For instance, at the banking organization Wachovia Corp., the organization's chief compliance officer explained, in an article in the November 25, 2003, issue of *SearchCIO.com*, his unit's relationship to the corporation's technology function:

> *The way our model works, accountability for compliance rests with either the business unit or the technology areas that are responsible for ensuring that they have systems, controls and procedures to ensure compliance on a day-to-day basis. My organization is*

more about oversight—making sure that there's an effective policy that is communicated and builds awareness.

Regardless of the specific organizational structure, it is critical that the organization's compliance and information technology functions

- Have identified their key compliance risks and vulnerabilities (see Box 8.2 for a detailed set of questions and issues that organizations should consider).
- Are managing these risks and vulnerabilities on a timely basis.
- Have adequate systems and technology capabilities (internal or external) to address their compliance risks and vulnerabilities effectively.

Privacy and Information Security

The past several years have witnessed staggering reports of information breaches. Laptop thefts, for example, have compromised the data privacy of hundreds of thousands of people. In 2006, an employee from the firm of Ernst & Young had his laptop stolen; it contained unencrypted credit and debit card information on 243,000 Hotels.com customers. In that same year, the U.S. Department of Veterans Affairs reported the theft of a laptop and an external hard drive that contained sensitive information on 26.5 million U.S. veterans.

Information Security Program and Policies

Given the range of legal, regulatory, and industry compliance obligations (and the significant risks associated with their violation), an organization's compliance initiative must include a comprehensive information security program. This initiative should address the key issues discussed here.

BOX 8.2   Thirteen Key Questions

A prerequisite for an effective information technology compliance framework is a comprehensive understanding of the organization's risk exposure, vulnerabilities, and control policies and practices in order to detect and correct any potential problems. Here are 13 key questions that organizations should ask themselves:

- What are the critical laws and regulations governing the organization's data and records systems?
- Are the organization's technology and practices consistent with federal and state laws and regulations, and with industry standards?
- Has the organization conducted a risk assessment to identify specific threats (internal or external) to its information system that could result in the loss of information or unauthorized access?
- Has the organization developed comprehensive compliance policies and procedures that provide guidance for the staff in developing and maintaining the organization's systems and technology?
- How effectively does the organization integrate technology and internal controls in key risk areas?
- What technology does the organization's compliance program employ to identify and monitor key compliance risks?
- What are the organization's key areas of privacy and security vulnerability? Are the organization's policies and practices adequate to meet these risks and requirements?
- How often does the organization audit its information technology for compliance with regulations?
- Are there specific business or staff functions that are particularly vulnerable to information and/or security risks?
- What are the organization's policies and practices regarding records retention?
- How do the compliance and information technology units coordinate their activities, e.g., is compliance involved in the development of or changes in the organization's systems and programs?
- Are significant system and program changes subject to a full universal acceptance testing (UAT)?
- Are the organization's compliance, legal, and audit units involved in the introduction of any new product or system that has an electronic component?

Organizational Structure. An effective program must identify the units and persons that have the specific authority and responsibility for meeting the organization's information technology security and regulatory compliance obligations.

Risk Assessment. Given the Federal Sentencing Guidelines for Organizations, Sarbanes-Oxley, and the myriad regulatory requirements, it is incumbent upon an organization to implement an effective information technology risk assessment process. Using as a framework the standards developed by the Information Systems, Audit and Control Association (ISACA) or a similar institution, the organization should

- Assemble a team representing the compliance, information technology, legal, audit, human resources, internal control, and finance units.
- Identify the critical vulnerabilities and weaknesses in the organization's records, communication, and information management and internal control systems.
- Take the appropriate measures to address and correct any deficiencies that are found.

Physical Security. This includes limiting physical access to systems and information, detecting intruders, perimeter control, and fire protection. It should also include appropriate background checks on employees, students, volunteers, temporaries, consultants, and contractors—anyone who has access to the organization's systems and information and may represent a potential risk.

Data Management and Classification. The organization should review its electronic information to determine the level of protection it may require. Using a classification system, the organization can assess the level of security controls it might require to prevent unauthorized access to confidential or critical information.

Confidentiality and Privacy

Organizations must develop a program to protect the confidentiality and privacy of data. Writing in the July/August 2006 issue of *Information Systems Security*, Rebecca Herold, an expert on information security and privacy, said, "An effective privacy governance program will not only make your customers happier, but it will also mitigate your exposure to regulatory noncompliance, lawsuits, bad publicity, and government investigations."

Records Management and Retention

To minimize compliance risk, organizations should establish a records management and retention program for either print copy or electronic information, including e-mails. In creating a records management and retention program, Jin Lee, an authority on records management, noted in the June 2005 issue of *DM Review*, "It's difficult for any company just to keep current with the wave of federal, state or industry-specific regulations that either directly or indirectly impact their record retention practices. . . . [R]egulators are rigorously enforcing books and records regulatory requirements."

Organizations must consider a number of issues concerning their current records management policies and practices, along with their anticipated requirements. For instance, what information needs to be archived, what data does the organization currently collect, who "owns" this information, how is it accessed, where is information currently stored [e.g., phones, personal digital assistants (PDAs), BlackBerries, removable storage devices, voice message machines, or laptops], who needs access to these data, what are the regulatory requirements for retention and storage, where are the organization's deleted files and backup tapes kept, and are these records easily retrievable?

Perhaps the best advice was offered by Paul French, writing in the January 2004 issue of *Law Practice Today*, who said, "In the relatively short history of corporate electronic data retention, earlier default corporate policies have been fairly straightforward—if in doubt, delete it. . . . [T]his is not a wise protocol. Nor is it wise or cost-effective to retain *all* electronic data. A responsible approach shifts the focus from 'what to destroy' to 'what electronic documents to retain.'"

E-Mail and Instant Messages

E-mail has become one of the most ubiquitous forms of organizational communication. Paul Chen, writing in the April 1, 2006, issue of *EDPACS*, noted, "As much as 60 percent of business-critical data now resides in e-mail, making it potentially the most important repository of data your company own." Myriad articles have been published on protecting and managing an organization's e-mail systems and records. It is critical that an organization establishes an e-mail policy that

- Governs the use of organizational e-mail for personal use.
- Establishes guidelines for archiving e-mails. (Can employees and others create a personal archive? How long can such archives be kept? Where should the information be stored?)
- Sets the format in which e-mails are to be saved.
- Quickly terminates access to the organization's e-mail system by ex-employees or temporary employees.

Business Continuity and Backup Policies

Regulators are increasingly requiring organizations to have business continuity plans and procedures to identify how the organization, including its information technology system, would function in the event of an emergency, such as weather, a terrorist attack, or a computer attack. Where are the organization's backup servers? Who has access to critical organizational information in case of disruptions? Is there an off-site facility that employees can use? Can data and systems be accessed from remote locations?

Internal Controls

Organizations should evaluate their internal controls, including password management, network and Internet access controls, security logging, identification and authentication devices, and data encryption. Has the information technology (or some other) unit built compliance-related requirements and controls into the systems and products that it develops and maintains? Who is testing, and ensuring, that the organization's products and systems have the proper controls in place and that they are performing as expected?

Rapid Response to Situations

Organizations should develop and implement procedures and train employees to make a rapid assessment of suspected security breaches: refer suspected criminal acts to law enforcement agencies, notify affected residents, and make appropriate public announcements to stakeholders and other interested parties to minimize the negative impact of the security breach.

Third-Party Relationships and Outsourcing

It is critical that organizations review their arrangements with all third parties that store, process, or transmit organizational information. A prudent organization should ask each such service provider for basic information about its capabilities and experience. In the case of information technology, organizations should specifically address the potential vendor's security measures. For instance, does the vendor encrypt its files, e-mails, and documents; does it have sophisticated firewall and intrusion detection systems; what are its backup capabilities; and has its internal controls and activities been audited pursuant to the Statement on Auditing Standards (SAS) No. 70 developed by the American Institute of Certified Public Accountants (AICPA)?

Compliance Technology Tools

In the 1970s, the rock singer Meat Loaf had a hit tune, "Paradise by the Dashboard Light." Three decades later, compliance officers are seeking the glow and virtues of compliance technology dashboards, although for somewhat more businesslike purposes. The growth of technology tools ranging from compliance dashboards to automated policy management systems has significant potential to allow compliance programs to gather, interpret, measure, and disseminate disparate strands of compliance-related information. Ernst & Young's *Corporate Regulatory Compliance Practices* found that a majority of the companies surveyed used technology to track compliance issues and management (67 percent), monitor compliance controls (62 percent), and handle regulatory reporting (60 percent).

The challenge for organizations is to use diverse technologies effectively and efficiently to meet their compliance obligations. In an article for Deloitte entitled *A Working Marriage*, Nancy Creedon and Ron Malur write of this challenge: "There is no silver bullet, no single technology platform that can manage all global compliance issues. There are a multitude of systems that address specific regulations and while tackling regulatory compliance by using several unrelated software packages is seductive, it is short-sighted."

Technology Components

The quest for an effective compliance framework requires the adoption of a holistic, multidimensional approach to technology utilization and compliance. Its goal should be the delivery of critical compliance information to key organizational decision makers as swiftly as possible. From compliance portals to business intelligence systems, the range of technology options available is staggering. The objective for an organization is to select those technologies that are most appropriate for meeting its compliance demands.

Compliance Dashboards. One of the most widely discussed software tools, the compliance dashboard, allows compliance and other organizational officials an opportunity to monitor the identified risks of specific activities (operations, finance, or market activities), often in real time. Built around an organization's key controls, dashboard systems establish metrics that an organization can monitor.

The attractiveness of the compliance dashboard was explained by the chief information officer of Daiwa Securities, Stephen McCabe, in an interview in the October 25, 2005, issue of *Wall Street and Technology*:

> *[Computer dashboards] are particularly helpful for a midsize firm such as ours, where you don't have 50 compliance people — you only have two. . . . For us, the dashboard is a one-stop shopping situation where viewers can more easily see the compliance status of the firm at any given time.*

While the potential for compliance dashboards has great allure for many organizations, a note of caution has also been raised. For instance, what is the quality of the data that feed the system? Are they reliable? Moreover, given the diversity of dashboard products on the market, as Michael Rasmussen, a computer specialist interviewed in *ITCi* explained, "[T]here is no single standard for information display, data integration reports, and system architecture standards."

Exception Reporting ("Red Flags"). Exception reporting software provides organizations with an automated methodology for identifying and monitoring critical results or events that fall outside of predefined conditions. With these systems, organizations can readily identify potentially significant or problematic events that are not consistent with routine or expected activities. Exception reports can be delivered via e-mail, PDA, phone calls, or some other means. While regulators generally value an organization's use of exception reporting, a word of caution was issued by one regulator. John Walsh, chief counsel of the SEC's Office of Compliance, Inspection, and Examinations, cautioned in an April 2006 speech:

> *Firms are increasingly relying on electronic exception reports as fundamental elements in their supervisory and compliance systems. That is great. These reports can be valuable and can play a very positive role. Nonetheless, you have to use them carefully. If you set their parameters too high, they could miss important red flags. For example, if you have an electronic report that monitors for investment time horizons, but you assume that only investors under age 50 have investment time horizons, you could miss a lot of red flags relating to the elderly.*

Education, Communication, and Training

A critical component of an effective compliance framework is an informed organizational staff that is aware of the organization's policies and practices regarding information technology, privacy, security, and record keeping. As discussed previously, an organization's intranet communication program can be very useful in helping managers and supervisors, as well as employees, to

- Answer questions regarding information and security policies and practices.
- Learn about the availability of training programs.
- Provide access to organizational resources that help address specific concerns, such as access to the organization's information security or compliance functions.
- Update employees on the latest news and developments regarding information security and compliance.

Summary

The quest to integrate technology into the organization's compliance program, while important, should never obviate or diminish the overall goals of an effective compliance program. Technology is a means to an end. Writing in the January 18, 2007, issue of *Bank Systems and Technology*, Steve Schlaman, a computer specialist, made the following comment on the appropriate value and role of technology in the compliance process: "Technologies are the enablers for compliance but do not define compliance. Technology should help demonstrate compliance, ease the burden of compliance activities or be used to facilitate the compliance process."

9

Compliance and Oversight: Risk, Monitoring, Audits, and Regulators

Regulatory compliance and risk are inextricably linked. As Bridget Hutter and Michael Powar wrote in *Risk Management and Business Regulation* (2000), "Regulation is one way in which risks are managed in modern societies." The role of government and its agents in regulating risk and behavior in all aspects of organizational life has increased dramatically, and with this growth has come significant and complex organizational compliance obligations.

Andrew Haynes, writing in the *Journal of Banking Regulation* (February 2005), described the challenges that compliance officers and programs face in managing compliance risk. He said, "Managing and mitigating the compliance risk of an organization is probably the most difficult challenge facing compliance managers. Compliance risk can be a consequence of employee misbehavior, external shock or systemic risk."

Compliance Risk

What is compliance risk? How does it different from other forms of organizational risk? Perhaps Justice Potter Stewart's famous words on

---

BOX 9.1   Definitions of Compliance Risk

The Basel Committee on Banking Supervision defines compliance risk as the "risk of legal or regulatory sanctions, material financial loss, or loss to reputation a bank may suffer as a result of its failure to comply with laws, regulations, rules, related self-regulatory organization standards, and codes of conduct applicable to its banking activities (together, '*compliance laws, rules and standards*')."

Writing in *Public Utilities Fortnightly* in September 2006, James Bowers and David Doot have a slightly different vision of compliance risk, seeing it as "threats to an organization's strategy, operations, financial condition, and reputation resulting from a failure to comply with laws, regulations, internal policies and procedures, ethical standards, and customer expectations."

Michael Kelsey and Michael Matossian, writing in *ABA Bank Compliance* in June 2004, proposed another definition of compliance risk: "The adverse consequences that can arise from systemic, unforeseen, or isolated violations of applicable laws and regulations, internal standards and policies, and expectations of key stakeholders including customers, employees, and the community, which can result in financial losses, reputation damage, regulatory sanctions, and, in severe cases, loss of franchise or rejected mergers and acquisitions."

---

pornography ("I will know it when I see it") apply equally well to a definition of compliance risk. There is no specific, universal definition of this term; different entities and persons have defined it in different ways (Box 9.1 gives several of these definitions). A common view is that compliance risk concerns an organization's risk of loss (sanctions, lawsuits, or damage to its reputation) as a result of its failure to comply with laws, regulations, rules, and internal standards of behavior and policies.

Regulatory Requirements

The need for organizations to address compliance risk as a key element of any compliance program can be seen in various regulatory requirements from both government agencies and standards-setting organizations.

Federal Sentencing Guidelines for Organizations

One of the underpinnings of an effective compliance and ethics program for an organization is the need to document and prioritize its compliance risks. This is not envisioned as a one-time event, but rather as an intrinsic component of an organization's compliance program. In considering the 2004 Amendments to the Federal Sentencing Guidelines for Organizations (FSGO), the advisory group said, "[R]isk assessments need to be made at all stages of the development, testing, and implementation of a compliance program to ensure that compliance efforts are properly focused and effective. "

As a consequence, the 2004 Amendments to the FSGO mandate that organizations "shall conduct ongoing risk assessment . . . to reduce the risk of violation of law identified by the risk assessment." The risk assessment process has a fourfold goal:

- Identify the scope and nature of any risks associated with a violation of law.
- Assess the organization's exposure to these risks.
- Examine how the organization will allocate its resources to address these risks.
- Determine that the organization's efforts to prevent and detect violations of law are commensurate with its current activities.

It is the intent of the FSGO that an organization's systematic risk assessment effort will help the organization to evaluate and, if necessary, restructure the elements of its compliance program to

- Remedy possible deficiencies.
- Add new elements, such as a training program, to address risk situations that might lead to violations of law.

The Federal Sentencing Guidelines for Organizations, however, do not specify the means by which organizations should undertake this requirement. As the advisory group stated in its recommendations,

"[T]he proposed guidelines and commentary provisions do not mandate how risk assessment studies need to be performed in order to comply with the Federal Sentencing Guidelines for Organizations. Each organization will need to scrutinize its operating circumstances, legal surroundings, and industry history to gain a practical understanding of the types of unlawful practices that may arise in future organizational activities."

Federal Regulators

From the U.S. Environmental Protection Agency (EPA) to the Federal Reserve System, U.S. government regulators are increasingly focusing on the compliance risk assessment as a key element of a compliance program and as a process that they have adopted in their own examination process. For instance, banking and securities regulators are increasingly moving beyond strict adherence to a specific regulatory requirement and focusing their attention on a more general assessment of the means by which an institution identifies and manages compliance risk. As the Securities and Exchange Commission's (SEC's) Office of Compliance Inspections and Examinations explained, in its "risk-focused examinations":

> *Examiners review risk conditions and responsive compliance controls at a sample of firms. This approach allows the staff to obtain a more comprehensive view of the particular risk, assess the gravity of the risk, evaluate the compliance performance of individual firms compared to that of their peers, and recommend regulatory solutions.*

Standards-Setting Organizations

In September 2004, the Committee of Sponsoring Organizations of the Treadway Commission (COSO) released its "Enterprise Risk Management—Integrated Framework" (ERM) guidance. The ERM framework builds upon COSO's earlier guidance on internal control and expands on the risk management component of that earlier guidance.

Enterprise Risk Management

Like its internal control framework, COSO's ERM framework provides organizations with a comprehensive, integrated, and consistent approach to risk management. COSO's approach seeks to protect organizations from large, unknown risks. The ERM framework requires that organizations establish a risk appetite, measure their actions and decisions against that risk appetite, and communicate the results. It examines whether management processes are in place and functioning. The organization's board of directors and audit committee have an oversight role of determining that appropriate risk management processes are in place and that these processes are adequate and effective. Finally, the ERM framework looks at risk not in discrete segments, but across an organization to identify and manage vulnerabilities that might not be apparent with a narrow perspective. To this end, it encourages organizations to move away from measuring discrete, individual risks (often referred to as "silos") to evaluating its "risk landscape" in the aggregate and treating risk in an integrated, holistic manner.

Governance and Compliance Risk

A critical element of creating effective organizational risk management is the active involvement of the board of directors and senior management in promoting and supporting a risk-aware culture. It is the board and senior management that set the values and expectations for risk-related behavior, and that establish a program to effectively identify and monitor risk, including compliance risk. Mark Anson and Cindy Ma, writing in *The Corporate Board* (September/October 2003), noted the critical role of the board of directors in the risk management process: "Effective boards insist on systematic efforts to identify and address recurring and newly emerging risks. They seek out information needed for making informed decisions and they execute their oversight duties with rigor, consistency, and expertise."

To this end, the board has a number of important duties and responsibilities with respect to compliance risk.

Oversight and Monitoring

An effective board of directors takes a proactive approach to compliance and risk issues. It receives periodic reports on emerging issues and on the effectiveness of the organization's compliance program in addressing these issues. It needs to act promptly when there are significant risk situations and control breakdowns. It ensures that the compliance program is involved in the review of new organizational strategies and product offerings to identify any potential risk exposures.

Creation of a Compliance Risk Program

The board of directors must ensure that the organization has established the appropriate structure and allocated sufficient resources to systematically identify, monitor, and address compliance risks. While the administration of this function can be delegated to staff, it is ultimately the board's responsibility to ensure that the organization has an effective compliance risk program in place. In addition to the elements mentioned earlier, the organization's compliance risk program should also address risk ownership.

Risk Ownership

Organizational policies must clearly identify each employee's role and responsibilities in managing organizational compliance risk. All employees must be made aware of their general and specific responsibilities regarding compliance requirements. Additionally, each specific compliance risk must have an owner(s).

- All risk owners must have the appropriate level of authority and resources to manage the risk.

- All risk owners must be aware that they are the designated owner. There is nothing more frightening to someone than realizing that he or she is the owner of a risk that he or she did not know about.

Communication and Training

A communication and training program should be developed to articulate the organization's risk policy, appetite, and tolerances, and the specific compliance requirements faced by the organization and by individual positions and functions.

Compliance Risk Assessment Process

Knowing which risks to take (or to avoid) and how to mitigate and monitor those that are accepted is one of the goals of a compliance risk assessment process. It offers a structured approach to

- Identifying the organization's key compliance risks and vulnerabilities
- Prioritizing these risks and vulnerabilities
- Allocating resources to address these concerns
- Identifying the controls in place to mitigate risk
- Planning for any changes or additions in policies, programs, systems, and people to address these risks

Conducting the Compliance Risk Assessment

Compliance risk assessments have become an increasingly important feature of organizational management. The Conference Board's *Universal Conduct* study found that 70 percent of the companies it surveyed undertook "periodic risk assessments" of their compliance risks (not surprising, given the mandate of the FSGO).

While compliance risk assessment has become a standard feature of organizational compliance programs, there is little uniformity in its form or application. Some organizations conduct their compliance risk assessments entitywide; others focus on a specific business or corporate function. Similarly, the frequency of the compliance risk assessment is also variable. Being mindful of the FSGO and other regulatory requirements, organizations may conduct risk assessments in a variety of ways: in conjunction with their annual review process, quarterly, monthly, or "as needed" in the event of a special circumstance, such as when marketing a new product, entering into a new business venture, or facing a regulatory development that might affect the organization.

Under the direction of the organization's compliance officer and/or chief risk officer, organizations have used various approaches for conducting compliance risk assessments. Examples include the creation of a risk committee or team composed of representatives from various units in the organization, the use of independent consultants, or even the use of questionnaires to query organizational units. As Box 9.2 cautions, it is critical that the organization does not overlook any potential compliance risks due to gaps in its organizational structure. Surveys conducted by the Conference Board and the Ethics & Compliance Officers Association (ECOA) have found that most risk assessments were conducted by in-house personnel, often with the involvement of a consultant or lawyer. In fact, the ECOA reported that 40 percent of its respondents' risk assessments fell under the attorney-client privilege.

BOX 9.2   Note of Caution

To avoid any potential problems in assessing its compliance risks, it is critical that the organization clearly define the roles and responsibilities of each of its risk-related management functions (e.g., internal audit, risk, finance, and compliance) to ensure that there are no gaps or redundancies in the oversight of its compliance risks.

For example, an organization's compliance program might not include tax laws within its sphere of operation. In this case, specialists in the tax department should address those issues in their own risk assessment.

Identifying Risk Factors

"In this initial step," Tillinghast-Towers Perrin advised in its 2000 monograph, *Enterprise Risk Management*, "a wide net is cast to capture all risk factors that potentially affect achieving business objectives. Risk factors arise from many sources—financial, organizational, and political/regulatory or hazards. The key characteristic of each is that it can prevent the organization from meeting its goals."

The two principal sources of data for capturing risk information are

- Interviews with key organizational managers, both business and staff, including the CEO, chief legal officer, chief information security officer, chief auditor, chief financial officer, and human resources director, among others. The goal is to obtain a diverse and candid analysis of the organization's goals and objectives, the risk(s) it faces in meeting these objectives, how the organization functions, and areas for possible improvement in its compliance and control structure and systems. An organization might also consider interviewing its external partners (e.g., insurers, customers, and industry association) for additional insight into its inherent and projected risks.

  The Investment Advisor Association, in its 2006 article "Conducting a Risk Assessment," advised companies to think "outside the box" when identifying risks. It said, "It is easy to spot risk areas that regulators have already identified. . . . [H]owever, firms must also assess new risk areas that could significantly affect client assets and firm viability."

- Reviews of internal and external documentation. These include audit and regulatory reports, self-assessments, strategic business plans, current operating policies and procedures manuals, regulatory or supervisory enforcement actions, technology and systems utilization, internal controls, and staff changes (e.g., turnover, terminations, and skill and experience gaps). In conducting its risk assessment, organizations should heed the advice of an SEC official (see Box 9.3).

> **BOX 9.3   Advice from a Regulator**
>
> In speaking to a group of compliance officers in 2006, John Walsh of the Securities and Exchange Commission gave the following advice regarding risk assessments:
>
> *In our examinations of the risk assessment process, we have seen two recurring themes. One, a number of you used checklists. No question: a good one can really help. Please remember though, a checklist is only a start. One of the more important assessments you should perform is whether your firm has any unique risk exposures due to its personnel, business model, structure or affiliations. If these exposures are not widely shared by your peers, they may not appear on a checklist.*
>
> *Two, some of you, at the end of your risk assessment, ended up with two documents: a checklist of possible risks; and a list of compliance policies and procedures; with no apparent connection between the two. Please remember: the Commission said your policies and procedures should be designed to address the risk you identified.*

The Risk Context

To understand the compliance risks inherent in the organization, it is critical to examine the broader context and environment in which the organization operates. Externally, for instance, the regulatory climate will have a significant impact on the organization's risk management. In heavily regulated industries, in periods of significant government and self-regulatory organization (SRO) oversight, or after a company or industry "risk event" (such as the failure of a major business or widespread corruption in an industry), an organization's appetite for risk may be greatly diminished if taking on additional risk means endangering its franchise or its public reputation.

The organization's internal structure and operations will also significantly affect its compliance risk.

The Organizational Structure. It is important to understand how the organization is structured and how decision making is carried out. These are key factors in understanding how the organization addresses its compliance risk. For instance, is decision making decentralized, or are all key policy and program decisions approved at the corporate level? If a legal or regulatory issue should arise, who in the organization is responsible for managing the issue? In a decentralized environment, does the management staff at various levels in the organization have the resources, knowledge, and expertise to address these issues? What types of issues are raised to higher levels in the organization to address, and when? Who deals with the regulators or other key stakeholders?

Appetite for Risk. What degree of risk is the organization willing to accept in pursuit of its goals and objectives? Some organizations pride themselves in "pushing the envelope" to the boundaries of acceptable legal and ethical practices in the pursuit of market share and profits, while others have minimal tolerance for risk and aggressive behavior. Each philosophic approach will have a significant impact on organizational policies and practices.

Organizational Compliance Risks

In addition to understanding the broad contextual environment, a comprehensive compliance risk assessment examines specific aspects of the organization's operations and managerial practices. While compliance risks can potentially be wide-ranging, among the most significant are the following.

Strategic Risks. Organizations function in a dynamic environment. Change is endemic in modern organizations — from new products and services to reorganizations, acquisitions, and cost containment strategies. Organizations need to be alert to and understanding of the myriad risks that can affect their strategic goals and objectives. It is these strategic goals that will ultimately shape the organization's operations, products, and services. Will the organization focus on Web-based products, a particular market segment, or a specific geographical region? Each choice presents a series of compliance-related issues and challenges for an organization.

Similarly, does the organization plan any strategic acquisitions? If so, does the acquiring organization have the resources, skills, culture, experience, and expertise to manage the new entity successfully or to integrate its operations into the existing organization? Will the acquiring company inherit any reputational or compliance risks associated with the acquired organization?

Legal and Regulatory Risks. At the heart of compliance responsibilities are the legal and regulatory requirements and risks that organizations must constantly address and assess.

Who is responsible for the oversight of these functions?
An organization should clearly delineate the responsibility for managing these risks and define the jurisdictional "boundaries" and roles for its chief legal officer and chief compliance officer. Beyond these two functions, what are the compliance risk responsibilities of the organization's other risk management functions, such as internal audit, finance, human resources, or health and safety? Equally important, the critical role of managers and supervisors in compliance oversight must be clearly understood. The organization must be able to identify any gaps in oversight that prevent effective management of these risks.

How effectively does the organization assess and plan for the impact of anticipated changes in law and regulation?
An effective compliance program anticipates changes and works with other key organizational units, such as legal, technology, communications, training, and business managers, to ensure a timely, orderly, and effective installation of any new process or policy to address changes in law or regulation.

Are the organization's policies and procedures current, adequately detailed, and specific to that organization?
The organization's compliance-related policies and procedures must reflect current law and regulation. All policies and procedures should be reviewed by counsel to ensure their legal adequacy. Organizations should ensure that all of their policy statements are consistent with one another, whether they are found in a manual, in a handbook, or on a Web site.

How does the organization monitor and anticipate legal and regulatory risks? What controls are in place?

It is critical that an organization continually monitor its legal and regulatory risks. Under Sarbanes-Oxley, the organization has a duty to promptly inform senior management and the board of directors of significant risk issues. Has the organization instituted an effective program of internal control to mitigate and monitor these risks? Who is responsible for the program, and how effective are the controls that have been instituted? What is the role of internal audit in monitoring legal and regulatory risks? Is there sufficient review and approval of new products and systems for compliance-related issues?

How does the organization train and inform employees?

An effective compliance program includes a proactive program to inform employees, volunteers, and others of changes in law and regulation and the implications of these changes for the organization and for each individual's job function. Who is responsible for this effort? What techniques are used to disseminate compliance information? Who are the recipients of the training and information? Are managers and employees trained to spot risk and compliance issues, and do they know where to report any such problems?

How and where does the organization capture, retain, and report key information?

While establishing an effective internal control or audit program is critical, how does the organization use the information generated from these and other sources to mitigate risk? What is the quality of the data generated by the business that assist in monitoring compliance? Who in the organization reviews and disseminates reports? Is there a system for escalating information to the board of directors and senior management?

How effectively do the organization's technology and systems manage and monitor these requirements?

Given the vast scope of potential legal and regulatory risks, does the organization have adequate systems and technology to monitor its operations and to identify and report risk issues? Governor Mark Olsen of the

Federal Reserve Board noted the importance of an organization's information systems in capturing key risk data.

> *Large complex banking organizations are typically supported by information systems that provide management with timely reports related to compliance with laws and regulations at the transaction level. Examiners will look to see whether these reports generally address monitoring and testing activities, actual or potential material compliance deficiencies or breaches, and new or changing compliance requirements. They will also assess whether reports are designed to ensure that information on compliance is communicated to the appropriate levels within the organization.*

Are these systems well designed and sufficiently tested to ensure that their processing is consistent with legal and regulatory requirements?

How knowledgeable, capable, and independent are the staff members responsible for compliance oversight?
An organization must feel confident that the employees to whom it has given the primary responsibility for the oversight of its legal and regulatory risks (legal, compliance, audit, risk management, or business managers) have the skills, knowledge, resources, and training to address these issues effectively. Moreover, is the compliance staff sufficiently independent of the functions it is reviewing to provide unvarnished assessments and unfiltered reports to senior management and the board of directors?

Managerial Risks. A factor that is frequently overlooked, yet critical to fully understanding an organization's compliance risk, is the organization's managerial style and culture. Managers and supervisors play a critical role in compliance risk. They set expectations, and they establish and reinforce standards of behavior. They create an atmosphere that condones or prohibits illegal or unethical behavior. Organizations need to examine their own values and culture to ensure that they have created a work environment that supports ethical behavior and discourages unethical behavior.

Human Resources Risks. Another frequently overlooked area of compliance risk involves the organization's human resources operations. This is an area of potentially significant risk to the organization if it is not managed properly.

What are the organization's policies and practices governing the hiring and promotion of employees?
Are the organization's hiring and promotion policies and practices compliant with federal and state laws and industry requirements? Does the organization have appropriate due diligence procedures for the vetting of new employees? A key element of the Federal Sentencing Guidelines for Organizations (Section 8B2.1) is the requirement that: "The organization shall use reasonable efforts not to include within the substantial authority personnel of the organization any individual whom the organization knew, or should have known through the exercise of due diligence, has a history of engaging in violations of law or other conduct inconsistent with an effective program to prevent and detect violations of law." As the advisory group succinctly noted in its commentary, "Organizations would logically want to ensure that those with significant responsibilities are law abiding and likely to act in accordance with company policies."

Have managers and employees been trained in managing and preventing harassment and sexual harassment issues?
How knowledgeable are the organization's managers and supervisors regarding applicable federal and state law governing harassment and sexual harassment in the workplace? Do they know how to manage employee-related issues when such issues are brought to their attention?

How does the organization manage its third-party employment relationships (such as those with consultants or temporary employees)?
Improper management of third parties can pose significant financial and legal risks for the organization. Have the organization's managers been trained in the proper management of temporary employees? Does the organization understand the tax and benefit risks of improper usage of third parties?

Are the organization's managers adequately trained in managing employees and appropriate disciplinary procedures?
Managers must understand the correct steps in conducting disciplinary actions involving employees: what to say and what not to say, what documentation to keep, and when to involve human resources in critical situations.

Has the organization reviewed its compensation policies and practices?
Compensation policies and practices can present significant potential risk for an organization, from backdating of stock options or failing to properly classify employees for overtime eligibility to giving employees incentives to engage in potentially improper behavior (e.g., overly aggressive sales practices).

Culture, Values, and Ethics. Values and culture create the framework for the organization.

- Has the organization issued a code of conduct pursuant to Sarbanes-Oxley, New York Stock Exchange, or other regulatory or SRO requirements? Is it a paper exercise?
- Do the actions of the board of directors and senior management reflect the values and ethics that are espoused?
- How aware are employees of the organization's values and ethics?
- How does the organization manage issues of ethical wrongdoing? Does it have a whistle-blower program or a system for reporting incidents anonymously?
- Has the organization instituted any training programs focusing on ethics and values?

Subcontractors, Consultants, and Vendors. Risk assessment must examine the role that third parties play in the organization's operations. In areas from systems and technology and human resources management to audit, legal, and even compliance-related services, the use of third parties is increasingly common. They are an intricate part of organizational operations that represents as great a risk, if not a greater one, as the organization's own staff.

Assessing and Prioritizing Compliance Risk

Having identified the potential universe of compliance risk facing the organization, the next task is to analyze and assess those issues that present the greatest risk. As the Advisory Group on the Federal Sentencing Guidelines for Organizations said in its commentary, "Organizations must periodically prioritize their compliance and ethics resources to target those potential criminal activities that pose the greatest threat in light of the risks identified."

The goal of ranking and prioritization of compliance risks is to

- Distinguish between major and minor risks.
- Evaluate each risk and its importance to the organization's goals and objectives.
- Assess the level of internal controls and testing frequency.
- Determine the resources required to manage the risk.

Techniques. Unlike more traditional methods of evaluating credit, financial, or market risks that use quantitative techniques such as Value at Risk (VaR) or Monte Carlo simulation, compliance risk assessment and evaluation is often a more subjective process. There are often no hard standards or criteria for measuring compliance risks. A June 2006 report by the Economist Intelligence Unit, *Bank Compliance: Controlling Risk and Improving Effectiveness*, noted a myriad of challenges that banks address and approaches that they take with respect to compliance risk.

> *Compliance risk tends to be intangible and thus hard to quantify or boil down to a few numbers. There is also a lack of historical data, ruling out for now the use of tools similar to those used to gauge market and credit risk. Even so, banks are developing more systematic ways to capture compliance risk, often using both qualitative and quantitative measures. These include using surveys and business line input to help grade compliance efforts and create matrices, score cards, heat and bubble maps, and*

various risk assessment scores. Other tools include internal and external benchmarking, audit trails and scenario testing.[1]

Organizations generally assess their compliance risks from two perspectives:

- The "likelihood of occurrence" of the risk (e.g., is it rare, possible, or almost certain?).
- The "significance" of the risk (e.g., is it minor, significant, or catastrophic?). "Significance" refers to the legal, regulatory, financial, and reputational consequences for an organization if it fails to manage the risk.

The quest for many organizations has been to develop ways to quantify these probabilities and create a ranking or hierarchy of risk. By using objective definitions, organizations seek to classify each of their compliance risks in a reasonably objective fashion (although these classifications always involve some degree of subjective interpretation and decision making).

In the case of likelihood of occurrence, an organization may assign a risk rating of 1 to 5 to each compliance risk (see Figure 2). As an example, an organization may wish to examine whether one of its employment practices, in this case the possibility of hiring illegal workers, poses a major compliance risk. Based on an assessment of its policies, practices, and internal controls, the nature of its business, and the volume and type of persons employed, the organization might rank the likelihood of this risk occurring on a scale on which 5 is high and 1 is low. Ideally, the organization's goal is achieve a 1 level of risk.

A similar analysis is then performed for the significance aspect of the risk. Using the example just cited, the organization will determine the significance for it if it does employ illegal workers, again on a scale with 5 as the highest, with major reputational or legal consequences, to 1, with little or no impact on the organization. In this fashion, the organization is able to understand the relative importance of each of its compliance risks, which will assist it in resource allocation and oversight planning.

Rating	Likelihood Description	Qualitative Description	Quantitative Description
5	High (certain)	Expected to occur in most circumstances	Likely to occur this year or at frequent intervals
3	Moderate (possible)	Might occur at some time	Likely to occur in the next three years
1	Low (unlikely)	May occur only in exceptional circumstances	Likely to occur once in 25 years

FIGURE 2. Sample Ranking of Likelihood of Occurrence

Thus, if, based on its history, its record of employment, its industry, and its policies and practices, the organization determines that there is a strong likelihood that it may hire illegal workers, and if it believes that the consequences for the organization would be significant (e.g., fines, disbarment from contracts, or damage to its public reputation), it will clearly focus its resources and compliance risk oversight in this area.

Risk Mapping. Another technique that organizations frequently use in assessing and reporting compliance risk is called "risk mapping" or a variation of this, such as the "heat maps" in Figure 3. Essentially, a risk map is a graphic depiction in which the organization, using the "likelihood of occurrence and "significance" criteria described earlier, plots each risk on a grid to show the potential danger posed by each risk. Risk mapping, in the words of the December 2001 *Journal of Accountancy*, "is a simple but powerful way to display the relationship between likelihood and consequences" of a risk. Significant risks that appear in the upper right corner (marked in dark gray) on the grid require immediate organizational attention. Frequently, organizations will overlay their internal controls over the risk map to ascertain how they can mitigate their risks.

Findings and Recommendations

It is tempting to believe that once an organization has gone through the process of identifying, prioritizing, and assessing its compliance risks, and

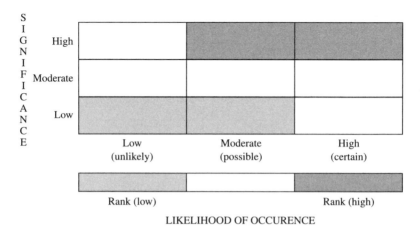

FIGURE 3. Sample Risk Map Format

even plotting them on a risk map, this is the end of the risk assessment process. In fact, it is only the beginning. The result is a baseline against which the organization, the board of directors, and senior management must decide which compliance risks to address, monitor, and manage. The findings of the compliance risk assessment will have a significant impact on the organization (and the consequences of compliance failure can be devastating; see Box 9.4):

- Does the organization understand the requirements and compliance risks it is responsible for?
- Does it have the internal capabilities to effectively address the compliance risks that have been identified?
- Are its compliance risks increasing or decreasing over time?
- Is the severity of the compliance risks increasing or decreasing?
- Are the organization's internal controls adequate to meet these risks?
- Who in the organization is going to be responsible for managing these risks?
- What investment of resources and management attention should be allocated to addressing these risks?

> **BOX 9.4   Consequences of Compliance Failure**
>
> As an organization assesses its compliance risks, it should be mindful of the consequences of compliance failure. Ironically, the least of these consequences might be the statutory fines associated with an infraction. Once an organization has been cited by government officials, there may be numerous other ramifications that dwarf any monetary penalty:
>
> - Failure to gain government permission to acquire or merge with another organization
> - Reputational damage that affects future sales and revenues
> - Increased regulatory scrutiny of all aspects of organizational operations
> - A potential drop in the stock price
> - Failure to attract and retain top employee talent

- Are any of the compliance risks so severe, and their initial assessments so negative, that they require notification of the organization's regulators?

Both the Conference Board and the ECOA studies of organizations' risk assessment practices, mentioned earlier, found that

- Approximately three-quarters of the respondents presented the results of their risk analyses in a written report.
- More than half provided the information derived from their analysis to the organization's senior management. (In the ECOA study, 27 percent of the respondents also sent the risk assessment analyses and results to the board of directors. Other recipients included compliance and ethics staff, business unit leaders, outside auditors, and risk managers.)

Compliance Monitoring and Audits

Monitoring and compliance audits are natural complements and follow-ons to the organization's risk assessment process.

Monitoring

A key function of an organization's compliance oversight activities is an ongoing program monitoring the organization's compliance requirements and activities, and potentially changing its risk assessment assumptions based on these monitoring activities. Compliance monitoring involves ensuring that the organization's internal controls are working properly and reviewing ongoing operations to respond to any potential issues that may have arisen. Compliance monitoring entails collecting and analyzing information from diverse sources:

- Exception reports
- Trends in customer complaints
- Employee hotline information
- Reports from regulatory examinations
- Key risk indicator threshold violations (e.g., a surge in reports of customer complaints to regulators)

In securities organizations, for instance, monitoring activities include surveillance of business transactions and communications to identify potential violations. As the Securities Industry and Financial Markets Association (SIFMA)'s *White Paper on the Role of Compliance* (July 2005) said, "[M]onitoring business activity facilitates ongoing compliance with firm policies and regulatory requirements by helping to identify at their early stages patterns of improper behavior or activities." Monitoring is not without its risks, however. The author remembers an encounter with an irate employee whose securities trading was being monitored as part of a routine insider trader monitoring program. His declarations of alleged "communist" tactics by one of the world's largest financial institutions were most ironic.

Compliance Auditing

After the organization has identified the major compliance risk issues facing it, made an initial assessment of its compliance risk exposure, and supplemented this assessment by ongoing monitoring of data concerning the effectiveness of its controls, the next level of protection for the organization is the compliance audit. It is an invaluable tool. In its *Compliance Examination Handbook*, the Federal Deposit Insurance Corporation (FDIC) succinctly described the role and value of the compliance audit as

> *An independent review of an institution's compliance . . . with laws and regulations and adherence to internal policies and procedures. The audit helps management ensure ongoing compliance and identify compliance risk conditions. It complements the institution's internal monitoring system. The Board of Directors of the institution should determine the scope of the audit, and the frequency with which audits are conducted.*

Benefits of a Compliance Audit. Writing in the 1996 *Food & Drug Law Journal*, George Burditt had an interesting comment on the value of compliance audits, especially with regard to an organization's relationship with its regulators: "A corporate compliance audit is clear evidence that the management of the company realizes its moral and legal responsibilities and intends to make certain that corporate policies are carried out properly, down to the smallest production line."

And the Legal Risks. A major dilemma that organizations confront when conducting compliance audits involves two potentially significant legal issues:

- Information gathered during the course of an audit may potentially be used against the organization during a regulatory proceeding, or it may be "discoverable" by parties in civil or even criminal litigation against the organization.
- The organization is required to "self-report" to regulatory or legal authorities any legal and compliance violations that a compliance audit may uncover.

Organizations have often used attorney-client privilege or the work-product doctrine to protect compliance audits (and even risk assessments) from legal discovery. The decision to maintain privilege rather than divulging information to regulators is a complex and sensitive issue that has significant legal and reputational risks.

M. Elizabeth Fast and Terri Thomas have emphasized the dilemma of attorney-client privilege in the current regulatory environment. Writing in the May/June 2005 ABA *Bank Compliance*, they state:

> *It is the government's view that protecting the long-standing privilege is less important that [sic] convincing a lawyer or client to reveal potentially damaging secrets. For the company's part, it has to decide whether it is in the best interests of its directors and officers to waive client-attorney privilege with the hope that the waiver will cause the government to look favorably upon the company's management.*[2]

Self-reporting has been promoted by government agencies from the Internal Revenue Service (IRS) to the EPA. Regulators have instituted various "voluntary disclosure" programs to encourage organizations to police themselves and to come forward with reports of violations. The SEC's "Seaboard Report" listed various criteria that it would use in considering possible credit for organizations with securities law issues for "self-policing and self-reporting."

Getting Started

Where to start in the compliance audit process? In performing a formal compliance audit, organizations should be cognizant of the professional standards of practice followed by other audit functions (internal audit departments or external audit firms). These standards, such as those promulgated by the Institute of Internal Auditors and the American Institute of Certified Public Accountants, should govern the planning, execution, documentation, and reporting of the compliance audit and its findings.

Planning is the first step in any audit review program. It is during this phase that the organization must determine how to address the compliance risks it has identified. Often, organizations will prepare an annual review plan, based upon an updated risk assessment, that delineates which of the specific compliance risk areas are to be addressed in the forthcoming year and which will be addressed in subsequent years.

Objective and Scope of the Compliance Audit

Given the breadth of the compliance risks described earlier in this chapter, it is critical that an organization clearly define the objective(s) of a compliance audit. Organizations must set a realistic scope for the review and have realistic expectations for what they can accomplish given their resources and capabilities. The objectives and scope of the compliance review may be based on several criteria:

- Risk assessments
- Regulatory requirements
- Previous compliance reviews and audits
- Patterns of weaknesses in the organization (e.g., traditionally low compliance with certain regulations, systems, products, or customer requirements)
- Previous incidents of wrongdoing
- Monitoring results
- Acquisition of a new entity
- Changes or additions of new products and services
- Length of time since previous compliance audits
- Volume and severity of customer complaints
- Changes in policies and practices since the last audit review
- Legal opinions about the organization's policies, practices, and services
- Resources available to do an evaluation review (e.g., focus one year on training and the next year on outsourcing relationships)

Format for the Audit

As with risk assessments, organizations use various formats and approaches to conduct compliance audits. These include self-assessment, peer reviews (internal and external), internal audits, external audits, "vertical" reviews of all risks associated with a specific process, and "horizontal" reviews of a specific risk across all products and processes.

Frequency

Organizations generally consider the following factors in considering the frequency of their compliance audits:

- The nature of the organization's operations and activities
- Significant organizational risks
- The results of the organization's monitoring processes
- The results of previous audits
- Regulators' requirements

In the absence of specific regulatory guidance, an organization should establish an audit approach and time frame that are consistent with its risk assessment, resources, and management risk appetite.

The Reviewers

Reviewers must have the experience, objectivity, and knowledge necessary to ask probing questions and ascertain the situation. Regulators have been quite clear about their views regarding the independence and qualifications of compliance audit reviewers. For instance, the Federal Reserve Board, in its *Bank Secrecy Act Anti-Money Laundering Examination Manual*, says that examiners must: "Determine whether the BSA/AML testing (audit) is independent (e.g., performed by a person (or persons) not involved with the bank's BSA/AML compliance staff) and whether persons conducting the testing report directly to the board of directors or to a designated board committee comprised primarily or completely of outside directors." Moreover, the examiners must: "Evaluate the qualifications of the person (or persons) performing the independent testing to assess whether the bank can rely upon the findings and conclusions."

The decision as to who will conduct the compliance audit is critical. The organization has several options:

- Establish a compliance audit function within the compliance program as an adjunct to its advisory and other functions.
- Establish a separate compliance audit function.
- Rely on the auditing and testing of other organizational risk management functions (e.g., internal audit).
- Utilize outside consultants or audit firms (see Box 9.5 for a precautionary note).
- Use teams of internal staff on a project basis.

The decision will ultimately be based on the organization's size, experience, industry, and other factors. In any case, the organization's dedicated compliance unit should be given the primary responsibility for overseeing, if not necessarily performing, all compliance audits.

Data Collection

In conducting an evaluation of the organization's compliance risks and activities, it is critical that reviewers have complete and unimpeded

---

BOX 9.5   A Word of Advice

In the March 1999 meeting between the Office of the Inspector General and the Health Care Compliance Association discussed in Chapter 5, participants noted that "one of the largest impediments that they encounter, however, is finding qualified personnel to conduct the audits. Several indicated that they had previously received improper advice from consultants who had conducted risk assessments and evaluations of their respective organizations. The recommendation from the participants was to conduct thorough interviews of consultants prior to contracting with them."

access to all pertinent documentation, systems, and individuals (internal or external).

Documentation. An important factor in demonstrating the organization's effectiveness at managing its compliance risk is documentation (for the organization's own internal purposes and to present to its regulators). Examples of audit documentation include

- Risk and control identification
- Testing and sampling methodologies utilized
- Audit results and conclusions
- Corrective action plans
- Due diligence efforts regarding business transactions
- Modification and distribution of policies and procedures
- Records of employee education, including the number of training hours, the courses offered, materials used, and the identities of the attendees
- Web sites

Interviews. Reviewers should speak with key staff members to ascertain their knowledge of regulatory requirements, review key controls, and identify their issues and concerns. If possible, reviewers should "walk through" the transaction process under review. (How is information gathered? Who signs and approves the transactions? What forms are used? Who handles or inputs data? What is the documentation process?) Reviewers should not limit their interviews to senior or even midlevel managerial staff. It is critical that they obtain a candid and complete picture of the function's operations from all perspectives.

Findings and Recommendations

As with the risk assessment, effective management of the compliance audit's findings and recommendations is critical. The organization needs to determine how it will manage any significant risks and problems that are identified and who is going to be responsible for addressing these issues, then set a time frame for their resolution and develop a corrective action tracking procedure and an approval process to ensure that the corrective actions are proper and effective. Effective resolution of identified issues is critical, as unresolved or poorly resolved issues will generally be viewed as "repeat" issues by a regulator and treated harshly.

The organization, in conjunction with counsel, will have to determine when it will disclose any significant compliance findings to its regulators, what information to present to the regulators, and what the potential ramifications for the organization (e.g., censure, fine, or criminal liability) of its disclosure are. It is axiomatic that an organization that finds a problem and does not fix it in a timely fashion may face significant legal or reputational consequences from its failure to act promptly.

Regulators

An important component of the organization's compliance program is maintaining an effective, cordial, and professional relationship with its external regulators: state, federal, and SRO. Regulators serve a vital public role, and their relationship with the organization can be productive. While the compliance program may not have an exclusive relationship with the organization's regulators (often the corporate counsel or other organizational attorneys may also have an ongoing relationship), it is critical that the organization be cognizant of several key points.

Know the Organization's Regulator

Understanding the role, mission, concerns, and priorities of a regulatory body is critical. Regulatory bodies see their role as protecting the interests of both the companies they regulate and the communities they serve. They can provide expert advice on a range of regulatory issues, and they can influence the implementation of legislation that is vital to the organization. Writing in the March/April 2005 issue of *ABA Bank Compliance*, Michael Mahler, an expert on regulatory relations, said of a bank's relationship with its regulators, "Our regulatory relationships are probably more like our relationships with hard-to-please in-laws than our relationship with our dearest loved one. But managing these relationships doesn't have to be unpleasant if we are willing to invest in these relationships."

Communicate Early

Do not wait for something to go wrong to open a dialogue with the organization's regulators. Develop an ongoing relationship with the regulators. Meet with them to discuss the organization, issues of concern, priorities, and strategies. Eric Rosenberg, a consultant and former senior regulatory counsel for a major investment company, advised, "[An] organization has got to know its regulators before a problem arises." Have regulators meet the organization's business managers to build trust and respect.

Establish an Open Relationship

Organizations and their compliance personnel should establish an open, respectful, and forthright relationship with their regulators. Rosenberg advised that compliance professionals must develop "a climate of openness, trust, and a feeling of credibility" between the organization and the regulators.

Craig Glazer, a commissioner at the Public Utilities Commission (PUC) in Ohio, in the February 15, 2000, *Public Utilities Fortnightly*, gave some insightful advice to avoid mistakes in doing business with his regulatory organization:

> *Conceding a point where you might have screwed up can be a successful tactic for achieving credibility on a bigger point. Don't be afraid to be honest. Regulatory relationships are like good marriages—they're for the long term. . . . Swallow hard on a bad decision and then begin immediately to mend the relationship.*

There is nothing more damaging to an organization than losing the confidence of its regulators. Once that is lost, even small, isolated incidents and infractions will be looked at entirely differently; past issues will be knitted together as part of a pattern where perhaps none existed. Once this confidence is lost, regaining it will be a long and painful process, and one that will be typically assigned to your successors.

Summary

It is crucial that organizations understand their compliance risks. An effective organization takes a proactive approach to identifying and managing these risks. Issues do not fade away. They must be identified and managed appropriately. Are the organization's compliance risks systemic or "one-off" events? Is the problem an obscure field location with little, if any, supervision? Does the organization's managerial structure have major deficiencies in its compliance oversight? Is the risk a senior manager who believes that his or her actions supersede law or organizational policy? Are the organization's compliance risk policies and programs obsolete, not having been updated to reflect changes in the organization's mission, population, products, or services? The list of possible issues is endless; the need for action is immediate.

Notes

1. © Reproduced by permission of the Economist Intelligence Unit.
2. In December 2006, U.S. Deputy Attorney General Paul McNulty announced major changes to the U.S. Department of Justice's (DOJ) policies as expressed in the 2003 Thompson memorandum (see Chapter 1). Among the changes was the requirement that federal prosecutors must obtain written approval from senior management in the DOJ before seeking a waiver of the attorney-client privilege and work-product protection as part of investigation into corporate misbehavior.

10

Compliance and Controls

An effective internal control system is a key component in the organization's web of protection. It addresses the myriad legal, regulatory, financial, and operational risks that organizations routinely confront: Is the organization hiring people in accordance with U.S. law and regulation? Are billing and coding in accordance with U.S. Department of Health and Human Services policy and practice? Do employees have conflicts of interest with respect to procurement operations?

Breakdowns in an organization's internal controls can have severe consequences. These can range from fines, loss of reputation, and lost business and funding opportunities to even imprisonment in the most severe cases. In testimony before the House Subcommittee on Oversight and Investigations, Robert Gramling, an official of the U.S. General Accountability Office, gave a cogent explanation of the meaning and importance of internal controls for an organization.

Internal control can be simply defined as the methods by which an organization governs its activities to effectively and efficiently accomplish its mission. More specifically, internal control is concerned with stewardship and accountability of resources consumed in the process of striving to accomplish an entity's mission with effective results. . . . [I]nternal control should be recognized as an integral part of each system that management uses to regulate and guide its operations.

Government Regulations

The development of internal control systems and their relationship to regulatory compliance issues is reflected in the evolution of federal legislation over the past 40 years. The Foreign Corrupt Practices Act of 1977, for instance, required public companies to develop internal control systems that accurately reported all transactions and assets. Similarly, the Federal Deposit Insurance Corporation Improvement Act (FDICIA) of 1991 tightened financial institutions' internal controls in reaction to the egregious financial failures of savings and loan associations and other financial institutions. In fact, FDICIA required the organization's chief executive officer and chief financial officer to report on the quality of the organization's internal controls. This served as a model for later legislation.

However, it was the spate of corporate wrongdoing in the late 1990s and early 2000s that caused the federal government's mandate for internal controls to reach its zenith with the passage of the Sarbanes-Oxley Act of 2002. That legislation, along with internal controls mandated by the Federal Sentencing Guidelines for Organizations (FSGO), federal regulators, and self-regulatory organizations (SROs), has placed a significant burden on organizations in terms of developing and documenting their internal control programs.

Sarbanes-Oxley Act of 2002

As previously discussed, the Sarbanes-Oxley Act of 2002 has been hailed (or vilified) as a monumental act of legislation to reform corporate governance practices in the United States. From an internal control perspective, two sections of the law are at the heart of Sarbanes-Oxley:

- Section 302 requires the organization's chief executive officer and chief financial officer to personally certify not only that they have personally reviewed the organization's required financial reports, but that the "signing officers are responsible for establishing and maintaining internal controls . . . have evaluated the effectiveness of the . . . internal controls . . . and have presented in the report their conclusions about the effectiveness of their internal controls."
- Section 404 mandates that a company make an annual assessment of its internal controls for financial reporting. It also requires that the organization have an independent auditor issue a separate report attesting to the organization's assertions concerning the effectiveness of its internal controls and procedures for financial reporting.

Despite the fact that Sarbanes-Oxley is focused principally on a relatively narrow, albeit powerful, range of organizations (i.e., publicly traded corporations), and on accounting and financial reporting in particular, its impact has been felt throughout the economy. The law's provisions for corporate governance and internal control have set the standard for organizational governance and management across an enormous swath of organizations: public, private, and nonprofit. In a September 2003 speech, William H. Donaldson, former chairman of the U.S. Securities and Exchange Commission (SEC), noted the importance of the internal controls provisions of the law.

> *For many companies, the new rules on internal control reports will represent the most significant single requirement associated with the Sarbanes-Oxley Act. . . . By requiring a report stating management's responsibility for internal control over financial reporting and management's assessment regarding the effectiveness of such control, investors will be better able to evaluate*

management's stewardship responsibilities and the reliability of a company's disclosure.

A classic example of the failure of internal controls and its impact on an organization is found in Box 10.1.

Federal Sentencing Guidelines for Organizations. While Sarbanes-Oxley focused on financial reporting, the Federal Sentencing Guidelines for Organizations have similarly addressed the need for internal controls to address compliance risk, although somewhat more obliquely. Section 8B2.1 of the FSGO states that to have an effective compliance and ethics

---

BOX 10.1 Embezzlement Facilitated by Inadequate Internal Controls

In 2005, the Federal Deposit Insurance Corporation's *Supervisory Insights* presented a case of egregious fraud when an organization's internal controls system failed to function properly. It is a lesson worth noting!

A retail institution in a small city held less than $500 million in assets. The bank was consistently profitable. During a two-year period, a senior executive officer exerted significant influence over the loan function as well as the bank's operations. He had an authoritarian management style and was responsible for administration of more than half of the loan portfolio. The bank's board of directors had granted the officer authority for a very high lending limit. Furthermore, the board usually reviewed and approved loans only after the fact, and delinquent-loan reports provided to the board were manually prepared by bank staff and subject to the officer's manipulation. The effects of the bank's inadequate internal controls and ineffective internal audit program were exacerbated by the officer's intimidation of employees and the bank's level of staffing, which did not keep pace with its significant asset growth. Moreover, although senior management officials began to notice irregularities in the officer's activities, they failed to notify the board of directors, regulators, or law enforcement authorities in a timely manner, allowing the misconduct to continue.

Through his misconduct, the officer acquired personal benefit of more than $1 million. However, the officer's misconduct combined with his efforts to conceal his activities resulted in losses of nearly $5 million to the insured institution. Moreover, his departure left a significant void in management. Subsequently, the bank merged with another institution and no longer exists as an independent entity.

program, "an organization shall establish standards and procedures to prevent and detect criminal conduct." In the guidelines' commentary, there is an application note that says, "'[S]tandards and procedures' means standards of conduct and internal controls that are reasonably capable of reducing the likelihood of criminal conduct." It is this reference that organizations cite as creating a need for broad-based internal control programs.

Internal Control Regulation and the Public Sector

The U.S. government's role in recognizing the importance of internal control is not limited to the private and nonprofit sectors. The use of internal control in the government's own operations dates back to the passage of the Accounting and Auditing Act of 1950, which established internal controls for the funds, property, and other assets for which an agency had responsibility. The act was subsequently amended by the Federal Managers Financial Integrity Act of 1992 (FMFIA), which required ongoing evaluations of and reports on the adequacy of the systems of internal accounting and administrative control of each executive agency, and the Federal Financial Management Improvement Act of 1996 (FFMIA), which ensures that federal financial management systems provide accurate, reliable, and timely financial management information to the government's managers.

Self-Regulatory Organizations: New York Stock Exchange

Reflecting the enhanced government mandate for internal controls, self-regulatory organizations have also identified the need for enhanced internal controls for organizations. For instance, the New York Stock Exchange's (NYSE's) Rule 342.23 requires members of the exchange to maintain adequate internal controls over their business activities and to include procedures for the independent verification and testing of those internal controls. According to the NYSE, "independent verification and testing" means testing samples to identify shortcomings, gaps, and inefficiencies in supervisory systems and procedures. Moreover, starting in 2006, NYSE-listed firms had to include in their annual compliance reports a summary of the organization's internal controls testing and any exceptions that were identified.

Standards-Setting Organizations: Committee of Sponsoring Organizations of the Treadway Commission

The past decades have seen a growth in the importance of U.S. and international private organizations in promulgating industry standards and practices. A number of these organizations have been active in developing standards that are increasingly playing a key role in compliance management functions. Of these, the Committee of Sponsoring Organizations of the Treadway Commission (COSO) is of prime importance in the area of internal controls.

In 1992, COSO promulgated its benchmark *Internal Control—Integrated Framework*." Mark Simmons, writing in *The Internal Auditor* (December 1997), said of COSO, "The 1992 COSO document, Internal Control-Integrated Framework, changed the way we look at internal control. . . . Traditional theories, which primarily addressed financial controls, were broadened substantially. The COSO Framework considers not only the evaluation of hard controls, like segregation of duties, but also soft controls, such as the competence and professionalism of employees."

COSO's prominence derives not only from its being the catalyst that changed the way organizations viewed their internal control functions but, equally important, from the endorsement of the Securities and Exchange Commission. In its implementing regulations for Sarbanes-Oxley, the SEC specifically cites COSO as an accepted internal control framework. COSO, it said, "satisfies [the] criteria and may be used as an evaluation framework for purposes of management's internal control evaluation." While COSO is not the only internal control framework (e.g., there have been other internal control frameworks developed in Canada, the United Kingdom, and Australia), the SEC's endorsement further solidified its prominence as the standard framework for the analysis of internal controls.

The COSO framework defines internal control, describes its components, and provides criteria against which control systems can be evaluated. It offers guidance for public reporting on internal control and provides materials that management, auditors, and others can use to evaluate an internal control system. Two major goals of the framework are to (1) establish a common definition of internal control that serves many different parties, and (2) provide a standard against which organizations can assess their internal control systems and determine how to improve them.

COSO defines internal control as a process, affected by an entity's board of directors, management, and other personnel, that is designed to provide reasonable assurance regarding the achievement of objectives in the following categories:

- Effectiveness and efficiency of operations
- Reliability of financial reporting
- Compliance with applicable laws and regulations

The Five Key Elements of the COSO Framework

The COSO framework for internal control systems consists of five interrelated components: (1) the control environment, (2) risk assessment, (3) control activities, (4) information and communication, and (5) monitoring. To assist smaller organizations in meeting their internal control requirements, COSO has published additional guidance (see Box 10.2).

Control Environment. The organization's control environment is the foundation for its internal control program. It is the integrity and ethical values maintained and demonstrated by the organization's management and staff. It is the organization's board of directors and senior management

> **BOX 10.2   Small Organizations and Internal Controls**
>
> Small and medium sized organizations often face legal, regulatory, and ethical challenges similar to those facing their larger organizational brethren, but frequently without the resources to meet their compliance needs. In recognition of this situation, in June 2006 COSO issued a three-volume guide for smaller public companies, *Internal Control over Financial Reporting—Guidance for Smaller Public Companies*, that addressed the internal control challenges that these organizations encounter.

setting the "tone at the top" through their endorsement of ethical standards and values, codes of conduct that are applicable to all persons in the organization. Susan Schmidt Bies, a governor of the Federal Reserve Board, spoke of the critical role of the organization's board of directors in the internal control system.

> *Although directors are not expected to understand every nuance of every line of business or to oversee every transaction, they do have responsibility for setting the tone regarding their corporations' risk-taking and establishing an effective monitoring program. They also have responsibility for overseeing the internal control processes, so that they can reasonably expect that their directives will be followed.*

Perhaps the role of the organization's control environment was stated best in the University of California's *Understanding Internal Controls*. It talks of the need for everyone in the organization, from the board of directors and senior management down through the organization, to understand their roles and responsibilities in an effective internal control program. The university said, "The control environment is the control consciousness of an organization. . . . An effective control environment is an environment where competent people understand their responsibilities, the limits to their authority, and are knowledgeable, mindful, and committed to doing what is right and doing it the right way. They are committed to following an organization's policies and procedures and its ethical and behavioral standards."

Risk Assessment. Fundamental to understanding internal control is the identification of the organization's objectives and the risks associated with those objectives. As part of this process, an organization should address several key questions:

- Have the organization's board of directors and senior management undertaken a process to determine its goals and objectives?
- How do these goals and objectives relate to the organization's mission statement and strategic initiatives?
- Has the organization undertaken a comprehensive and ongoing risk assessment process?
- Has the organization assessed the impact and costs of potential risks, both quantitatively and qualitatively?
- Has the organization determined how it will manage the potential risks it has identified?

Control Activities. Control activities are policies, procedures, techniques, and mechanisms for managing or reducing risk. These activities occur at all levels and functions of the organization. They include approvals, authorizations, verifications, segregation of duties, reconciliations, performance reviews, maintenance of security, and the creation and maintenance of related records that provide evidence of the execution of these activities. Control activities may be applied in a computerized information system environment or through manual processes.

The breadth of control activities is as expansive as an organization's mission, goals, and risk situation. They span the spectrum of organizational management from top-level supervisory reviews of performance management to stockroom inventories. Controls are generally classified as either preventive or detective (or sometimes a combination of both). Ultimately, each control must be shaped to meet the specific needs and risk situation of a particular organization.

- *Preventive controls.* Preventive controls are designed to prevent an error or exception *from* occurring. They are proactive measures that organizations can take to mitigate risks and errors. Here are some examples:

- *System edit checks.* These are computerized edit checks that are built into information systems to ensure that data input is valid and within the authority of the person entering the information.
- *Separation of duties.* Duties and responsibilities are divided among different people to reduce the risk of error or fraud. For instance, in a payroll operation, one person authorizes a transaction and another person inputs the information. No one person controls all the aspects of a transaction.
- *Password procedures to restrict access.* Passwords giving access to information systems must be considered confidential information that cannot be shared. They should be changed periodically.
- *Authorization processes.* Authorization involves the delegation of authority. It may be applicable to departments or individuals. For instance, an individual may not be able to conduct a transaction, such as purchasing supplies, without the specific permission, signature, or approval of an individual with approval authority.
- *Detective controls.* Detective controls are designed to detect an error or exception *after* it has occurred. As the University of California says of detective controls, "[They] play a critical role providing evidence that the preventive controls are functioning and preventing losses."
  - *Physical inventories.* An organization should establish an inventory control process for key assets. Periodic counts of all assets should be made by a person independent of the purchase and authorization process, and compared against the number of items on record.
  - *Maker/checker.* Analogous to the segregation of duties control, the maker/checker control requires someone to review or check all transactions to ensure that they are free of

error and within prescribed limits before the transactions are processed.

Information and Communication. For an organization to control its operations effectively, it must have relevant, reliable, and timely information. Managers need operational, financial, and compliance-related data to determine whether they are addressing their organization's objectives and compliance risks effectively. Effective communication occurs when information flows smoothly throughout the organization. A change in a process, product, policy, or system in one unit, for example, must be communicated throughout the organization so that appropriate changes in internal controls in other critical areas can be made. In additional to internal communication, organizational managers must be able to obtain information from external stakeholders, such as regulators or nongovernmental organizations (NGOs), that may have a significant impact on the organization's achieving its goals.

In its *Guide to Understanding Internal Controls*, the University of California poses several important questions that organizations should consider when evaluating the effectiveness of their information and communication processes.

- Does the organization get the information it needs from internal and external sources in a form and time frame that is useful?
- Does the organization get information that alerts it to internal or external risks (e.g., legislative or regulatory changes and developments)?
- Does the organization get information that measures its performance—information that tells it whether it is achieving its operations, financial reporting, and compliance objectives?
- Does the organization identify, capture, process, and communicate the information that others need (e.g., information used by its customers or other departments) in a form and time frame that is useful?

- Does the organization provide information to others that alerts them to internal or external risks?

Monitoring. An effective internal control program provides for the ongoing testing and monitoring of controls. The testing and monitoring of controls is a critical determinant of whether the organization's internal controls, especially those designed to mitigate its highest-rated compliance risks, are properly designed or being properly administered. Testing and monitoring of controls can be done by various means: self-assessment, internal audits, compliance or control unit reviews, or peer review. The scope and frequency of separate evaluations will depend primarily on the assessment of risks and the effectiveness of ongoing monitoring procedures.

The Internal Control Program

An effective internal control program is a critical management tool that helps organizations identify their compliance risks, weaknesses, and vulnerabilities. The COSO framework provides a valuable road map by which organizations can develop such a program. Successful implementation of an internal control framework includes four key components: governance, risk assessment, identification and assessment, and testing and monitoring of controls.

Compliance and Internal Audit

The organization's compliance and internal audit functions have a symbiotic relationship. The compliance function, with its focus on the organization's adherence to legal, regulatory, and internal standards, and the internal auditing function share the mutual goal of protecting the organization. Raymond O'Connor, writing in the February 1989 issue of the *Internal Auditor* described this relationship.

> *Each is a staff function responsible for protecting the officers of the corporation from liability resulting from inappropriate*

corporate activities. Both positions provide an oversight function in the area of compliance. Both are responsible for planning and executing audits of compliance with applicable rules and regulations of government agencies and of self-regulating professional associations.

The key difference between the two functions lies, in O'Connor's view, in their authority and responsibility. Compliance officers, either individually or working with the organization's internal control specialists, have the authority and responsibility to ensure that appropriate internal controls are in place and are working effectively to mitigate compliance risk to the organization. They are "part of the control structure." Internal auditors have the responsibility to identify areas where there are "potential risks due to weaknesses in internal controls, corporate procedures, and compliance with those procedures." As an independent body, their role is to evaluate and report on the organization's control structure.

Compliance and Line Management

Internal controls are ultimately the responsibility of the organization's management. As the International Organization of Supreme Audit Institutions (INTOSAI) declared in its 2001 *Internal Control: Providing a Foundation for Accountability in Government,* "Managers should realize that a strong internal control structure is fundamental to control of an organization and its purpose, operations and resources. Responsibility for providing an adequate and effective internal control structure rests with an organization's management." Senior management of the organizational unit should

- Identify the organization's unique compliance risks.
- Ensure that the appropriate policies and procedures to manage these risks are in place.
- Conduct periodic self-assessments to ensure that the controls are working properly.

It is the compliance (or internal control) unit's responsibility to ensure that management officials

- Are aware of their compliance risks.
- Are managing their compliance risks appropriately.
- Have an effective internal control process (through testing and review of organizational processes and policies).

Identification and Assessment

The identification and assessment of an organization's internal controls are based on a detailed and comprehensive assessment of the organization's compliance risks, such as

- Inventorying the organization's compliance risks
- Assessing the level of these risks (high, medium, or low)
- Linking each compliance risk to a control activity
- Describing how controls are monitored and tested to ensure their effectiveness

The goal of internal controls is to effectively manage the compliance risks that have been identified. Given limitations of time and resources, many organizations focus their attention on the highest compliance risks first, and then address medium and low-rated risks in successive order with less frequency, or as the need demands. Using detective and preventive control activities, the organization should assess each identified risk against its current control policies and procedures.

The employment example used in Chapter 9 illustrates this process. An organization has identified the employment of persons not authorized to work in the United States as a high risk. This determination was based on an inventory of the organization's compliance risks: a review of its employment policies and practices, government opinions, the attitude of senior management toward hiring, the number and types of persons employed, the status of the organization's management training program, and government audit practices.

Using this analysis, the organization reexamines its employment policies and procedures to determine how it can effectively control this compliance risk and documents its findings. For instance, it might institute controls on the keeping of government-mandated records, or it might create a log that tracks the completion and receipt of all required information. Ultimately, these and other controls will form the basis for its controls testing process.

A similar control analysis should be completed for all the organization's compliance risks. The goal is to develop an inventory of all the organization's control activities. When this inventory has been completed, the organization will be able to assess, through testing, the strengths and/or weaknesses in its internal control program:

- Gaps in its current controls activities
- Out-of-date control policies and procedures that are inconsistent with current law and regulation
- Overlapping control activities between organizational units

Once these gaps or weaknesses in the organization's internal controls are identified and assessed, the organization can undertake a corrective action strategy to fix the control weaknesses and to ensure that its compliance risks are appropriately addressed.

Testing and Monitoring

Testing the organization's existing control procedures to identify weaknesses or deficiencies is a critical component of an internal control program. It is an early warning mechanism that notifies the organization that there may be potential problems with its protective measures. Regulators place significant importance on organizations' testing of their internal controls. Speaking at a conference of bank compliance officers in 2006, Mark W. Olsen, a member of the Board of Governors of the U.S. Federal Reserve System, said:

> *An essential part of the internal control framework is periodic testing to determine how well the framework is operating, so that*

any required remedial action can be taken. The frequency of testing should be risk-based and should involve, as appropriate, sample transaction testing, the sample size being determined by volume and the degree of risk of the activity.

Key Questions for Testing an Organization's Internal Controls. Effective testing of an organization's internal control program requires a number of determinations. Many of these decisions will be influenced by the nature of the risk, organizational resources, the size of the organization, and the organization's regulators and their examination programs and philosophy:

- How will the testing be conducted (e.g., using manual or automated systems)?
- What are the criteria for "effectiveness" or "failure"?
- Will the controls be assessed against a framework such as COSO?
- Who will conduct the testing process (e.g., compliance, a third party, internal audit, line management, or the control unit)?
- What type of testing will be employed (e.g., transaction, periodic, or forensic)?
- How frequently will the controls be evaluated (daily, quarterly, monthly, or at some other interval)?
- How will the test results be assessed and reported (pass/fail or numerical ratings)?
- Who will establish a corrective action plan if weaknesses or deficiencies need to be addressed?
- Who will ensure that the corrective action plan is implemented?

A Brief Overview of the Testing Process. While internal control testing programs vary depending on the scope and nature of the transactions to be reviewed, there are some generic features that are applicable to most internal control review programs.

- *Identifying the compliance risks and key controls to be tested.*
- *Determining the criteria or standards against which the controls and transactions will be tested.* What is the organization's risk

tolerance, if any? Using the employment example given earlier, an organization may determine that the standard for that control is, "No person who is not authorized to work in the United States will be employed by the organization." If the control testing finds that people who do not meet this standard are being employed, then a serious vulnerability in the organization's compliance policies and processes has been identified and must be addressed immediately.

- *Determining the testing methodology to be utilized.* It might include sampling of data and transactions, interviews with employees, and observation of the processes (if applicable). The key is to obtain a sufficient amount of information on which to base a reasonable judgment concerning the effectiveness of the control process.

- *Determining who will conduct the testing.* There are a number of options that organizations may employ: self-assessment, internal audits, compliance or control unit reviews, or peer reviews. The organization's compliance program may do the testing of a department's controls, or it may delegate this responsibility to the business unit's control function or another risk management function. In some larger organizations, such as banks and broker-dealers, it is not uncommon to have a control officer specifically assigned to a business unit (the control officer may report to financial control or risk management). Control officers are business generalists who look at a broad range of risk issues, including legal and regulatory compliance risks. The control generalists will either coordinate or perform a self-assessment and testing of the business controls.

- If the organization's compliance program decides to delegate the testing of controls to the business control officer or to some other risk management function, the compliance unit is still responsible for ensuring that the controls and the test focus on key compliance risk issues. Alternatively, the compliance program may do the testing itself or use a combination of both approaches to reduce the duplication of activities and the burden to the business. Finally, compliance may also utilize, to some degree, business self-testing as long as the organization thoroughly considers the less independent nature of such reviews.

- Regardless of which option it chooses, an organization must be cognizant of the ultimate sin in control testing. It should never allow control tests to be conducted by the person who regularly performs the activity under review.
- *Documenting the internal control testing.* A record should be created that details the testing procedures, the persons involved, the key controls analyzed, and the results of the testing review.
- *Analyzing the results of the review.* Were any weaknesses or deficiencies in the organization's internal controls identified? If so, were they significant or minor? What were the causes of the control weaknesses: a single event or a continuing process? Was there a breakdown in policy, procedures, systems, or technology? Was the cause a human error? Was the weakness the result of lack of information, training, skills, or experience? Could it have caused significant harm to the organization if not identified and promptly corrected? Do the results warrant escalation to senior management and possibly the regulators?
- *Developing a follow-up or corrective action plan.* It is critical that prompt action be taken to address the review's findings and recommendations. This should include establishing specific time frames for the correction of the issues and appropriate tracking, review, and approval of corrective actions.

Summary

An effective compliance program incorporates a well-developed internal control program. Carolyn Sigg and Paul Fiorelli, writing in the February

2002 issue of *Internal Auditor,* perhaps best summarized the value of internal controls and compliance:

> [I]nternal control is a process. It is a means to an end, not an end in itself. A strong internal control system can be a powerful statement to employees and outside contractors about a company's commitment to responsible corporate conduct. Controls help prevent and discover unethical or lawful behavior.

11

Evaluating Compliance

A modern compliance program is a complex activity that affects many critical aspects of an organization's operations. A compliance evaluation helps an organization identify any outstanding gaps in the compliance program's mission, service, performance, or operations. As the compliance program is the organization's safeguard, any weaknesses or imperfections in its design and execution must be promptly identified, assessed, and corrected. The organization must determine if these weaknesses are systemic or the result of happenstance, or if they are associated with a particular process, individuals, function, or region. Has an identified weakness been ongoing, or is it a one-time occurrence? Regulators expect organizations to take proactive measures to identify and ameliorate flaws in their compliance programs.

Evaluating an organization's compliance program, however, can be a daunting task. There are few hard criteria for evaluating the effectiveness of a compliance program. The criteria are often amorphous goals: How does an organization define an enhanced or effective "compliance initiative"? What criteria or metrics should an organization use to measure "integrity," "culture," or "ethics" in a meaningful or productive fashion?

This problem in measuring compliance program effectiveness was noted by several different sources:

- In a 1999 General Accountability Office (GAO) report: entitled "Early Evidence of Compliance Program Effectiveness Is Inconclusive," the federal oversight agency said that it was difficult to measure compliance program effectiveness because of the lack of comprehensive baseline data and the existence of many other factors that could affect measurement results.
- A 2005 study of global compliance programs, *Protecting the Brand*, by PricewaterhouseCoopers found that 78 percent of the 73 companies surveyed thought that compliance added value. However, the study reported that "none had yet developed a systematic measurement approach. . . . [R]espondents indicated . . . that measuring the value was difficult because it depended on inverse logic, i.e. non-compliance events not happening. As one European respondent noted, an insurance policy is only really appreciated when something goes wrong."
- This limitation was similarly noted by the Health Care Compliance Association (HCCA). In the preamble to its *Evaluating and Improving a Compliance Program*, the HCCA said:

Due to the complexity and volume of health care regulation and the relative infancy of compliance programs in health care organizations, management and governing bodies frequently have questions about compliance programs. Are they focused on the right issues? Is the program addressing our principal risks? How much should [we] spend? Are we deriving maximum value from our efforts? How do we evaluate the quality and effectiveness of our program?. . . In short, this document is provided by the HCCA as a tool to help an organization determine whether the resources it devotes to compliance are effectively, efficiently and appropriately utilized.

Criteria for Compliance Effectiveness

A number of government agencies have sought to establish criteria for compliance effectiveness. Some of these, such as the Federal Sentencing Guidelines for Organizations (FSGO) and the U.S. Department of Justice's *Principles of Federal Prosecution of Business Organizations*, have general applicability, while others are specially targeted to a specific area of regulation. The U.S. Department of Health and Human Services, for example, has attempted to quantify compliance effectiveness. It has embarked on a project to adopt a standard for effective compliance. Starting in 2004, it initiated a Compliance Effectiveness Pilot. The study's results are expected to be released in late 2007.

Despite these developments, evaluating the effectiveness of a compliance program is a challenge. There are no "bright lines" that clearly demarcate what is an effective compliance program. Rather, it is the aggregate actions of the organization that demonstrate its willingness to address compliance initiatives and its commitment to doing so. As representatives of the U.S. Department of Health and Human Services said in a 1999 report, "Building a Partnership for Effective Compliance," "The OIG [Office of the Inspector General] considers the attributes of each individual element of a provider's compliance program to assess its 'effectiveness' as a whole."

Federal Sentencing Guidelines for Organizations

The U.S. Sentencing Commission's Advisory Group, convened in 2003 to review and propose changes to the original 1991 FSGO, explicitly recommended that organizations evaluate the effectiveness of their compliance programs. The advisory group recommended that the following language be included in the proposed Section 8B2.1:

> *Due diligence and the promotion of an organizational culture that encourages a commitment to compliance with the law within the meaning of subsection (a) minimally require the following steps: . . . (b) to evaluate periodically the effectiveness*

of the organization's program to prevent and detect violations of law.

In its commentary, the advisory group explained that the organizations must review "the sufficiency of managerial practices comprising an organization's compliance program to ensure a reasonable likelihood of success in preventing and detecting violations of law." It did not delineate the specific form or fashion of this self-evaluation. Instead, it said, "Differently focused monitoring and auditing practices may be used to assess the effectiveness of an organization's compliance program, although other periodic evaluation methods may be used as well." It did note, however, that in larger organizations, separate evaluations of compliance performance would usually be required and should be conducted by persons independent of the compliance function. In smaller organizations, periodic evaluations of compliance in the course of day-to-day business operating practices would be adequate.

Office of the Inspector General of the U.S. Department of Health and Human Services. In a March 1999 meeting between the Office of the Inspector General and the Health Care Compliance Association, government representatives identified a number of factors used in evaluating the effectiveness of an organization's compliance efforts:

- The funding and legitimate support provided to the compliance function by management, as well as the background of the individual designated as the compliance officer
- Whether "buy-in" to the organization's compliance program by the organization's employees and contractors is influenced by the adequacy of training and the availability of guidance on policies and procedures
- Evidence of open lines of communication and the appropriate use of information lines to address employee concerns and questions
- A documented practice of refunding of overpayments and self-disclosing incidents of noncompliance with program requirement

The Need for Evaluation

In the words of the U.S. Department of Justice's *Principles of Federal Prosecution of Business Organizations*, the fundamental question that an organization has to ask itself is, "Does the corporation's compliance program work?" or to put it another way, "Does the compliance program add value?" To answer these questions, organizations are using various methods (from self-assessments to outside consultants) and criteria to evaluate the key areas of compliance to gather both qualitative and quantitative information to assess "effectiveness." These analyses look at this effort from two perspectives:

- Techniques that organizations have used to measure compliance program effectiveness
- Criteria that have been adopted as measures or key performance indicators of compliance program effectiveness

Techniques for Evaluating Compliance

Given the broad and nascent nature of compliance, it is not surprising that organizations have sought various techniques and strategies to quantify and assess their compliance program's effectiveness. These evaluation methods are still evolving and rely heavily on a combination of qualitative and quantitative measures. Christine Parker, an authority on compliance programs, commented in a 2002 paper, *Is There a Reliable Way to Evaluate Organisational Compliance Programs?* "The methodologies for evaluating corporate compliance management are critically under-developed at present."

Techniques for evaluating the effectiveness of compliance programs have ranged from employee surveys to assessing compliance-related reports received through e-mail and hotlines (Box 11.1 provides some basic rules for conducting a compliance evaluation). Brian Sharpe, in an article in the May/June 2003 issue of *Ethikos*, described a two-stage process used in Australia to measure compliance program effectiveness

> **BOX 11.1   Conducting a Compliance Evaluation**
>
> While a variety of techniques have been used to assess compliance effectiveness, organizations, at a minimum, should follow several basic rules in conducting a compliance evaluation:
>
> - The same principles that are used in conducting a compliance risk assessment and audit (as defined in Chapter 9) apply to conducting a compliance evaluation: planning, documentation, interviewing, data analysis, and preparing findings and recommendations.
> - Organizations should consider conducting a compliance evaluation at least every two years (or less if regulations require).
> - The independence and expertise of the reviewers is critical to the integrity of the evaluation and its findings and recommendations.

that involves the use of "rigorous key performance indicators" to evaluate the performance and a scorecard to measure effectiveness. Writing in *Nursing Homes* (August 2004), Lawrence Fogel and Joseph Watt described a three-phase process that they call "compliance program assessment (CPA)" in which an independent consultant, in conjunction with the organization's staff, evaluates the effectiveness of an organization's compliance program.

Assessing Compliance Effectiveness

Regardless of the methodology used, evaluations of compliance program effectiveness seek essentially the same basic range of information. This information can be categorized as generic measures and organization- and program-specific information. In conducting the compliance evaluation, a note of caution is warranted (see Box 11.2).

Generic Measures

In this category, organizations are evaluating the strategic outcomes and effectiveness of their compliance programs.

> **BOX 11.2 A Note of Caution**
>
> During the course of a compliance evaluation, it is possible that the organization may uncover potentially harmful information. If there is any doubt, immediately contact counsel (either internal or external) to review the information and to determine the most appropriate course of action.

- Are concerns about compliance and breaches of law, regulations, and ethics being addressed effectively?
- Is the organization "safer" as a result of the compliance program?
- Is the organization complying with the Federal Sentencing Guidelines for Organizations and other regulatory guidance?
- Are employees less likely to engage in illegal or unethical behavior?
- Has the organization's compliance program effectively responded to compliance failures or issues that have arisen? If not, why not, and how can this be corrected?
- Are employees more likely to report illegal or unethical behavior?
- Is the organization's compliance program considered a "player" in the organization's power structure and control functions?
- Does the organization's compliance program have the authority to delay or stop the introduction of any new product, system, or organizational change that may have significant ramifications for the organization until any issues it presents are resolved?
- Has the compliance program added value? Is it worth the cost? Are there any alternatives?

Establishing Benchmarks

In an effort to define key criteria for evaluating organizational compliance effectiveness, organizations have sought to establish benchmarks, sometimes referred to as key performance indicators (KPIs), for compliant behavior, such as the number of complaints an organization receives, employee retention rates, or number of regulatory inquiries. While they are attractive as a simple measure of compliance effectiveness, KPIs present several issues. One of the difficulties is the task of trying to measure negative impact (e.g., the lack of fines or penalties). The 2006 Economist Intelligence Unit report on compliance benchmarking asked participants the following question, "How do you establish benchmarks for measuring your compliance effectiveness?" The diverse answers again reflected the imprecise nature of establishing compliance evaluation criteria: 56 percent reported "information meetings with regulators"; 40 percent cited "benchmarking against industry surveys"; 38 percent said "achievement of compliance objectives against budget"; 37 percent said "benchmarking against specific financial institutions"; and 35 percent said "informal meetings with industry peers."

Organization- and Program-Specific Measures

In this category of information, the organization seeks to identify and assess the institution's ethical and cultural behavior, its senior management, its board of directors, and the overall compliance program to ensure that they are managing compliance risks effectively and promoting ethical behavior.

Governance and Senior Leadership. As discussed in previous chapters, it is the organization's board of directors and senior management that are the focal point for compliance and ethics in the organization. They establish the values, ethics, priorities, and resources that govern the organization's compliance program.

To evaluate the role of the board of directors and senior management in the compliance process, the regulators' views are an important starting point. As noted earlier, the U.S. Department of Justice's "Principles of Federal Prosecution of Business Organizations," delineate the various criteria that federal prosecutors may use in evaluating whether compliance programs are effective in detecting and preventing misconduct.

The principles ask the following questions of the organization's board of directors and senior management:

- Do the corporation's directors undertake an independent review of proposed corporate actions rather than unquestioningly ratifying officers' recommendations?
- Are the directors provided with information sufficient to enable the exercise of independent judgment, and are internal audit functions conducted at a level sufficient to ensure their independence and accuracy?
- Have the directors established information and reporting systems in the organization that are reasonably designed to provide management and the board of directors with timely and accurate information sufficient to allow them to reach an informed decision regarding the organization's compliance with the law?
- Has the corporation provided sufficient staff to audit, document, analyze, and utilize the results of the corporation's compliance efforts?
- Are the corporation's employees adequately informed about the compliance program and convinced of the corporation's commitment to it?

In a 2004 speech, Mary Ann Gadziala, associate director of the Office of Compliance Inspections and Examinations of the U.S. Securities and Exchange Commission (SEC), discussed the SEC's comprehensive compliance examination for broker-dealers and what it looks for in an effective compliance program. As Gadziala explained, the SEC's compliance examinations are different from traditional audits.

> *What are we reviewing and what are we finding in those exams? SEC compliance examinations are enterprise-wide, covering all broker-dealers within an enterprise. They are top-down reviews of compliance over all business operations. As such, they are different from typical examinations that are bottom-up reviews*

more focused on specific rules and the firm's compliance with its own procedures. In the comprehensive compliance exam, we evaluate the compliance "culture" at the enterprise—that is the overall environment in which compliance issues are handled at the firm.

The Compliance Organization

The evaluation of the organization's compliance function should address a number of critical issues:

- What are the resources (budget, staff, systems and technology, and training funds) provided for the compliance program? Are they adequate for the compliance program? If not, where are they deficient?
- Does the chief compliance officer have a visible role in the organization?
- Does the chief compliance officer report to the organization's senior management and board of directors?
- Are the compliance structure and compliance reporting relationships appropriate for the organization's needs and requirements? Possible issues are: Should compliance staff be full-time? Should compliance staff be located in new or different businesses or at different levels in the organization? For instance, the Office of the Inspector General of the Department of Health and Human Services asks of compliance personnel who work part-time, "[D]o [they] compromise the goals of the programs by virtue of their other duties in the organization"?

Further insight into the evaluation of a compliance structure can be seen in Mary Ann Gadziala's comments on effective compliance structures. She explained, "Examiners will look for clear lines of authority, accountability, and specificity of assigned responsibilities. Documentation and complete and accurate records are critical." Specific questions on compliance structures include

- What are the compliance programs at the firm? Do they cover all businesses?
- Is compliance independent from business, both in reporting and compensation? Do compliance programs have access to top management and the board?
- Does compliance have adequate resources, systems, and reports?
- Do compliance personnel have appropriate expertise and experience? How are they trained? Are they adequately compensated?
- Does compliance have the ability to respond to and coordinate with all relevant regulators?

Karen Stensgaard, writing in the April 2002 issue of *Internal Auditor*, gave advice to auditors in evaluating a compliance program's effectiveness. In examining the compliance structure, she suggested: "When assessing the effectiveness of the structure in place, auditors should consider whether it meets the organization's particular compliance needs. . . . The structure should be appropriate to the organization's size, compliance requirements, and history of regulatory issues."

Compliance Committee

Compliance committees have become an important component of many organizations' compliance programs. Evaluation of compliance committees should address the following issues:

- Is the committee fully staffed as defined in the organization's compliance mission statement? Does it include the appropriate members of the organization? If not, what changes need to be made?
- Does the committee meet on a regular basis?
- Is there an agenda for its meetings? What level of issues and concerns does the committee review?
- What are the power and authority of the committee?

- Does the committee set goals for itself, and has it achieved them for the most recent time period? If not, what were the impediments and how can they be overcome?

Compliance Operations

A key issue is the effectiveness of the compliance-related programs and services being provided by the organization's compliance function. Policy development, communications, training, auditing, self-assessments, investigations, whistle-blowing programs, and monitoring are vital components of a modern organizational compliance program. Deficiencies and weaknesses in these operations must be identified and addressed promptly to avoid significant problems.

Policies and Procedures. Well-developed and well-executed organizational compliance policies and procedures are a core function of a compliance program.

- Has the company established a code of conduct?
- Have written policies and procedures been established that address all critical compliance risk areas?
- Are organizational policies and procedures updated on a regular basis to ensure that they address critical organizational risks effectively? How does this process work? Who manages it?
- Are the organization's policies easily accessible, readable, and translated into different languages, if necessary?
- Has the organization matched its paper documentation with its intranet or Internet postings to ensure the consistency of the material?

As the Office of the Inspector General of the Department of Health and Human Services asks in its *Program Guidelines for Nursing Facilities* (2000), "Do employees: experience recurring pitfalls because issues are not adequately covered? Do they have trouble understanding the policies?"

Education and Training. Education and training programs that address key compliance risks effectively are critical to an organizational compliance program. Evaluation of these programs should address the following questions:

- Does the organization regularly assess its training needs and requirements (compliance issues and regulatory requirements) for all its units and for functions at all levels within the organization, including senior management and the board of directors?
- Does the organization have a structured training program with a person(s) who is accountable for training needs and delivery?
- Does the organization regularly evaluate the effectiveness of its compliance-related training?
- Have employees in high-risk functions received compliance training?
- Does the organization provide orientation and in-service training for all employees?
- Has the organization identified any significant gaps in training for employees and volunteers (scheduling, scope of courses, training methodology)?
- Does the organization track and document all training (orientation, in-service training, hours of training)?
- Have employees who have failed to attend mandatory training been disciplined?
- Are training instructors sufficiently qualified and experienced to deliver effective training?

Communications. An effective communications program uses the spectrum of modern communications techniques and technologies to inform employees and others of compliance and ethical concerns. It is a key component of a modern compliance program. Evaluation of the communications program should include the following:

- How effectively are the organization's policies, standards, guidelines, and practices being communicated?

- Are regulatory developments and relevant case law routinely communicated to compliance and other organizational control functions?
- Does the compliance program regularly communicate and coordinate with business managers on new products, systems, and organizational changes that may have significant ramifications for the organization?

Monitoring and Auditing. It is crucial that the organization's compliance program proactively and effectively identify and monitor its key compliance risks. Evaluation of the compliance program's monitoring and auditing program should address these questions:

- Does the organization routinely conduct compliance audits of its key compliance risk areas?
- Has the organization developed a schedule for audit reviews that is based on specific compliance risk and vulnerability criteria?
- Have the results of previous compliance audits and/or deficiencies been reviewed and corrected?
- Are compliance reviews focused on all pertinent units and departments? Are senior management and the board of directors notified of reviews in a timely fashion?
- Is the staff conducting the compliance audits objective and independent from the areas of the organization they are reviewing?
- How does the organization respond to issues raised during its monitoring and audit operations? Are written corrective action plans required? Who follows up on the plans?

Ethics. It is critical to assess whether the organization's resources are being used effectively and efficiently to address issues of integrity, ethics, and conduct. Evaluation of the organization's ethical and cultural frameworks should address the following:

- Has the organization conducted an employee climate survey to identify ongoing cultural or integrity issues?

- Have the number and types of incidents of noncompliance by the organization's employees have been reduced?
- What has been the organizational response to incidents of noncompliance?
- How effective is the organization in identifying risk situations that have led or could lead to potential areas of organizational misconduct?

Investigation and Whistle-Blowing Programs. Investigations and whistle-blowing programs are symbolic of the organization's employees' concerns and commitment to legal and ethical behavior. Evaluations of these programs should address these questions:

- Has the organization established a hotline mechanism or some other effective mechanism for reporting violations?
- Are hotline calls regularly reviewed for trends and patterns (e.g., types of incidents reported, locations, frequency, and resolution of issues)?
- How is information handled? Who follows up on hotline calls?
- How promptly are issues addressed, and who tracks the response?
- Do employees fear retaliation?
- Has the organization taken appropriate action against employees, volunteers, contractors, or others who have violated the organization's policies, practices, and standards of conduct?
- Does the organization track and document all disciplinary measures: type of offense, disciplinary actions taken, frequency, business, and location?
  - Have appropriate sanctions been applied to compliance misconduct?
  - Are sanctions applied consistently, regardless of the employee's level in the corporate hierarchy?
  - Have double standards bred cynicism among employees?

Role of Business Managers. One area that is frequently overlooked in assessing the effectiveness of a compliance program is the role of the business managers. While boards of directors, senior managers, and compliance personnel and related functions are the primary focus of evaluation, the first-level and middle-level managerial structure is often overlooked. Business managers must not only be knowledgeable about the key laws and regulations affecting their operations and products, but, equally important, know when to seek advice and guidance from the organization's compliance program.

Costs. Attempts at quantifying and measuring the effectiveness of compliance programs are still in their infancy. The same goes for evaluating the cost-effectiveness of compliance. In the 2004 *Annual General Counsel Roundtable* survey of 75 general counsels of major organizations, it was reported that 56 percent of the companies did not measure the cost of compliance programs. None had measured their return or value.

A February 2006 report by the Securities Industry and Financial Markets Association (SIFMA), *The Costs of Compliance*, reflected the difficulties in measuring the cost of compliance. In its survey, the SIFMA did not limit cost measurements to the activities of an organization's compliance department, but looked at a broad range of organizational functions that had some compliance-related function, such as risk management, internal audit, and the legal department. As the survey remarked, "The essence of compliance is embedded in the concept of 'supervision,' where business management, not the compliance department, has ultimate responsibility to ensure that every element of the firm adheres to all regulatory and legislative mandates."

Perhaps PricewaterhouseCoopers summarized it best. Noting the difficulties in measuring costs, its 2004 report, *The Future for Compliance—An Efficient and Effective Commercial Operation*, explained: "Cost of compliance is a difficult area to examine, primarily because it is defined in a number of ways and used in diverse contexts by different organizations."

Postevaluation Actions

In many respects, this is the most crucial component of evaluating compliance effectiveness. After the information has been gathered, analyzed, and compiled into a report, the organization must decide on the most appropriate course of action to address any weaknesses or deficiencies that may have been identified. At a minimum, senior management and the board of directors (or the appropriate committee) should be informed of the findings and consulted with concerning the findings and the proposed course of action.

Organizations have several options to consider in addressing issues raised during a compliance assessment.

Revise Policies and Procedures

Appropriate changes must be made in policies and procedures to correct systemic errors. This may include the introduction of new monitoring systems or technology and outsourcing (or even insourcing) of certain compliance-related functions that may not have been appropriately managed.

Training

Additional training can be provided in specific areas where gaps in knowledge or skills have been identified.

Communications

The method of dissemination of critical compliance-related information can be revised or expanded. This may include the use of new compliance technologies and strategies, or assurance that employees and others can communicate with the organization's board, senior management, and the organization's whistle-blowing program about incidents of compliance risk or wrongdoing.

Compliance Structure and Staff

The evaluation results may demonstrate a need for the organization to restructure its compliance program or redeploy compliance personnel to serve the organization more effectively. The compliance staff may need to have new skills and knowledge, or more effective coordination between compliance and other key organizational control units may be needed.

Disciplinary Action

Based on the severity and pattern of the actions, it may be necessary to take disciplinary action against certain individuals for violations of policies and procedures, or for lapses in ethical judgment. In any decisions that may involve termination of employment or reduction in salary and/or benefits, consult with the human resources department.

Revise the Review Focus

The results of the compliance review may indicate the need to change the objectives, scope, and methodology of the next compliance evaluation.

Summary

The need and rationale for organizations to monitor and evaluate the effectiveness of their compliance function and program are self-evident and well documented. The challenge for organizations, and for their compliance programs, lies in the intrinsic nature of compliance. In an organizational world that demands answers in concrete, definable terms, compliance is a concept that does not easily lend itself to measurement and quantification. This is going to be the challenge for the compliance community as it enters the next decade.

PART IV

THE FUTURE OF
COMPLIANCE

12

Compliance, Going Forward

There is a saying, "It's tough to make predictions, especially about the future." The past two decades have witnessed such an extraordinary growth in organizational compliance awareness and programs that no one knows with certainty what the future holds for compliance. Today, an industry and a profession that barely existed 20 years ago plays an important role in a growing number of public, private, and nonprofit organizations ranging from financial services, defense, and health services to universities and colleges. The sweep of legislative, judicial, and administrative actions, as well as the spate of organizational wrongdoing over the past two decades, has spurred the growth of this industry and led to an organizational focus on ethics and integrity that has transcended any one particular segment of the U.S. and international economy. This growth, however, has not come without struggles and internecine conflicts. This chapter examines some of the possible future directions for compliance.

Brief Retrospective

As we have seen, the concept of compliance was born of a confluence of various elements: corruption, judicial and legislative actions, the extraordinary growth of technology and communications that has revolutionized organizational operations and transcended national boundaries, growing social activism, and a focus on ethics and organizational behavior. The advent of the Federal Sentencing Guidelines for Organizations (FSGO), the growth of self-regulation, the passage of Sarbanes-Oxley, and the proactive compliance steps taken by federal agencies have been some of the measures that have created a national focus on legal and regulatory compliance. Whistle-blowing and hotline programs have become the norm for organizations in all sectors of the economy.

A Profession with Growing Pains

This focus on compliance brings to prominence a nascent profession and industry that are struggling to clarify their role and identity: One senior compliance officer remarked that compliance is currently in the same organizational position that environmental health and safety or quality control programs were 20 years ago: a relatively new organizational function that is striving to achieve credibility and acceptance.

The struggles that compliance faces are varied:

- There is a never-ending professional conflict as to whether a values-based or a rules-based approach is better for achieving organizational compliance.
- For many small and medium-sized organizations, the reality is that compliance is a way of conducting business, not an organizational function. For most organizations in the United States, having a formal compliance program is simply not realistic. They do not have the resources (funds, time, staff, or expertise) to undertake such a venture. They manage the best they can, relying on the external resources that are available and hoping that nothing unfortunate happens.

- There is a struggle to define the boundaries of the profession. What is "compliance"? As noted throughout the book, there is still a degree of confusion about the role of a compliance program in an organization. The program's boundaries are often not clearly defined in many industries. Turf battles between compliance, audit, internal control, legal, and risk management are not uncommon.
- There is a struggle concerning where compliance should report within the organization. Should it report to the organization's chief legal officer or directly to the chief executive officer? Is compliance a subset of the organization's risk management function?
- Will the concept of "governance, risk, and compliance" gain momentum as a major strategic direction for organizational compliance programs?
- A popular motif is the never-ending quest to "go beyond compliance." Compliance is often viewed as a "check the boxes" function that needs to transcend the prosaic tasks of complying with particular laws and regulations and focus on changing the essence of the organization's values, culture, and ethics. And yet, the need to check the boxes and comply with the specific rules and regulations has not evaporated. How can these divergent views and aspirations be reconciled?
- In a world that demands organizational accountability, how does compliance prove its value? How do organizations and their compliance programs measure and justify the costs of compliance?

At the Crossroads

In many organizations, compliance programs came about because of the demands from regulators for change and from legislative reforms, such as Sarbanes-Oxley, that placed significant governance requirements on organizations. As with any nascent profession, there are questions about the future of compliance. In the years since the passage of Sarbanes-Oxley and FSGO, has the impetus for reform and change started to slowly deteriorate? A compliance officer for a major corporation lamented, "The post-Enron compliance spirit is sputtering out." Will compliance reach its zenith in the near future? If so, what are the implications for compliance programs?

Even the Federal Sentencing Guidelines for Organizations, the bedrock of modern compliance programs, are subject to questions about their future. Apart from the issues raised by the *Booker* and *Fanfan* court decisions, Peter Henning, in the *Yale Law Journal Pocket Part* (2007), questions whether the FSGO are effective any longer in changing organizational culture. As Henning says, "The moment has arrived to put them to rest as a worthy effort whose time simply has passed."

In interviews with compliance officers and people associated with the compliance profession, there is a general belief that the compliance function is, in the words of one observer, "here to stay." They point to the reality that corporate social responsibility initiatives, with their focus on ethics and transparency, have become an established fact of organizational life. For instance, major U.S. companies routinely publish an annual report on their corporate citizenship activities—a development unknown a decade ago! The question that many people focus on, and that Figure 4 illustrates, however, is the ultimate evolution of compliance programs.

Growth of "Principles-Based" Regulation

One of the key developments that might influence the future development of the compliance function is the emergence of "principles-based" regulation in the United States. As noted in Chapter 2, the controversy over rules-based vs. principles-based legislation has sparked much debate as to whether compliance programs need to manage the seemingly infinite number of rules and regulations, as opposed to taking the more "relaxed" approach adopted under a principles-based regime. Comments made by leading government officials in 2007 signaled a potential change in government regulation. For instance, Henry Paulson, Jr., secretary of

FIGURE 4. Crossroads

the treasury, speaking at a conference on capital markets competitiveness, cited the need to revisit the U.S. regulatory structure. He said, "We should also consider whether it would be practically possible and beneficial to move toward a more principles-based regulatory system, as we see working in other parts of the world."

The rules-based approach is often seen as a metaphor for traditional compliance programs, with their focus on monitoring, policy, audit, and training programs. The evolution to a principles-based approach is viewed as more appropriate for a "values-based" climate, with its emphasis being placed on ethics, integrity, culture, and communications, not on specific adherence to particular rules and regulations. The latter responsibilities are the domain of specific organizational functions such as finance, human resources, and audit. John Lenzi, a senior compliance officer for Altria Group, Inc., says, "Employees across demographic groups are looking for shared values in an organization. They are looking for a company that provides an environment built on values that they can trust. A company that is ethical and undertakes a 'holistic approach' to managing organization culture will inevitably attract and retain the best talent."

Regulations Are Not Changing

While some compliance officials see a change in the regulatory landscape, others do not share the same vision. Roy Snell of the Society of Corporate Compliance and Ethics pointed out that the U.S. Department of Justice is not going to stop investigating, that Sarbanes-Oxley is only one of many laws that regulate organizational behavior, and that enforcement is not going to disappear in the future.

Evolving Role of the Compliance Officer

The vision of the future role of the organizational compliance officer is as diverse and amorphous as the topic or compliance itself. Will the compliance officer ultimately be transformed into a "chief corporate social responsibility" position that interrelates the issues of corporate social responsibility, governance, ethics, and compliance? Or will it evolve into a "corporate ethics and responsibility" position that focuses on issues of ethics, integrity, and creating a corporate culture that fosters compliant behavior? In the latter scenario, many of the functions currently managed by compliance programs (e.g., audit, training, and policy) would be the responsibility of other organizational control functions, such as financial control, security, or legal.

Professionalism and Certification

One possibility that might emerge is the need for a cadre of professional compliance officers, similar to what is found in other professions such as accounting and law. However, as noted in Chapter 5, while compliance officers in particular industries, such as banking and health care, have compliance certifications, the compliance industry is at odds concerning the definition of the scope and boundaries of a professional compliance officer's role.

Internationalization of Compliance

In our global world, regulatory issues transcend national or regional boundaries. Anti-money-laundering, antitrust, environmental health and safety, operational risk, data privacy, and information dissemination are issues that are as problematic in Beijing, New Delhi, Buenos Aires, or Brussels as they are in New York or San Francisco. With burgeoning corporate scandals (and compliance regulation) in Europe and the growth of corporate governance requirements in Asia, especially in China and India, and in the emerging markets, the opportunities for compliance programs are accelerating. For instance, the new Markets in Financial Instruments Directive (MiFID), effective November 2007, will have a significant compliance impact on many EU financial services organizations.

Arthur Mitchell, general counsel for the Asian Development Bank, speaking at a meeting of Asian lawyers in 2006, expressed the value of regulatory compliance programs for Asian companies:

> *Compliance may even be its own reward. Companies that are able to demonstrate consistently high standards of self-governance might expect less scrutiny from the regulators as a kind of "regulatory dividend." Compliance is necessary to ensure a global enterprise's very survival.*

It was reported in the January 26, 2006, *Financial Daily* that a survey conducted in Asia and Australia showed growing awareness of regulatory compliance. It reported that companies are expected to increase their spending on regulatory compliance significantly over the next several years. To quote one person, "Asia is waking up to the relevance of international compliance requirements such as Sarbanes-Oxley and Basel II to the region. . . . [A]ssurance must be given to international customers and partners that you can work at the same level as they do."

The Road Ahead

For organizational compliance programs and their staff, the future is dependent on three critical factors, some of which are within their control and others beyond their ability to manage.

- The continued emphasis by the organization's board of directors and senior management on visibly supporting and demonstrating the organization's commitment to ethics, transparency, and values. Equally important, there is a need for the organization's leadership to publicly recognize the importance of the compliance program by elevating its head to senior executive status (commensurate with the organization's other control functions) and providing continued financial support of the compliance program.
- The continued support and encouragement of organizational compliance programs by the universe of regulators, both government and private. Their influence in promoting organizational compliance and ethical programs is invaluable.
- The continued need by the compliance community to demonstrate its leadership, vision, and skills by working successfully with its key constituencies. Compliance is a growing and evolving profession that has great potential; however, internecine conflicts over strategies and tactics can only diminish the profession's outlook.

Resources

This section provides information on major organizations involved in compliance and ethics in the public, private and nonprofit sectors. Given the breadth of compliance-related issues, the section cannot identify compliance organizations for specific industries, but rather concentrates on those organizations that span businesses and organizations within different sectors.

General

Ethics Resource Center (ERC)

www.ethics.org

This is a Washington, D.C.–based organization that is devoted to independent research and the advancement of high ethical standards in public and private organizations. The ERC sponsors research on ethics, ethical behavior, and ethical issues. It sponsors the National Business Ethics Survey and hosts the ERC Fellows Program for senior organizational executives.

The Business Roundtable Institute for Corporate Ethics

www.corporate-ethics.org
The institute is an independent center, established in partnership with the Business Roundtable, that focuses on the issues of ethical behavior and business practice. It hosts seminars, provides executive education programs, and conducts research.

The Ethics & Compliance Officers Association (ECOA)

www.etheecoa.org
This is a professional organization focused exclusively on ethics and compliance officers. It conducts seminars, research, surveys, and studies on issues of interest to the ethics and compliance community.

Open Compliance and Ethics Group (OCEG)

www.oceg.org
The OECG is a nonprofit organization that helps companies align their governance, risk, and compliance activities. It publishes a wide variety of material on the topic and hosts periodic seminars on the subject.

The Society of Corporate Compliance and Ethics (SCCE)

www.corporatecompliance.org
The SCCE holds an annual institute that is a primary education and global networking event for corporate compliance and ethics professionals. It also offers a certification program for compliance professionals.

Nonprofit and Philanthropic Organizations

BBB Wise Giving Alliance

http://www.give.org

The alliance establishes standards covering governance and oversight, effectiveness, finances, and fund-raising and informational material that are used to evaluate national charities.

Independent Sector

http://www.independentsector.org
Independent Sector is a leadership forum for charities, foundations, and corporate giving programs that provides, in addition to its other responsibilities, guidance to nonprofit organizations on issues regarding governance, ethics, and compliance.

BoardSource

http://www.boardsource.org/
BoardSource works with the boards of directors of nonprofit organizations to strengthen an organization's governance and operational capabilities. It provides consulting services and educational and training programs.

Public Sector

Government Regulations

www.Business.gov
Business.gov is the official business link to the U.S. government. It is managed by the U.S. Small Business Administration in partnership with 21 other other federal agencies. It is an invaluable source of compliance information for businesses dealing with the federal government.

The Council for Excellence in Government

http://www.excelgov.org/
A nonprofit organization, the Council for Excellence in Government works to improve the performance of government at all levels through stronger public-sector leadership and management.

ICMA (International City/County Management Association)

www.icma.org

The ICMA is the professional and educational organization for chief appointed managers, administrators, and assistants in cities, towns, counties, and regional entities throughout the world. It provides technical and management assistance, training, and information resources to its members and to the local government community.

Auditing and Internal Controls

The Institute of Internal Auditors

http://www.theiia.org/

This is a professional organization that provides extensive guidance, standards, certification, and training pertaining to corporate governance and management, including conducting audits and risk assessments.

American Institute of Certified Public Accountants

http://www.aicpa.org/

The professional association of public accountants provides extensive information on a wide range of topics relating to organizational management and compliance, including standards for managing audits.

Index

ABA Bank Compliance, 154, 216, 238, 243
ABA Bankers News, 169
In re Abbott Laboratories Derivative Shareholder Action, 82
Access to hotline program, 185
Ad hoc compliance officer, 133
Administration:
    compliance costs, 143
    of hotline, 182–183
    training and education programs, 164
AFL-CIO, 24
Agencies, investigation reporting, 195–196
    (*See also* Federal agencies)
Allen, William T., 81
Alliance Capital Management, 17–18
Altria Group, Inc., 70, 120–121, 292
American Bar Association, 122, 187
American Express, 186
American Institute of Certified Public Accountants (AICPA), 211, 298
Amnesty International, 25
Anderson, Howard, 197
Angelides, Philip, 24
Annual General Counsel Roundtable, 2004, 282
Annual Profile of Health Care for 2007, 143
Anonymous complaints, whistle-blowing, 185, 189–190
Anson, Mark, 219
Aon Corporation, 89
Asian Development Bank, 293

Assessment:
    of compliance risk, 221–235
    evaluating compliance program effectiveness, 272–282
    for internal control program, 260–261
    of risk assessment, 115, 208, 255
    training and education needs, 161–163
Assigning responsibility for investigations, 193–194
Attorney-client privilege, 195, 238
Audit committees, 87–88, 93–94
Audits:
    assessing compliance effectiveness, 280
    compliance risk, 236–243
    internal control program, 258–259
    internal controls, 263–264
    nonprofit oversight, 94–95
    policies, and Board of Directors, 92
    of public sector organizations, 50
    resources, 298
Australian Institute of Criminology Research and Public Policy Series, 47
Authorization process, internal controls, 256
Availability of hotline program, 185

Backup policies, information security, 210
"Bad news," delivering, 129
Balch, Oliver, 26
Bank Accounting & Finance, 89

Bank Compliance: Controlling Risk and Improving Effectiveness, 231–232
Bank Secrecy Act Anti-Money Laundering Examination Manual (BSA/AML, Federal Reserve Board), 240
Bank Systems and Technology, 214
The Banker, 26
Basel Committee on Banking Supervision, 43, 71, 216
BBB Wise Giving Alliance, 296–297
Benchmarks for assessing compliance effectiveness, 273–274
Berresford, Susan, 48
Bertelsmann Family Feud Ethics Game, 171
Beyond Compliance: The Trustee Viewpoint on Effective Foundation Governance (Center for Effective Philanthropy), 92–93
Bies, Susan Schmidt, 42, 254
BizEd, 83–84
Board Governance Survey for Not-for-Profit Organizations, 2006 (Grant Thornton), 73
Boards of directors:
   audit committees, 87–88
   compliance committees, 88–89
   compliance program coordination, 128–129
   compliance program evaluation, 274–275
   compliance reporting to, 122–123
   compliance risk, 219–221
   expanded compliance roles and responsibilities, 85–86
   institutional shareholder influence on, 23
   investigation reporting, 195
   key questions, 89–92
   leadership and culture, 85–92, 96
   nonprofit sector oversight, 94–96
   personal qualities of members, 86–87
   Sarbanes-Oxley Act (2002), 11, 83–84
   structure of, 87–89
   training and education programs, 166–167
   whistle-blowing information, 190–191
BoardSource, 94, 297
Bonus, determination of, 142
The Book of the States, 74

Bowers, James, 216
BP, 186
Braithwaite, John, 59
Brown, H. Lowell, 13
Budgeting (*See* Costs and budgeting)
"Building a Partnership for Effective Compliance" (DHHS), 269
Burditt, George, 237
Burlington Indus, Inc. v. Ellerth, 10
Burrows, Melinda, 152
Bush, George W., 11, 100
Business and Society Review, 139–140
Business continuity, information security, 210
Business managers, assessing compliance effectiveness, 282
Business Roundtable Institute for Corporate Ethics, 296
Business Trends Quarterly, 200
Business units, compliance program coordination, 131
Business.gov, 297

California Corporate Disclosure Act, 18
California Data Protection Act, 201
California Management Review, 70
California Public Employees' Retirement System (CALPERS), 24
Canada, information security, 201
Canadian Centre for Occupational Health and Safety, 156
Canadian Office of Consumer Affairs, 44–45
Capdevila, Chris, 200
In re Caremark International Inc. v. Derivative Litigation, 10, 17, 81–82
Center for Effective Philanthropy, 92
Centralized compliance program structure, 119
Certification of CCO, 292–293
Charter of compliance programs, 110–113
Chemical Manufacturers Association CMA, 41
Chen, Paul, 209–210
Chief compliance officer (CCO):
   accountability, 136
   compliance program charter, 113

Chief compliance officer (CCO) (*Cont.*)
    compliance program coordination,
        128–129
    compliance program role, 134–141
    evolving role of, 292
    as guidance for regulators, 109
    power of, 135
    professionalism and certification,
        292–293
    protections for, 137–138
    qualities of effective, 136–137
    resignation decision, 138
    resources, 135–136
    skills and experience, 133–134
Chief executive officer (CEO) and chief
        financial officer (CFO):
    compliance program coordination,
        128–129
    compliance reporting to, 121
    as guidance for regulators, 109
    Sarbanes-Oxley Act (2002), 83
Chief legal officer (CLO), 122
Civil society organizations (*See*
        Nongovernmental organizations
        [NGOs])
Classification, information security, 208
Classroom teaching method, 170
Cleveland Plain Dealer, 11
Clinton, William J. "Bill," 204
Code of conduct specific compliance
        training curricula, 168
Code of ethics, Sarbanes-Oxley Act
        (2002), 12
Codes of conduct:
    defined, 64
    developing, 67–70
    ethics, 64–70
    growth of, 65
    NYSE, 66
    SEC, 65–66
    skepticism regarding, 66–67, 69
Committee of Sponsoring Organizations
        of the Treadway Commission
        (COSO):
    communication, 257–258
    compliance risk, 218–219
    control activities, 255–256
    control environment, 253–254
    detective controls, 256–257

    framework for internal controls,
        253–258
    internal controls, 252–258
    leadership and culture, 85
    monitoring, 258
    prominence, 253
    risk assessment, 255
    risk management, 42
    standards, 202
Communication:
    assessing compliance effectiveness,
        279–280
    codes of conduct, 69–70
    compliance risk, 221
    global telecommunications and the
        Internet, 27–28
    information technology (IT), 213–214
    postevaluation actions, 283
    by regulators, 244
    strategies for, 158–161
    training and education, 162–163
    whistle-blowing policies, 181
Compensation, 72, 91, 142, 230
Complaints, investigating, 160–161, 195
Complaints, whistle-blowing, 189–190
Compliance:
    barriers to, and ethics, 59–61
    creating multidimensional compliance
        framework, 204–206
    vs. ethics, as concept, 56, 63–64
    future of, 287–294
    information technology (IT) tools,
        211–213
    internationalization, 293–294
    motivation for, 57–59
    principle- vs. rule-based, 46, 63–64
    resources, 295–298
Compliance and Governance, 187
Compliance and procedures manuals, 158
*Compliance and the Compliance Function
    in Banks* (Basel Committee), 43–44
Compliance committees, 129–130,
    277–278, 283
Compliance dashboards, 211–213
Compliance effectiveness, assessing,
    272–282
    benchmarks, 273–274
    cautions, 273
    compliance committee, 277–278

Compliance effectiveness, assessing
(*Cont.*)
compliance operations, 278–282
compliance organization function,
276–277
generic measures, 272–273
organization-specific measures,
274–276
program-specific measures,
274–276
Compliance Effectiveness Pilot (DHHS),
269
Compliance Examination Handbook
(FDIC), 237
Compliance-Focused Environmental
Management System—
Enforcement Agreement Guidance
(CFEMS), 110
Compliance management, 3–52
corporate social responsibility, 21–22
Defense Industry Initiative (DII) as
prototype, 6
evolution of, 5–6, 33–35
federal agency expansion, 12–17
as federal mandate, 31–32
federal oversight, 18–20, 200
global telecommunications and the
Internet, 27–28
institutional shareholders, 22–24
internal corporate compliance systems,
37–38
judicial decisions, 6–10
legislative response, 10–12
NGOs, 24–26
nonprofit sector, 19–21, 47–49
overview, 31–33
private sector, 21, 38–47
public sector, 50–51
scandals increase focus, 3–5, 72
state oversight, 17–21
Compliance Management Systems
(FDIC), 130, 146
Compliance officers and staff:
certification and licensing, 140–141
compliance program budgeting,
143–144
full-time or part-time, 139–140
skill and experience, 133–134
types of, 132–133

Compliance policies and procedures,
151–158
characteristics of effective, 156
drafting, 153–156
FSGO, 152
implementing, 156–157
industry-specific, 152–153
key elements, 153–154
language clarity, 154–155
reviewing existing, 157–158
"Compliance program assessment" (CPA),
272
*Compliance Program Guidance for
Pharmaceutical Manufacturers*
(DHHS), 153
Compliance programs, 105–150
budgeting, 141–144
charter, 110–113
coordinating, 127–131
design, 106–108
evaluating, 267–284
expenses, 143
features, 113–116
goals of, 105–116
internal controls, 263–264
outsourcing, 124–127
role of chief compliance officer,
134–141
size of organization, 144–149
staffing, 131–141
structure, 108–110, 116–123
Compliance programs, evaluating,
267–284
assessing compliance effectiveness,
272–282
effectiveness criteria, 269–270
need for evaluation, 271
postevaluation actions, 283–284
problems, 268
techniques, 271–272
Compliance risk, 215–245
assessment of, 221–235
auditing, 236–243
consequences of failure, 235
data collection, 241–242
defined, 215–216
governance, 219–221
monitoring, 236
program creation, 220

Compliance risk (*Cont.*)
  regulators, 218, 243–245
  regulatory requirements, 216–218
  reviewers, 240–241
  standard-setting organizations, 218–219
  starting, 238–239
Compliance risk assessment, 221–235
  conducting, 221–222
  findings, 233–235
  goals, 221
  organizational risks, 225–230
  prioritizing, 231–233
  recommendations, 233–235
  risk context, 224–225
  risk factor identification, 223
  techniques for, 231–232
Computer-based training
    (*See* E-learning)
Comstock, Amy, 74–75
Con Edison, 62
Conference Board:
  compliance programs, 128, 132
  compliance risk, 221–221, 235, 238
  hotline, 183–184
  training programs, 161, 167–168
  whistle-blowing, 179, 197
Conferencing information technology
    (IT), 160
Confidentiality, 87, 185, 208–209
Contracting for services (*See* Outsourcing)
Control Objectives for Information
    Technology (COBIT), 202
Controls (*See* Internal controls)
Cooley Alerts, 201
Cooperation in ethics compliance,
    58–59
Coordination:
  of compliance programs, 127–131
  whistle-blowing information, 188
The Corporate Board, 219–220
Corporate Compliance Principles
    (National Center for Preventive
    Law), 106, 111, 135–136
Corporate governance:
  and compliance, 78
  compliance risk, 219–221
  multidimensional compliance
    framework, 204–205
  reforms, 95–96

(*See also* Boards of directors; Senior
    management)
*Corporate Governance and Compliance
    Hotline Benchmarking Report*,
    184, 188
Corporate Governance Rule Proposals,
    2002 (NYSE), 84–85
*Corporate Regulatory Compliance
    Practices* (Ernst & Young), 118–119,
    131, 157, 211
Costs and budgeting:
  assessing compliance effectiveness, 282
  for compliance programs, 141–143
  multiple regulations as challenge,
    202–203
  of regulatory compliance, 33
  for training and education programs,
    164
The Costs of Compliance (SIFMA),
    143, 282
Council for Excellence in Government,
    297
Council of Better Business Bureaus, 40
Craig, Valentine V., 40
Credit rating agencies, 44
Credit Union Magazine, 167
Creedon, Nancy, 212
Culture:
  creating ethical culture, 70–72
  cultural framework of organization,
    61–63, 70–72
  organizational, for compliance
    program design, 107–108
  organizational compliance risk, 230
Curricula, training and education,
    167–168, 172

Daiwa Securities, 212–213
Dashboards, compliance, 211–213
Data collection, compliance audit, 241–242
Data protection (*See* Security of
    information)
Decentralized compliance program
    structure, 119–120
Defense Contract Audit Agency
    (DCAA), 18
Defense Federal Acquisition Regulations
    Supplement (DFARS), 110
Defense industry, 110

Defense Industry Initiative (DII), 6, 110, 148, 170
Deficit Reduction Act, 109
Delaware Journal of Corporate Law, 13
Deloitte, 212
Design:
  of compliance programs, 106–108
  e-learning, 171–172
  training and education programs, 164–165
Deterrence approach, ethics compliance, 57
Devaney, Earl R., 74
Directors (*See* Boards of directors)
Directors & Boards, 77, 86
Directors and officers (D&O) insurance, 138
Directorship, 191
Disciplinary postevaluation actions, 284
Distribution of hotline information, 187–188
DM Review, 209
Documentation, 173, 242
Donaldson, William H., 249
Doot, David, 216
Draft Principles for Effective Practice (Panel on the Nonprofit Sector), 48
Drafting policies and procedures, 153–156
Duke Law Journal, 32, 41
Duty separation, internal controls, 256
Dworkin, Terry Morehead, 175–176

E-Government and Regulation (Urban Institute), 36
E-learning, 169–172
E-mail information security, 209–210
Economist Intelligence Unit, 231, 274
Edelman Trust Barometer, 26
Education (*See* Training and education)
Edwards, Chris, 61
Effectiveness criteria, evaluating compliance program, 269–270
Employees (*See* Staffing)
Enforcement, 59, 69
Enron, 5, 72, 77, 290
Enterprise Risk Management (ERM), 42, 218–219, 223
Enterprise Risk Management—Integrated Framework (COSO), 42, 218–219

Environment:
  environmental services industry, 110
  risk environment and compliance program, 106
EPPACS, 209–210
Equator Principles, 26
Ernst & Young, 118–119, 131, 157, 206, 211
Ethics, 55–75
  assessing compliance effectiveness, 280–281
  barriers to compliance, 59–61
  codes of conduct, 64–70
  commitment to, and self-regulation, 46
  vs. compliance, as concept, 56, 63–64
  compliance program, 115
  creating ethical culture, 70–72
  cultural framework of organization, 61–63
  motivation for compliance, 57–59
  nonprofit sector, 72–73
  organizational compliance risk, 230
  overview, 55–56
  policies, and Board of Directors, 91
  principle- vs. rule-based compliance, 46, 63–64, 290–292
  public sector, 74–75
Ethics & Compliance Officers Association (ECOA), 8, 222, 235, 296
EthicsPoint, 180
Ethics Resource Center (ERC), 176, 180, 295
Ethics specific compliance training curricula, 168
EthicsWorld, 176
Ethikos, 271
European Union, information security, 201
Evaluating and Improving a Compliance Program (HCCA), 268
An Evaluative Framework for Voluntary Codes (Canadian Office of Consumer Affairs), 44
Evans, Ruth, 125
Examination-specific compliance training curricula, 168
Exception reporting, 213
Executive Action, 197
Exit interviews, 160

External agency investigation reporting, 195–196
External documentation and compliance risk, 223–224
External investigations, 192
External training programs, 173

Fairness in ethical culture creation, 71
False Claims Act (FCA), 177–178
Fannie Mae, 96
Faragher v. City of Boca Raton, 10
Fast, M. Elizabeth, 238
FDA Enforcement Manual, 168
FDIC Banking Review, 40
Federal agencies:
    expansion, with compliance focus, 12–17
    Inspector General Act (1978), 14
    investigation reporting, 195–196
    punitive actions, 13–14
    regulatory agencies, 15–17
    U.S. Department of Justice, 14–15
Federal Deposit Insurance Corporation (FDIC):
    compliance committees, 130
    compliance management, 4, 130, 146
    compliance policies and procedures, 152
    compliance risk, 237
    customer complaints, 160–161
    internal controls, 250
Federal Deposit Insurance Corporation Improvement Act (FDICIA), 248
Federal Energy Regulatory Commission (FERC), 15–16
Federal Financial Management Improvement Act (FFMIA), 251
Federal Managers Financial Integrity Act (FMFIA), 251
Federal Mine Health and Safety Act, 177
Federal oversight, 18–20, 200
    (*See also specific federal agencies; specific legislation*)
Federal Reserve Board, 240
Federal Reserve Systems, 261–262
Federal Sentencing Guidelines for Organizations (FSGO):
    amendments to, 8–10, 38, 41, 56, 70, 79–80, 163, 177, 217

codes of conduct, 65–66
compliance effectiveness, 269–270
compliance policies and procedures, 152
compliance risk assessment, 217–218, 231
development of, 6–10, 15
elements of, 37–38
ethics compliance, 56, 61–62, 70
features of compliance program, 113–116
future of compliance, 290
as guidance for regulators, 108
internal control program, 248, 250–251
internal corporate compliance systems, 37–38
investigation reporting, 196
leadership and culture, 79
organizational compliance risk, 229
risk management, 41–42
section 8B2, 165, 229, 250, 269
training programs, 161, 165–167
whistle-blowing, 176–177
Federal Trade Commission (FTC), 36
Financial Daily, 293
Financial Industry Regulatory Authority (FINRA), 40, 109
Financial services industry, 109, 152
Fiorelli, Paul, 264
Fitch Ratings, 44, 92
Fogel, Lawrence, 272
Follow-up:
    hotlines, 187–188
    internal control tests, 264
    investigations, 196
    whistle-blowing information, 188
Food & Drug Law Journal, 62, 237
Foreign Corruption Practices Act, 4, 248
Fortune, 27–28
Foundation News & Commentary, 48
French, Paul, 209
Frequency of compliance audit, 240
Fried, Fank, Harris, Shriver & Jacobson, 82–83
The Future for Compliance—An Efficient and Effective Commercial Operation (PricewaterhouseCoopers), 282

Gadziala, Mary Ann, 275–276
GE, 187
General counsel, compliance reporting to, 121

General resources, 295–296
Generic compliance training curricula, 168
Gilman, Stuart, 176, 180
Gilson, Ben, Jr., 72
Glassman, Cynthia A., 16
Glazer, Craig, 244
Global Institutional Investor Study (ISS), 23
Global Policy Forum, 25
Goals:
  assessment of compliance risk, 221
  of compliance audit, 239
  compliance program charter, 112
  of compliance programs, 105–116
Good Manufacturing Practices (GMP), 173
Governance (*See* Corporate governance)
Governance, risk, and compliance
    (GRC), 203
Government:
  internal controls, 248–251
  nongovernmental organizations
    (NGOs), 24–26
  regulation resources, 297
  state government compliance focus,
    17–20, 201
  (*See also specific topics*)
Gramling, Robert, 247–248
Grant Thornton, 73
Grassley, Charles, 123
Greenspan, Alan, 101
Grundfast, Joseph, 89
Guide to Understanding Internal Controls
    (University of California), 254,
    257–258
*Guide to Writing an OHS Policy
    Statement* (Canadian Centre for
    Occupational Health and Safety),
    156–157

Hanson, Kirk, 77
Harassment and organizational
    compliance risk, 229
Harvard Business Review, 64
Harvard Law Review, 65–66
Haynes, Andrew, 215
Health Care Compliance Association
    (HCCA), 118, 268, 270
Health services industry, 108–109, 153
Henning, Peter, 290
Herold, Rebecca, 208–209

Higher education, Sarbanes-Oxley Act, 20
History of organization, compliance
    program design, 106–107
Holmstrom, Bengt, 22
Hotel.com, 206
Hotlines:
  as communication method, 160
  information distribution and follow-up,
    187–188
  instituting, 179–180
  international operations, 189–190
  key features, 185–186
  operations, 182–184, 189–190
  proliferation of, 179
  usage, 188–189
HR Focus, 186
Human resources risk, 229–230
Hutter, Bridget, 215

*The Impact of Regulatory Costs on Small
    Firms*, 33
Implementation:
  compliance policies and procedures,
    156–157
  hotlines, 179–180
  whistle-blowing programs, 179–187
Improving Regulatory Compliance
    (Braithwaite), 59
Independence:
  of Board of Directors, 90
  of investigators, 193–194
Independent compliance program
    structure, 118
Independent Sector, 20, 49, 73, 94, 297
Individual responsibility, ethics
    compliance, 58
Industry codes, voluntary, 44–45
Industry-specific:
  compliance policies and procedures,
    152–153
  guidance for regulators, 108–110
Information management:
  compliance risk, 223–224
  organizational compliance risk, 227
  quality of, and Board of Directors, 90
  whistle-blowing programs, 187–188
  (*See also* Information technology [IT])
*Information Security Governance: What
    Directors Need to Know* (IAA), 204

Information Systems, Audit and Control
    Association (ISACA), 202, 208
Information Systems Security, 208–209
Information technology (IT), 199–214
    communication, 213–214
    compliance tools, 211–213
    creating multidimensional compliance
        framework, 204–206
    e-learning, 169–172
    federal regulatory requirements, 200
    international regulatory requirements,
        201
    key questions, 207
    multiple regulations as challenge,
        202–203
    organizational compliance risk,
        227–228
    outsourcing, 211
    perspectives on, 199
    privacy, 206–211
    security of information, 206–211
    standards for, 202
    state regulatory requirements, 201
    training, 213–214
Inquiry tracking:
    hotline program, 185–186
    whistle-blowing programs, 188–189
Inspector General Act (1978), 14
Institute of Internal Auditors (IAA), 204, 298
Institutional shareholder compliance
    focus, 22–24
Institutional Shareholder Services (ISS), 23
Institutionalization of compliance, 47
Instructional techniques, 169–171
Integrity (*See* Ethics)
Integrity programs, 121
Internal Auditor, 252, 258–259, 265, 277
*Internal Control: Providing a Foundation
    for Accountability in Government*
    (INTOSAI), 259–260
Internal Control—Integrated Framework
    (COSO), 85, 252
*Internal Control Over Financial
    Reporting—Guidance for Smaller
    Public Companies* (COSO), 254
Internal control program, 258–264
    assessment, 260–261
    audit functions, 258–259
    compliance functions, 258–259

identification, 260–261
key questions, 262
line management, 259–260
monitoring, 261–262
testing, 261–264
Internal controls, 247–265
    compliance program, 115
    fraud example, 250
    government, 248–251
    importance of, 247–248
    information technology (IT), 200
    program for, 258–264
    public sector, 251
    resources, 298
    security of information security,
        information technology (IT), 210
    self-regulatory organizations (SROs),
        251–252
    standard-setting organizations, 252–258
    from standard setting organizations, 41
Internal corporate compliance systems,
    37–38
Internal documentation and compliance
    risk, 223–224
Internal investigations, 192, 194
Internal Revenue Service (IRS), 13, 20, 238
International City/County Management
    Association (ICMA), 99, 298
International codes of conduct, 21–22
International Electrotechnical
    Commission (IEC), 202
International operations:
    compliance, 293–294
    regulatory requirements and
        information technology (IT), 201
    whistle-blowing programs, 189–191
International Organization for
    Standardization (ISO), 43–44, 202
International Organization of Supreme
    Audit Institutions (INTOSAI), 259
Internet and Web sites:
    for communication, 158–159
    compliance-based information on, 148
    compliance focus, 27–28
    development of, 27
    Web conferencing information
        technology (IT), 160
    Webcasting, 160
    (*See also* E-learning)

Interviews:
  compliance audit, 242
  exit interviews, 160
Intranet communication, 158–159
Investigations, 191–196
  assessing compliance effectiveness, 281
  assigning responsibility, 193–194
  compliance program, 116
  conducting, 194–195
  follow-up, 196
  internal vs. external, 192, 194
  key questions, 192
  process of, 192
  prompt responses to, 191
  reporting, 195–196
  whistle-blowing information, 188
Investigators, independence and
      qualifications, 193–194
Investment Advisor Association, 223
Investment Company Act, 11
Is There a Reliable Way to Evaluate
      Organisational Compliance
      Programs? (Parker), 271
Issuance of compliance policies and
      procedures, 155
IT Governance Institute, 202
ITCi, 213
It's Not Your Father's Hotline
      (EthicsPoint), 180

Johnson & Johnson, 197
Joint Commission on Health Care and
      Accreditation of Health
      Organizations (JCAHO), 40
Joseph, John N., 191
Joseph, Joshua, 139
Journal of Accountancy, 233
Journal of Banking Regulation, 215
Journal of Health Care Compliance, 64,
      133–134, 137, 148–149, 189, 191
Journal of Investment Compliance, 125
Judicial decisions, 6–10, 290

Kaplan, Steven, 22
Kelliher, Joseph T., 15
Kelsey, Michael, 216
Key performance indicators (KPIs) for
      assessing compliance effectiveness,
      273–274

Key players, compliance program design,
      107
Key program elements, training, 164–169
Key questions:
  boards of directors, 89–92
  compliance program structure, 116–117
  information technology (IT), 207
  internal control program, 262
  investigations, 192
Key votes by trade unions, 24
Khan, Irene, 25
Kirkpatrick, David, 28
Kleinman, Bill, 191
Knerr, Anthony, 86
Krawiec, Kimberley, 8
Kusserow, Robert, 189

Language in compliance policies, 154–155
Law, collapse of belief in, 61
Law & Society Review, 59
Law Practice Today, 209
Leadership and culture, 77–101
  boards of directors, 85–92, 96
  compliant culture creation, 97–99
  ethical culture creation, 71
  Federal Sentencing Guidelines for
      Organizations (FSGOs), 79
  Greenspan on, 101
  legal and regulatory basis, 79–84
  nonprofit organizations, 92–96
  overview, 77–78
  public-sector organization, 99–100
  self-regulatory organizations (SROs),
      84–85
  senior management, 96–99
Leading Corporate Integrity: Defining the
      Role of Chief Ethics and
      Compliance Officer, 141
Learning Management Systems (LMS), 173
Lecture method of training, 170
Lee, Jim, 209
Legal and regulatory basis:
  compliance risk, 237–238
  leadership and culture, 79–84
  organizational compliance risk, 226–227
  outsourcing, 127
  training and education programs, 162
  voluntary codes, 45
  (See also under Compliance)

Legislative response, 10–12
  (*See also specific legislative acts*)
Lenzi, John, 292
Line management, internal control
    program, 259–260
London School of Economics, 55
Loomis, Tamara, 4
Los Angeles Times, 26
Louisville Water Company, 100

Ma, Cindy, 219
Mahler, Michael, 243–244
Maker, internal controls, 256–257
Malicious complaints, whistle-blowing, 190
Malur, Ron, 212
Management (*See* Compliance
    management; Senior management)
Managerial risk, 228
Markets in Financial Instruments
    Directive (MiFID), 293
Marsh & McLennan, 89
Matossian, Michael, 216
May, Peter, 59
McCabe, Stephen, 212
McCartney, William, 32
McNally, J. Stephen, 93
McNulty, Paul, 245n2
Merrill Lynch, 17
The Metropolitan Corporate Counsel, 78
Millstein, Ira, 83–84
Misconduct, reporting, 176
Mitchell, Arthur, 293
Monitoring:
    assessing compliance effectiveness, 280
    compliance program, 115
    compliance risk, 220, 236
    COSO internal control, 258
    internal control program, 261–262
    organizational compliance risk, 226
Motivation for compliance, ethics, 57–59

National Advertising Division (NAD),
    40–41
National Association of College and
    University Business Officers, 10
National Business Ethics Survey (ERC),
    176, 180
National Center for Preventive Law, 106,
    111, 135–136, 141, 193, 195

National Coalition for Corporate
    Reform, 23
National Environmental Investigations
    Center (NEIC), 110
National information technology (IT)
    Transfer and Advancement Act, 41
National Labor Relations Act, 177
National Underwriter, 136
Negative publicity effects, ethics
    compliance, 58
New Media Information Technology (IT)
    (Pavlik), 28
New York Law Journal, 4
New York Stock Exchange (NYSE):
    codes of conduct, 66
    Corporate Governance Rules, 66
    as guidance for regulators, 109
    internal controls, 251–252
    leadership and culture, 84–85
    Rule 342.23, 251
    self-regulation, 39–40
    whistle-blowing information, 190–191
New York Times, 51, 74
Newsletters, as communication method, 158
9th Annual Survey (Health Care
    Compliance Association), 118
Nongovernmental organizations (NGOs),
    24–26
*Nonprofit Governance and the Sarbanes-
    Oxley Act* (Urban Institute), 95
Nonprofit Integrity Act, 21
Nonprofit sector:
    audit committee functions, 93–94
    board oversight, 94–96
    compliance, 19–21
    enhanced federal oversight, 20
    enhanced state oversight, 21
    ethics, 72–73
    leadership and culture, 92–96
    private sector, 47–49
    resources, 296–297
    Sarbanes-Oxley impact, 19–20
    self-regulation and compliance, 47–49
Nursing Homes, 272

O'Connor, Raymond, 258–259
Olsen, Mark W., 227, 261–262
Ombudspersons, 186–187

Open Compliance and Ethics Group (OCEG), 296
Operating units, 131
Operation of hotlines, 182–184, 189–190
Optimize, 121, 137
Oracle Corporation, 89
Organisation for Economic Co-Operation and Development (OECD):
  codes of conduct, 21
  compliance management, 33, 35, 50
  ethics compliance, 57–58, 60–61
Organization-specific measures, compliance effectiveness, 274–276
Organizational context, compliance program design, 106
Organizational risks, assessment of, 225–230
Organizational Sentencing Guidelines: The New Paradigm for Effective Compliance and Ethics Programs, 9
Orientation training programs, 166
Ortquist, Steve, 137
Orvitz, Michael, 82
Outsourcing:
  compliance programs, 124–127
  hotlines, 183
  information technology (IT), 211
  internal controls, 263–264
  organizational compliance risk, 229–230
  quality and compliance outsourcing, 126
Oversight:
  compliance risk, 220
  federal, 18–20, 200
  nonprofit sector, 94–96
  organizational compliance risk, 226, 228
  private sector, 21
Overview of the Compliance Examination (FDIC), 152

Packard Commission, 6
Paine, Lynn Sharp, 64
Panel on the Nonprofit Sector, 47–48
Parker, Christine, 47, 271
Passwords, internal controls, 256
Paul, James A., 25
Paulson, Henry Jr., 290–291
Pavlik, John, 28
Personal Information Protection and Electronic Documents Act (PIPEDA), 201

Philanthropic resources, 296–297
Policies and procedures:
  assessing compliance effectiveness, 278
  compliance program evaluation, 278
  compliance risk, 220–221
  organizational compliance risk, 226, 229
  whistle-blowing, 181
Policy Brief, 2005 (OECD), 50
Postevaluation actions, compliance program, 283–284
Powar, Michael, 215
Practical Lawyer, 152
Prerequisites, compliance program charter, 110–111
PricewaterhouseCoopers, 73, 88, 93, 268, 282
Principle-based compliance, 46, 63–64, 290–292
Principles of Federal Prosecution of Business Organizations (DOJ), 14–15, 108, 269, 271, 274
Privacy, 206–211
Private sector:
  compliance, 39–47
  credit rating agencies, 44
  nonprofit, 47–49
  oversight by, 21
  self-regulating organizations (SROs), 39–41, 46–47
  standard-setting organizations, 40–44
  voluntary industry codes, 44–46
Privatization and compliance, 51
Professionalism of CCO, 292–293
Profile of Health Care Compliance Officers, 2007, 138, 164–166, 169
Program Guidelines for Nursing Facilities (OIG), 278
Programs:
  compliance programs, 105–150
  integrity programs, 121
  internal control program, 258–264
  whistle-blowing, 175–191
Prompt response to investigations, 191
Protecting the Brand (PricewaterhouseCoopers), 268
Public Company Accounting Reform and Investor Protection Act, 10–11

Public sector:
    compliance, 50–51
    ethics, 74–75
    internal controls, 251
    leadership and culture, 99–100
    resources, 297–298
Public Utilities Fortnightly, 216, 244
Punitive actions by federal agencies, 13–14

Qualifications of investigators, 193–194
A *Quest for Excellence* (Packard
    Commission), 6

Rasmussen, Michael, 213
Recommendations and compliance risk,
    233–235
Records management and retention, 209
Redmond, Arlene, 186
Reducing the Risk of Policy Failure
    (OECD), 33, 35
Regulation:
    compliance audit, 242–243
    compliance program relationships,
      115–116
    compliance risk, 216–218, 243–245
    constant changes in, 33–35
    enforcement, 33–36
    multiple regulations as challenge,
      202–203
    outsourcing, 126
    reporting, 123
    self-regulation, 34–36
    (*See also* Compliance management)
Regulators, 123, 126, 218, 243–245
Regulatory-specific compliance training
    curricula, 168
Reporting:
    compliance program structure,
      120–123
    investigations, 195–196
    misconduct, 176
    whistle-blowing, 181–182, 190–191
Resolution Trust Corporation, 4
Resources:
    committed, in compliance program
      charter, 113
    for compliance, 295–298
    training and education, 163

Responsibility and accountability:
    compliance risk, 222
    ethical culture creation, 72
    ethics compliance, 58
    for hotlines, 184
    multidimensional compliance
      framework, 205–206
    organizational compliance risk, 228
    responsibility for investigations, 193–194
    use of public funds, 100
Responsible Care Program, CMA, 40–41
Review:
    compliance audit, 240
    existing policies and procedures, 157–158
    postevaluation actions, 284
    reviewers and compliance risk, 240–241
Richards, Lori A., 78, 126
Riggs Bank, 55–56
Risk assessment:
    compliance program, 115
    compliance risk, 224–225
    information security, 208
    internal control, 255, 262
    risk factor identification, 223
Risk environment and compliance
    program, 106
Risk management, 42, 90
Risk Management, 186
*Risk Management and Business
    Regulation* (Hutter and Powar), 215
Risk mapping, 233–234
*Risk Regulation, Management and
    Compliance* (London School of
    Economics), 55
Rosenberg, Eric, 244
Ruddell, Kirk, 148
Rule-based compliance, 46, 63–64, 290–292
Rundorff, William, 154

*Sarbanes-Oxley: Relevance and
    Implications for Non-Public
    Healthcare Organizations*
    (PricewaterhouseCoopers), 93–94
Sarbanes-Oxley Act (2002):
    audit committees, 88
    codes of conduct, 65–66
    COSO internal control framework,
      252–253
    credit rating agencies, 44

Sarbanes-Oxley Act (2002) (*Cont.*)
and FSGO, 79
information technology (IT), 200
internal control program, 248–251
leadership and culture, 83–84
as legislative response, 10–12
nonprofit sector, 19–20, 93
OMB impact, 19
requirements, 11
section 11.07, 179
section 301(4), 88, 178
section 302, 200, 249
section 404, 12, 44, 200, 249
section 406, 65
section 802, 200
section 806, 178
whistle-blowing, 178–179, 190–191
Scandals, 3–5, 72, 77–80
Schaub, Alexander, 46
Schlaman, Steve, 214
Sczyrba, Meg, 169
SearchCIO.com, 205–206
Securities Act (1933), 11
Securities and Exchange Commission
(SEC):
codes of conduct, 65–66
compliance outsourcing, 126
compliance program evaluation,
275–276
compliance programs, 128–129
compliance risk, 218, 224
COSO internal control framework,
252–253
exception reporting, 213
as guidance for regulators, 109
internal control program, 249–250
leadership and culture, 78
Leniency Guidelines, 16–17
self-regulation, 39
and state government compliance,
17–18
Securities Exchange Act (1934), 11
Securities Industry and Financial Markets
Association (SIFMA), 112, 236, 282
Security Compliance Council, 199, 203
Security of information:
backup policies, 210
business continuity, 210
confidentiality and privacy, 208–209
e-learning, 172
e-mail, 209–210
hotline program, 185
information technology (IT), 206–211
instant messages, 209–210
internal controls, 210
programs and policies, 206–208
rapid response, 211
records management and retention, 209
security programs and policies,
206–208
Seidman, Dov, 121, 137
Self-regulating organizations (SROs):
internal controls, 251–252
leadership and culture, 84–85
private sector, 39–41, 46–47
Self-regulation, 34–36, 48–49
Self-Regulation in the Alcohol Industry
(FTC), 36
Self-reporting, 237
Semiautonomous compliance program
structure, 118–119
Senior management:
compliance program charter, 111
compliance program coordination,
128–129
compliance program evaluation,
274–275
compliance risk, 219–221
leadership and culture, 96–99
reporting misconduct, 176
Sarbanes-Oxley Act (2002), 11–12
training and education programs,
166–167
Separation of duties, internal controls, 256
Shapiro, Sidney, 32, 41
Shareholder compliance focus, 22–24
Sharpe, Brian, 271
Sigg, Carolyn, 264
Silverman, Michael G., 1–2
Simmons, Mark, 252
Size of organization:
compliance programs, 144–149
internal controls, 254
training and education, 163
Skills:
compliance officers and staff, 133–134
staffing and self-regulation, 46–47
(*See also* Training and education)

Small Business Compliance Policy (EPA), 146

Smith, Jennifer, 133

Snell, Roy, 292

Social Funds, 23

Society of Corporate Compliance and Ethics (SCCE), 292, 296

Sonnenfeld, Jeffrey A., 56

Spitzer, Eliot, 17

Sporkin, Stanley, 186

Staffing:
compliance costs, 143
for compliance programs, 131–141
internal controls, 263–264
organizational compliance risk, 227
postevaluation actions, 284
skills and self-regulation, 46–47
(*See also* Compliance officers and staff)

Stakeholders for compliance program design, 107

Standard-setting organizations:
compliance program, 121
compliance risk, 218–219
information technology (IT), 202
internal controls, 252–258
nonprofit sector, 49
private sector, 40–44

Standards for the Establishment and Operations of Ombuds Office, 187

State government compliance focus, 17–20, 201

The State of U.S. Corporate Governance: What's Right and What's Wrong (Holmstrom and Kaplan), 22

State oversight, 17–21

Statement on Auditing Standards (SAS), 211

Stensgaard, Karen, 277

Steuer, Joseph T., 93

Stewardship, of Board of Director members, 86

Stier, Edwin, 197

Strategic risk, 225–226

Structure of compliance programs, 116–123
compliance program charter, 112
industry-specific, 108–110
key questions, 116–117

postevaluation actions, 284
reporting, 120–123
standards and integrity programs, 121
types of, 117–120

Structure of organization
for compliance program design, 107
compliance risk, 224–225
information security, 207

The Struggle to Manage Security Compliance for Multiple Regulations (Security Compliance Council), 199

Stubblefield, Carole, 78

Supervisory Insights (FDIC), 250

Tabuena, Jose, 133

Targeted training and education programs, 168–169

Technical compliance officer, 132

Techniques for evaluating compliance program, 271–272

Tenet Healthcare Corporation, 123

Testing:
internal control program, 261–264
training and education, 173

Third-party relationships (*See* Outsourcing)

Thomas, Terri, 238

Thompson, Larry D., 14–15

Thornburgh, Richard, 3

Tillinghast-Towers Perrin, 223

Trade unions, influence of, 24

Training and education, 161–173
assessing compliance effectiveness, 279
assessing needs and requirements, 161–163
codes of conduct, 69–70
communication methods, 158
compliance program, 115
compliance risk, 221
documentation, 173
e-learning, 170–172
external programs, 173
information technology (IT), 213–214
instructional techniques, 169–171
key program elements, 164–169
organizational compliance risk, 227, 230
postevaluation actions, 283

Training and education (*Cont.*)
  Sarbanes-Oxley Act, 20
  testing and tracking, 173
The Treasury Board of Canada, 99
Trust, ethics compliance, 58–59

U.N. Global Compact with Business, 22
United States v. Booker, 9
United States v. Fanfan, 9
Universal Conduct: An Ethics and
  Compliance Benchmarking Survey
  (Conference Board), 128, 161, 221
University of California, 254, 257–258
Urban Institute, 36, 95
U.S. Customs and Border Protection, 35
U.S. Department of Health and Human
  Services (DHHS):
  compliance committees, 129
  compliance effectiveness, 269–270,
    276, 278
  compliance management, 51
  compliance policies and procedures,
    153
  compliance programs, 108, 118
  punitive actions by, 14
U.S. Department of Justice (DOJ)
  compliance effectiveness, 269,
    271, 274
  compliance focus, 14–15, 108
  investigations, 292
  leadership and culture, 84
U.S. Department of Veterans Affairs (VA),
  206
U.S. Environmental Protection Agency
  (EPA), 13, 35, 43, 146
U.S. Federal Register, 31
U.S. Food and Drug Administration
  (FDA), 35–36, 162, 168, 173
U.S. Government Accountability Office
  (GAO), 18, 31–32, 247, 268
U.S. Occupational Safety and Health
  Administration (OSHA), 35, 41, 162
U.S. Office of Compliance, 51
U.S. Office of Government Ethics, 74
U.S. Office of Management and Budget
  (OMB), 19, 100
U.S. Office of the Controller of the
  Currency, 162

U.S. Office of the Inspector General
  (OIG):
  compliance audit, 241
  compliance committees, 129
  compliance effectiveness, 269–270,
    276, 278
  compliance management, 51
  compliance policies and procedures,
    153
  compliance programs, 108, 118, 145–147
  federal oversight, 18
  punitive actions by, 14
  reporting, 123–124
  small and rural health-care providers,
    144–145
U.S. Sentencing Commission, 8–9, 79,
  269–270
  (*See also* Federal Sentencing
    Guidelines for Organizations
    [FSGO])

Values:
  for compliance program design,
    107–108
  organizational compliance risk, 230
  (*See also* Ethics)
Vanderbilt Journal of Transnational Laws,
  176
Vendors (*See* Outsourcing)
Video presentations, 160
Video training programs, 169–170
Voluntary industry codes, 44–46

Wachovia Corp., 205
Wall Street and Technology, 212
Wall Street Journal, 72, 186
Walsh, John, 213, 224
In re Walt Disney Company Derivative
  Litigation, 82–83
Washington Post, 36, 56
Washington University Law Quarterly, 8
Watt, Joseph, 272
Web-based training (*See* E-learning)
Web conferencing information
  technology (IT), 160
Web sites (*See* Internet and Web sites)
Webcasting, 160
Whistle-blowing, defined, 175–176

Whistle-blowing programs, 175–191
    assessing compliance effectiveness, 281
    background, 177–179
    importance of, 176
    information management, 187–188
    inquiry tracking, 188–189
    instituting, 179–187
    international operations, 189–191
    postevaluation actions, 283
White Paper on the Role of Compliance
    (SFIMA), 112, 236
Williams, Randy, 186

Wolf, Rick, 62
Wolfowitz, Paul, 74
Work-product privilege, 238
A Working Marriage (Creedon and
    Malur), 212
World Bank, 74
World Economic Forum (Davos,
    Switzerland), 25
World Trade Organization (ETO), 21, 25
WorldCom, 3, 5

Yale Law Journal Pocket Part, 290

About the Author

Michael G. Silverman has three decades of global experience in strategic planning, program management, compliance, risk assessment, and policy development in both the private and public sectors. His diverse experience includes 16 years as a senior compliance and human resources officer for Citigroup's global businesses, serving as a senior consultant to U.S. and state governments, managing several government agencies, and lecturing on policy, compliance, ethics, and risk management. Michael currently heads a consulting practice that specializes in helping organizations manage risk and compliance, corporate ethics, and corporate governance. He is on the faculties of both the FINRA (formerly NASD) Institute of Professional Development, where he conducts a one-day symposium on managing risk, compliance, and controls, and Columbia University's School of International and Public Affairs, where he teaches a graduate-level course on compliance management and ethics and administers a workshop program in international banking and finance. Michael has spoken and presented workshops on compliance and ethics at the University of Pennsylvania/Wharton (Multinational Research Advisory Group), the American Bankers Association (Annual Compliance Conference), and the Ballard Spahr/Ethics Alliance Conference on Business Ethics.

In his capacity as a senior compliance and human resources officer for Citigroup, he has had extensive experience, both in the United States and internationally, in the development and administration of risk management and compliance programs. Michael has worked on global audit programs specifically aimed at monitoring business compliance practices, and also on the development of risk assessment and internal control programs. He has created several global training programs for management staff in the areas of policy development, compliance, and ethics. He has worked extensively on issues pertaining to corporate ethics, social responsibility, whistle-blowing programs, and transparency. Michael also served as a business information security officer for Citigroup and chaired its Investigative Review Board program in the United States that addressed issues of employee wrongdoing.

Michael joined Citigroup (then Citibank/Citicorp) in 1986 as a senior human resources policy consultant responsible for developing Citibank's U.S. and international human resources policies. He developed the first consolidated set of human resources policies for Citibank's U.S. businesses. Prior to joining Citigroup, Michael worked as a consultant to various public, private, and nonprofit organizations, including the U.S. Department of Commerce and the New York State Assembly, on strategic planning and policy development initiatives. In the public sector, Michael has managed two government agencies at the state and county levels. He has lectured on public administration and policy development at Temple University and City University of New York.

Michael holds a B.A. degree in political science and a Masters Degree in public administration from Temple University. His professional and civic interests have ranged from serving as a member of the American Bankers Association's Human Resources Committee and a fellow at the Ethics Resource Center (Washington, D.C.), to being a volunteer business consultant to the NYC Partnership, a management advisor for God's Love We Deliver, and a volunteer trail maintenance worker for the Sierra Club.